PRAISE FOR *LET US PLAY*

"As a transgender person myself, I often encounter comments questioning whether transgender athletes should be allowed to compete. *Let Us Play* serves as a reliable resource to effectively counter ignorance and reinforces the message that transgender people rightfully belong in sports—and in the world. *Let Us Play* is for anyone seeking to understand the strengths and challenges of being transgender, being an athlete, and how many people embody both identities. I'm proud to join in and shout, 'LET US PLAY!'"

—MILES MCKENNA, author of *I Am NOT a Vampire*

"Harrison Browne has been an inspiration to many of us, on and off the ice, and has personally made me a better ally to any and all gender diverse friends, colleagues, and teammates. More urgent than ever before, *Let Us Play* is a crucial playbook that athletes and nonathletes alike can use to help make sports an inclusive place for all."

—MEGHAN DUGGAN, three-time Olympian
and Olympic gold medalist, USA Women's Hockey

"There has never been a more important time to elevate the stories and truths of transgender people in sport. Whether you're a sports fan, an ally, or someone navigating their own path toward self-acceptance, *Let Us Play* will shed light on the unique challenges trans athletes face."

—CHRIS MOSIER, transgender athlete and activist

"*Let Us Play* would be a vital, incisive book in any era, but of course this is not just any era. In a time when gender diversity in sports is being banned at the federal level, we need to understand the issue beyond the bigoted caricatures emerging from the sewers of US politics. In the hands of the Browne siblings, we get a new understanding of the issue in all its complexity by hearing the voices of those who have to navigate this never-more-perilous space. This book is a gift. Let's make sure it gets into the hands of those who need it. The Brownes' message matters because it's also a reminder that however complex their arguments may be, the message is a simple one: everyone should have the right to play."

—DAVE ZIRIN, sports editor, *The Nation*

"Much has been said about trans athletes, but not enough has been said by trans athletes. I knew those who opposed trans athletes were steeped in misguided fear, but this book gave me the language and research to articulate why that is. Trans athletes have always been here; the moral panic about them is a newly invented and stoked diversion. *Let Us Play* is about more than trans athletes; it's about gender in sports and the ways in which misogyny, sexism, and rigidity are ruining the joyous experience of athleticism for everyone."

—GABE DUNN, coauthor of *I Hate Everyone But You*

"Blending deeply personal experience with accessible political context and history, *Let Us Play* is a generous and necessary resource for navigating some of our most urgent sociopolitical issues."

—CHASE JOYNT, author of *Vantage Points*

"Harrison Browne is not only an incredible athlete but a leading figure in raising awareness and battling transphobia. His story of perseverance and the courage to be oneself will inspire anyone who reads it."

—ERIC RADFORD, Olympic gold medalist, figure skating

"Finally, a thoughtful deep dive into the intersection of sports and trans experiences! Tackling one of the most contentious and critical issues in sports today—the human right for gender diverse athletes to compete—Browne and Browne expose the moral-panic machine and challenge readers to envision a future in which all athletes are free to play without prejudice. *Let Us Play* is not just a call to action—it's a vital road map for equality in sports and beyond."

—AMOS MAC, coeditor of *Original Plumbing:*
The Best of Ten Years of Trans Male Culture

"Get your head out of your phone and stop doomscrolling. Read *Let Us Play* instead."

—JAY ONRAIT, sports anchor

"I've always believed that the best way to combat ignorance and bigotry is through education, and Harrison Browne and Rachel Browne do just that in *Let Us Play*. While fear-driven narratives have clouded discussions about trans and nonbinary athletes, this book demystifies the debate by confronting the misinformation that fuels the opposition, while providing actual facts to inform your thinking. This book is an invaluable resource for anyone interested in the future of sports, gender equality, and the ongoing fight for inclusivity."

—COLIN MOCHRIE, actor and comedian

LET US
PLAY

QUEER ACTION/QUEER IDEAS

A unique series addressing pivotal issues
within the LGBTQ movement

BOOKS IN THE QUEER ACTION SERIES

*Come Out and Win: Organizing Yourself,
Your Community, and Your World*, by Sue Hyde

*Family Pride: What LGBT Families Should Know
About Navigating Home, School, and Safety in
Their Neighborhoods*, by Michael Shelton

*Out Law: What LGBT Youth Should Know About
Their Legal Rights*, by Lisa Keen

BOOKS IN THE QUEER IDEAS SERIES

*At the Broken Places: A Mother and Trans Son Pick Up
the Pieces*, by Mary Collins and Donald Collins

*Beyond (Straight and Gay) Marriage: Valuing All
Families Under the Law*, by Nancy D. Polikoff

The Economic Case for LGBT Equality, by M. V. Lee Badgett

*From the Closet to the Courtroom: Five LGBT Rights Lawsuits
That Have Changed Our Nation*, by Carlos A. Ball

*Gaga Feminism: Sex, Gender, and the
End of Normal*, by J. Jack Halberstam

God vs. Gay?: The Religious Case for Equality, by Jay Michaelson

*Love's Promises: How Formal and Informal Contracts Shape
All Kinds of Families*, by Martha M. Ertman

The Queering of Corporate America, by Carlos A. Ball

*Queer (In)Justice: The Criminalization of LGBT
People in the United States*, by Joey L. Mogul,
Andrea J. Ritchie, and Kay Whitlock

*Reclaiming Two-Spirits: Sexuality, Spiritual Renewal &
Sovereignty in Native America*, by Gregory D. Smithers

LET US PLAY

WINNING THE BATTLE
FOR GENDER
DIVERSE ATHLETES

HARRISON BROWNE
& RACHEL BROWNE

QUEER ACTION/QUEER IDEAS
A SERIES EDITED BY MICHAEL BRONSKI

BEACON PRESS, BOSTON

BEACON PRESS
Boston, Massachusetts
www.beacon.org

Beacon Press books
are published under the auspices of
the Unitarian Universalist Association of Congregations.

28 27 26 25   8 7 6 5 4 3 2 1

This book is printed on acid-free paper that meets the uncoated paper
ANSI/NISO specifications for permanence as revised in 1992.

Text design and composition by Kim Arney

*Library of Congress Cataloguing-in-Publication
Data is available for this title.*
Hardcover ISBN: 978-0-8070-4534-3
E-book ISBN: 978-0-8070-4535-0
Audiobook: 978-0-8070-2078-4

The authorized representative in the EU for product safety and
compliance is Easy Access System Europe 16879218, Mustamäe tee 50,
10621 Tallinn, Estonia: http://beacon.org/eu-contact

Dedicated to Tommy, Libby, Sunny,
and any trans kid who feels alone.
You are loved.

CONTENTS

Introduction: She Shoots, He Scores   ix
A List of Terms   xxi

CHAPTER 1   The Moral Panic Machine   1

CHAPTER 2   A Brief History of Gender Diverse Athletes   17

CHAPTER 3   Fairness Fallacy   33

CHAPTER 4   The Hormones Question   45

CHAPTER 5   Panic at the Olympics   63

CHAPTER 6   The Myth of Saving Women's Sports   79

CHAPTER 7   School Battleground   103

CHAPTER 8   Voices from Inside the Locker Room   119

CHAPTER 9   The Trials and Tribulations of the
NCAA and College Sports   133

CHAPTER 10   The Future Is Trans   147

Appendix   161
Acknowledgments   165
About the Series   167
Notes   169
Index   195

SHE SHOOTS, HE SCORES

"You ready?" the doctor asked as he took a seat across from me in his office, syringe poised. "Yep," I replied tentatively. "Okay. One, two, three." He jabbed my outer right thigh an inch and a half deep into my muscles. It all felt so sudden. Even though I'd spent a long time mentally preparing for this, I'd never had a shot in my leg before. Almost immediately, it felt achy. Then my ears started ringing. It was a vivid point of no return. I watched as the doctor pushed the thick liquid into my body—testosterone. As soon as that first drop of testosterone hit my bloodstream, I said goodbye to my life as a professional hockey player and my identity as an elite athlete. It hurt.

As a kid, I always played women's sports. I really didn't think too much about how men and women are divided in athletics. I played on the women's and girls' side without question. As someone who was born a girl and lived my childhood as one, I didn't know there were any other options. I was celebrated as a woman athlete, and the more I accomplished, the deeper it became interwoven with my own identity, how people viewed me, and ultimately, my place in the world. Hockey was also my happy place, and it was where I learned to push myself and thrive alongside other people in a team environment. It was home. In less than a decade, I had gone from putting on my very first pair of hockey skates (and falling flat on my face) to being selected to represent my country on Team Canada in the 2011 Under-18 Women's World Championship in Stockholm, Sweden.

To understand the crossroads I was at before I took testosterone in 2018 after my professional hockey career, we must go back to my days as a college athlete. At the time that I entered college, in 2011, professional women's hockey players were getting paid nothing; they were all essentially volunteers. The pinnacle of achievement in women's hockey at that time was either playing for the national team and representing your country in international competitions or getting a coveted full-ride scholarship at an American college. I had achieved both and knew I was locked into women's hockey for at least four years while I completed my college studies. I had worked my entire life for this, so the thought of jeopardizing it to undergo gender-affirming surgery or take hormones wasn't remotely fathomable. While I was playing hockey for the University of Maine Black Bears, I wasn't aware of any trans college athletes or any policy for trans inclusion that existed. But, in any case, I wasn't looking for such answers, as I had decided to remain closeted—to the general public, at least. It turns out there was indeed an NCAA policy that was in place at the time that had been implemented in 2011, just before I enrolled.[1] That policy, considered "groundbreaking," was created after a basketball player on the women's team at George Washington University named Kye Allums came out as a trans man, becoming the first trans NCAA Division I athlete.[2] "I decided to do it because I was uncomfortable not being able to be myself," Allums told reporters. I didn't know about Allums's story until after I had come out, but I wish I knew about it sooner. Maybe I wouldn't have felt so isolated in my own struggles. Allums and I share so many similarities: he identified as gay in high school and realized he was trans shortly after starting college. We were both stressed about coming out as trans to our family members and friends. He too was worried that doing so would jeopardize his college scholarship. He also delayed hormones so that he could continue playing on his team.

The 2011 NCAA policy allowed transgender student-athletes to participate as long as their use of hormone therapy remained consistent with the association's policies and medical standards. The policy also stated that a trans man (assigned female at birth, or AFAB) student-athlete who received a medical exception for treatment with testosterone may compete on a men's team but is no longer eligible to compete on a women's team without changing the team status to a mixed team. A mixed team—made up of both men and women—is eligible only for men's championships. And a trans woman (assigned male at birth) student-athlete who is undergoing testosterone suppression may continue to compete on a men's team but may not compete on a women's team without changing the team to a mixed team status. That requirement remains in place until they have completed one calendar year of documented treatment. All of this seemed so complicated to me, especially as I was navigating intense hockey schedules and my studies for my business degree at the same time. In the grand scheme of life, four years—just four playing seasons—isn't a lot of time to make the most out of this small window in my sports career. I couldn't get distracted by anything, not even myself.

College was also a time for me to figure out who I was free from the watchful gaze of my parents and the microscope of my small, conservative hometown. I was living on my own for the first time and surrounded myself with like-minded people, and I gained confidence to express myself in a more masculine way—it was liberating. My college teammates became my second family, and I soon trusted them with my biggest secret. In my second year, I came out to my team and coaches as a transgender man and had my first taste of living my life as Harrison within my hockey locker room. I still wasn't sure that I could compete on the women's side as a trans man, so beyond coming out to those people, I didn't come out publicly out of fear that I could lose my scholarship and not be allowed to play anymore. I thus lived a double life for my entire college career—being Harrison in one aspect and someone I wasn't in every other way. It was agonizing and disorienting. For trans men and AFAB nonbinary elite college athletes, often their only option is to transition socially (when a trans person changes aspects about themselves, separate from medical treatments, to align with their gender identity), as they are beholden to strict policies. Those considering a medical transition with hormones will most likely take testosterone, a banned substance for athletes who play on women's teams, as it's seen as providing an unfair competitive advantage. (Later, I'll explain why this reasoning isn't necessarily correct).

It was at the end of my sophomore year that I knew I had to do something with regard to my gender dysphoria and my desire to live openly as a trans man. But as I've said, hormones were absolutely out of the question. I didn't know that, beyond letting my teammates know my secret, there were other officially sanctioned ways for me to be Harrison, a man, in my league. That wouldn't be revealed until the school's compliance officer called me into her office one day in late spring, after our season had ended in a disappointing way. (My team had been eliminated from the playoffs after the first round—it still stings to think about the breakaway I missed in overtime against Boston

College, the top-seeded team in the Hockey East conference. It would have been the upset of the century, and even my best friend still nags me about it to this day.)

I wasn't sure why the compliance officer had called me in. We started chatting and she mentioned that one of my teammates—who remained anonymous—had told her that I was transgender. My anonymous teammate wasn't being intentionally malicious, as far as I could tell, but I was stunned and a bit confused as to why I had been outed without my consent. The compliance officer, however, was completely nonchalant about me being trans and wanted to support me in my social transition while reminding me about the NCAA's testosterone policy; I assured her I wasn't planning on taking the hormone. She also said I could have my own locker room if I wanted and change my name and pronouns on the roster. I decided not to take her up on either of these options. I wanted to get ready for games and practices alongside my teammates; the locker room is a place of joy and camaraderie. It didn't feel like a "women's room" to me—it's simply where I felt most comfortable. As for publicly changing my name and pronouns, I just wasn't ready yet. I was too scared of how I might be perceived by those outside my little hockey bubble and how my parents would react, as I still wasn't out even to them at this point.

Looking back, I realize how important it is for trans and nonbinary student-athletes to have those options, whether or not they take them. These choices provide a baseline of institutional acceptance and acknowledgment for gender-diverse athletes at all levels, something that is becoming even more important amid the anti-trans backlash that is only getting worse these days. The process of transitioning socially is something that's often left out of the conversations about trans and nonbinary people in general and for athletes specifically. The focus is usually on the physical and medical aspects of transitioning. At the beginning of my journey in the public eye after I came out publicly, my body was all journalists really focused on. I was asked numerous times about surgeries and other very intimate things—it was jarring and violating. They likely would have never asked cisgender athletes such personal and specific questions. For many trans folks who don't undergo surgery or take hormones, it can be isolating and leave them feeling like they aren't valid members of the community. In recent years, I've been having conversations about this with Athlete Ally, a group based in New York that supports LGBTQ+ athletes who compete in sports at all levels, from recreational to elite. Anna Baeth, Athlete Ally's director of research, told me, "It is exceedingly uncommon that college athletes are going to undergo hormone replacement therapy, any sorts of surgeries, while they're in school." And there's a big void right now in college-level sports both in terms of the policies and overall awareness by coaches and administrators, and in terms of supporting athletes who seek to transition at least socially.

Filling this void will make things more comfortable and inclusive for all athletes and help people understand that there's more than one way to be trans. The only examples of transgender people I was aware of before I came out were folks who had transitioned physically and medically. I didn't fit into that category yet. I didn't think I would be accepted as a man in society, let alone in men's athletics, as someone who didn't necessarily look or sound like one. Had I been able to see more out trans people that had only socially transitioned, it would have empowered me to come out sooner and live my truth at an earlier age. But more importantly, it would've given me the knowledge that I can absolutely be myself while still playing my sport. I thought it had to be one or the other, but it can and should always be both.

By the time I was playing Division I hockey for the University of Maine in the NCAA, I was grappling with my gender identity and what being a transgender man meant for my future in the sports world. I was a woman athlete, I was on the women's college hockey team and, in every space, from classrooms to parties, that was my identity. I wanted to be seen as just an athlete, without the "woman" in front of it, but that could never be. When I was around my teammates, we did everything together from eating meals to attending classes, and every time I was surrounded by them, by default I was assumed to be "one of the girls" or "ladies." Everything from my scholarship to my friendships hung in the balance as I worked through the realization that I actually wasn't like the rest of my team; I was a man and I was transgender.

I knew hormone therapy—in my case, testosterone—is what I wanted and ultimately needed in order for society to view me as a man. It's important to note that this is my personal journey and my own unique vision for my future. Not all trans people follow this path or feel the need to "pass" as cisgender to others, and that is completely valid. Not every trans person undergoes a medical transition. But for me, it was vital to be seen and accepted as a man. That meant changing my physicality through testosterone: my voice would drop because my vocal cords would thicken; my Adam's apple would grow; I'd grow facial and body hair in new places; my face shape, hairline, and muscles would change. I was warned that hormones would make my skin break out like crazy, but I accepted and even welcomed that, knowing it would be my rite of passage as someone going through testosterone-driven puberty. I was looking forward to the day I could wake up and look in the mirror and see *me*, the me I'd been suppressing for a decade to stay in women's hockey. But I had no idea how to even begin accessing hormones.

I had seen some trans men on YouTube who shared their experiences and medical journeys in the US, but I didn't know any trans people personally. The whole process seemed so intimidating and out of reach. I felt alone and anxious. Transgender healthcare wasn't something I learned about in school, talked about with my friends, or even encountered in the media. There were very few online resources available that applied to Ontario, my home province in Canada, and I didn't know how my doctor would react to being asked about testosterone or even to the fact that I was transgender. I'm from a relatively conservative city and family where issues regarding LGBTQ+ people never really came up and, if they did, they were mostly frowned upon. The only thing that gave me real confidence to proceed with medically transitioning was the support I had from my hockey teammates at college, the Black Bears, to whom I had recently come out as trans.

Women's hockey, for the most part, is an extremely LGBTQ+ friendly sport globally, much more so than the men's side. Most of the teams I played on over the years had many lesbian and bisexual women on them. Since women's hockey is filled with queer people—and, well, women—it's a sport with individuals who have dealt with being discriminated against based on who they are as a person. As I walked into my locker room one day in my junior year, I was getting mentally prepared for a special team meeting before one of our practices. I don't remember who exactly planned the meeting, but I think it was one of my teammates. This was my moment to come out to my entire team as trans for the very first time. To finally be my true self in hockey among my teammates. I wasn't even nervous. Most of my fellow players were queer, so I knew they would understand me on some level, even though I would be the only openly trans member of the team. Acceptance isn't a new concept to them. "I'm still the same Brownie," I said, referring to my hockey nickname. "But can you use he/him pronouns for me?" Even though most of my teammates didn't understand intimately what being transgender was, they could understand other elements of what I went through. Although I wasn't exactly sure how my teammates would react to now having a man among them, I knew deep down that they would accept and support me. At the end of the day, we were a team. Their reaction to my coming out was pretty anti-climactic, to be honest, and we just continued getting ready for our practice as always. At the moment we hit the ice, not that much had changed. Sure, some of them poked fun at me later when I started letting my underarm hair grow freely, but I put them in their place!

Being Harrison, a man, in my hockey locker room and on the ice allowed me to really figure out who I was and how I wanted to be perceived. A huge weight had been lifted off my shoulders, and I felt free to express myself in ways that I never had the courage to before, such as cutting my hair short for the first time and wearing men's clothing and sports bras to flatten my chest—all things that count as socially transitioning. This can include someone changing their name, their pronouns, their hairstyle, clothing, and so on. Although socially transitioning alleviated some of my gender dysphoria and anxiety, I was still keeping part of myself hidden.

By 2016, when I was playing professionally in Buffalo, New York, with the Buffalo Beauts of the NWHL, I didn't want to hide anymore and decided to come out publicly as a trans man through an ESPN article that went viral and began an intense cycle of international news coverage. This media firestorm was stressful, but it prompted the hockey world to develop a type of cheat sheet for how to refer to me: my new first name, Harrison, was now on the roster, and there was widespread knowledge that I used he/him pronouns. The same couldn't be said of the non-sports world. I always had to stop and correct people who referred to me by my old name or she/her pronouns, many of whom were confused or dismissive. Being constantly misgendered and bound by an assigned-female legal name is what prompted me to retire from women's hockey sooner than I would have if I wasn't trans. Shortly after I announced my retirement through the *New York Times*, I finally mustered up the courage to call my doctor's office to talk about hormone therapy and explore taking the substance that would officially ban me from women's hockey and alter the course of my life.[3]

My family doctor is the same one who delivered me at birth in 1993 and ceremoniously announced, "It's a girl!" before handing me over to my parents. So, naturally, when the receptionist asked what the appointment was for, I froze. After a deep breath I sputtered, "I'm trans and I want to go on testosterone!" To my relief, the receptionist had no reaction and booked me without further question. Luckily, there was a new physician at the office who just happened to specialize in transgender healthcare and was filling in for my regular doctor, who was on leave. Most doctors aren't well versed in transgender health issues, let alone have experience working with actual trans patients. I felt incredibly fortunate to be cared for by someone who understood my specific needs, and that I didn't have to go on a wild goose chase for hormone therapy.

There were still several hurdles to go through, however. First, I had to speak with the doctor about my medical and gender history and get a formal diagnosis of gender dysphoria, a term that describes the sense of unease a person might have because of a mismatch between their sex assigned at birth and their gender identity. That diagnosis was more of a formality since I'd already been living openly as a man for four years. Next, I had to undergo multiple blood tests to assess my existing hormone levels. I was checking off the boxes quickly. Finally, I got my hormone prescription at the pharmacy and took it back to the doctor, who administered it the first few times until I learned to do the weekly injection myself. I remember thinking that my life was about to start. I had been envisioning this day from the moment I realized I was trans. At the same time, I was about to lose my identity as an athlete. I sat on the chair in my doctor's office, heart pounding and knees bouncing, as I watched him ready the injection. He plunged the needle into the small vial to draw up the golden liquid.

While it was crucial, and even lifesaving, for me to abandon women's hockey so I could finally begin to live as my true self, it was still excruciating to have to make that call. This is a reality for far too many transgender and nonbinary competitive athletes who often must sacrifice their authentic selves for their sport. In 2018, the year I made the difficult decision to stop playing hockey and pursue hormone therapy for my physical transition, the NWHL at that time did not allow trans men to take testosterone and continue to participate. Three years later, in September of 2021, the NWHL had changed its name to the (gender-neutral) Premier Hockey Federation (PHF) and updated its trans policy so that players like me were no longer prohibited from taking testosterone while they were playing. This was the first trans policy of its kind to not focus on hormones, and the first policy to mention nonbinary athletes as well. It was a pivotal moment in professional sports, not to mention a bold move at a time when transgender participation was facing increased hostility and scrutiny. This groundbreaking change came too late for me and my hockey career. If I had been allowed to take testosterone in the years that I was part of that league, I still might be playing the sport I love.

It's now been over a decade since I came out as trans to my team; more than eight years since I came out publicly; and more than six since I retired from professional women's hockey and went on testosterone. Although I no longer play in competitive leagues, hockey will always be the love of my life, and I'm dedicated to defending the inclusion of all players in all sports.

I was feeling more and more defeated by the worsening tide of anti-trans rhetoric and legislation, and wanted to find the best course of action to do something about it. My time in professional athletics had come to a close and I had entered the world of storytelling through acting and writing, so it made perfect sense for me to team up with my sister Rachel, an investigative journalist, to highlight the ongoing and crucial efforts being made for trans inclusion. Together, we have been wading into the latest frontier for trans rights to explain what's at stake and share stories from athletes and allies who are left out and maligned. The remainder of this book will not take a direct autobiographical approach as I've done here, but instead will examine gender-diverse athletes as a collective group facing a situation that is both dire and contains hints of optimism and resilience. You'll hear about inspirational world-class gender-diverse athletes including my friend Quinn, the Canadian professional soccer player and Olympic gold medalist; Laurel Hubbard, who represented New Zealand at the Olympics in weightlifting; and Andraya Yearwood, a high school track star from Connecticut, to name just a few.

Today, gender-diverse people, athletes and non-athletes alike, are facing an unprecedented threat to their very existence. This includes their right to play sports on the team of their choice. And the worsening struggles of trans athletes is occurring while their access to proper healthcare is being eroded.[4] We can't talk about these two issues as if they're separate. They are deeply connected.

It's never been more important to debunk the misinformation and misunderstanding regarding trans athletes in order to improve our society as a whole and pave a peaceful path for future athletes of all genders and sexual orientations. The sports world has become the newest battleground over the fight for true equality. What happens in sports reflects how tolerant we are as a society. Why is inclusive participation in sports so important when not everyone is an athlete? It's important because when we exclude trans people in one area of society, it sets a dangerous precedent to exclude trans people in other areas. We aren't seen as full members of society unless we have the same exact rights as everyone else, and that includes sports. We're not seen as human if we don't have access to the right bathroom. We're not seen as human if we don't have access to healthcare. We're not seen as human unless we have access to the same places as everyone else. This is about so much more than sports, and I'm about to show you why.

A NOTE ON METHODOLOGY

This book is unique in that it not only features portions that describe Harrison's personal point of view and experiences as a transgender hockey player, but is also by two authors, Harrison Browne and Rachel Browne. Our writing process has been deeply collaborative from the beginning, in a way that combines our voices and expertise. As an investigative journalist, Rachel has utilized her reporting and research skills to underpin Harrison's anecdotal and subjective takes on the topic. Through Harrison's connections in the sports world, we conducted our interviews together and endeavored to include perspectives from a range of athletes, from amateur to professional. Debates about gender diverse athletes typically lump them together into one, dimensionless category, but every transgender athlete's experience is unique, and painting as complicated and diverse a picture as possible is imperative to understanding and improving the status quo.

We wanted to take on this project, especially at this time, to tackle the misinformation that's affecting not only adult athletes and the policies to which they are beholden, but also trans and nonbinary children and youth who are experiencing the degradation of their right to play sports and have access to the same opportunities for joy and health as all other kids. Now is the time to take action before it's too late, and that includes equipping allies and communities with knowledge and specific approaches for inclusion and safety for all. We hope this book will challenge our own biases when it comes to athletes and sports, and, at the same time, dismantle prejudice toward gender diverse people in all areas of life. The first step is a simple but crucial one.

Not knowing the proper pronouns and basic terminology or failing to show empathy about using them can be the biggest barrier to reaching a consensus. If your goal is to make inroads and create pathways for empathy on this topic, it's important to get this right and to call out incorrect and harmful language. For Harrison, engaging with people who advocate the banning of trans women from sports was nearly impossible for this reason. It was like being forced to speak a different language, one that caused harm and put up walls. This happened during one of our interviews with Fair Play For Women, a leading voice in the UK for the exclusion of trans women athletes in the women's division of sports. The group has also been at the forefront of the outcry over trans women inmates being allowed to serve jail time in women's prisons. The group boasts that it consults with governing bodies in the UK and worldwide about their policies for trans athletes.[5]

When we spoke to one of the campaign managers at Fair Play For Women, what struck us was how she flipped terminology for trans women athletes. Instead of using the terms "transgender women" or "trans women," she shifted to using phrases like "male who identifies as trans."[6] As a trans man, Harrison felt dehumanized by such language because he is not a woman who identifies as a man, he *is* a man. Plus, gender is not defined by one's assigned gender at birth. This harmful rhetoric stems from a perspective that considers the rare instances of trans women attacking cis women in gender-segregated areas such as prisons and shelters as indicative that trans women pose the same threat as cisgender men. Groups like Fair Play For Women point to such instances and say these are men pretending to be women to hurt women, and that same fear-based mentality is then applied to all transgender women athletes—all trans women. While we of course welcome disagreement and genuine curiosity, what has become clear is that it's impossible to have meaningful debates when people and groups are unable to accept basic terminologies and respect someone's identity in all aspects of their life. It's disrespectful and it's denying basic humanity on all levels. These types of microaggressions make it difficult to even start the conversation, let alone begin to achieve any kind of common ground.

In addition to getting pronouns right, we want to help you understand other basic terminology that will come up throughout the book and in your own everyday conversations. Below, we have compiled a List of Terms that is nowhere near exhaustive but could be a helpful starting point. As terminology is evolving all the time, these definitions are subject to change, even from the time we've compiled them. We encourage you to stay up-to-date and consult trusted authorities for the latest understanding and usage of these concepts.

A LIST OF TERMS

AFAB/AMAB: Abbreviations for "Assigned Female at Birth" and "Assigned Male at Birth."

Ally: Someone who acts in solidarity with LGBTQ+ and marginalized people even if they do not share their same identities. For example, a heterosexual cisgender man who fights for the rights of transgender folks.

Biological sex: Commonly refers to one's genitalia or reproductive organs with which they were born that are typically categorized as either male or female.

Cisgender: Having a gender identity that matches the sex they were assigned at birth.

Gender binary: The term for the widely held, yet arbitrary, notion that there are only two classifications of gender: man or woman.

Gender diverse: Refers to people who do not identify as either exclusively men or exclusively women. Can also refer to the broader category of people whose gender identities fall outside the gender binary.

Gender identity: The innate and deeply felt sense of or identification with one's gender, which may match or may not match their assigned birth sex.

Heteronormative: Refers to the problematic assumption that the default or "correct" sexuality is heterosexuality.

Misogyny: Discrimination and/or hatred against women because they are women.

Nonbinary: Term for someone whose gender does not fall exclusively into the categories of man or woman.

Patriarchy: The systems of power and social organization that empower cisgender men over everyone else.

Queer: A catchall term for the gender identities and sexual preferences that fall outside the heteronormative gender binary.

Sexuality: One's sexual preference toward other people—i.e. straight, gay, bisexual, pansexual, asexual, and so on.

Transgender: The term for people who identify with a gender different from their sex assigned at birth. Many transgender people refer to their gender identity using the binary of woman or man, while others consider themselves to have fluid genders and thus do not fit into either of the gender binary options.

Transphobia: Fear and disdain of transgender people that manifests as hatred and discrimination.

LET US
PLAY

CHAPTER 1

THE MORAL PANIC MACHINE

In June 2023, a nine-year-old girl in Kelowna, British Columbia, showed up for her track and field meet at the Apple Bowl, the local stadium.[1] The girl's two mothers, Heidi and Kari Starr, watched proudly from the bleachers as their daughter began competing in the shot-put event. Earlier that day, she had competed in the discus event—in which participants see who can hurl a heavy disc the furthest—and came in second place, earning a blue ribbon.[2] When the girl stepped up to compete in the fourth-grade final event, right before her throw, a grandfather of another athlete started yelling at her. "Hey, this is supposed to be a girls' event, and why are you letting boys compete?" he exclaimed from the crowd. The man continued, "Get that boy off the field," and called for her disqualification from the event.

Many of the other participants and parents asked the man to stop, but he was relentless, saying he wasn't going anywhere because his granddaughter was competing. Since there were no security officials at the event, one of the girl's mothers urged the organizers to remove the man for being so disruptive and disrespectful. During the altercation, the man's wife accused Heidi of being a "genital mutilator, a groomer, and a pedophile," all terms that are being promulgated by the far right in its rhetoric against LGBTQ+ people. This includes Florida governor Ron DeSantis's then press secretary, who had tweeted a year earlier that anyone who was opposed to the state's "Don't Say Gay" bill was "probably a groomer."[3]

Heidi reiterated to the man that her daughter is actually cisgender, assigned female at birth, and uses she/her pronouns. She also happened to have a pixie haircut, which she got a few months earlier. Still, the man persisted, and demanded proof in the form of "certification" that her daughter was indeed assigned female at birth. He also pointed at another girl with short hair who was competing and said, "Well, if she is not a boy, then she is obviously trans." Heidi and Kari's daughter, who hasn't been named publicly, felt devastated because people had mistaken her for a boy in the past.[4] "But no one has taken it as far as he did," the girl later recalled. After she made two shot-put throws, she and her team moved to another field to get away from the man. "My first two throws weren't that good because I was crying and hurt because of what he said. I think I could have gotten a ribbon if this had not happened," she said.[5] Luckily, she made a better final throw, buoyed by the positivity she felt from the crowd, in spite of the man who had been harassing her and her teammate. "There were a lot of bystanders supporting me and it was making me feel more confident and safer."[6]

Staff finally intervened and the man—who happened to be a former amateur wrestler—was banned from all future events in the school district. The Royal Canadian Mounted Police, which has jurisdiction over the area, received a number of messages from other people who were concerned about the incident. "It is important to our community to speak out against discriminatory behaviors, and research shows that social support is an important protective factor for those experiencing marginalization, racism, or discrimination," RCMP Constable Mike Della-Paolera said after the incident.[7]

The man's calls for proof and his questioning of the gender of this young girl, coupled with his use of loaded terminology that comes from right-wing news outlets, is a manifestation of the tide of hateful transphobia that has extensive impacts. His behavior, and the ideologies underpinning it, also perpetuates the surveillance and assault of children's bodies, both cisgender and transgender. What this incident shows is the real-life impacts of the moral panic that is swirling around trans people and trans athletes. Further, the impacts of this moral panic are seen and felt well beyond trans people themselves. This anti-trans mania affects cisgender people, including (and especially) cisgender women and girls, as well as the family members, friends, and communities of which trans people are a part.

Kyle Frackman, a scholar who researches queer and trans history and culture, explains how incidents like these are emblematic of deeply rooted and surging fears around shifting sexual and gender norms and expectations worldwide. "When marginalized groups gain more visibility, it tends to provoke fear and anger among majority groups who often feel that they lost something when someone else gains something," Frackman told the *Vancouver Sun* after the incident.[8] "Now, cultural backlash focuses on trans people as a supposed threat to social order, like people of color and other LGBTQ people have been in the past. Cultural reactions often supposedly aim to protect children when in fact there is no threat to anything but [to] what some view as proper."[9]

There have been countless moral panics throughout history, all targeting misunderstood, marginalized, and vulnerable people in the name of safety, purity, and, of course, morality. Understanding this phenomenon and its historical antecedents is crucial to understanding and properly engaging with the current moment.

According to American and Israeli sociologists Erich Goode and Nachman Ben-Yehuda, a moral panic is "the outbreak of moral concern over a supposed threat from an agent of corruption that is out of proportion to its actual danger."[10] In the words of renowned British sociologist and criminologist Stanley Cohen, moral panics occur when a "condition, episode, person or group of persons emerges to become defined as a threat to social values and interests."[11] The targets of a moral panic are almost always symbolic, and the modus operandi driving them is the desire to preserve the traditional heteronormative family and reinforce stereotypical gender roles.

Thus, one of the criteria for a moral panic is an outsized or disproportionate response to an issue. Consider, then, this furor over trans athletes now participating in sports in the context of their low numbers, which haven't suddenly increased. Although available data is scant regarding the exact number of transgender students in high school, let alone transgender student-athletes, we can at least arrive at a rough estimate.[12] A CDC study published in 2019 estimated that 1.8 percent of high school students are transgender, meaning there are roughly 270,000 transgender students in US high schools.[13] But only 14 percent of transgender boys and 12 percent of transgender girls play sports, according to a report by the Human Rights Campaign.[14] Using these numbers, we can say it's statistically possible that there are only some thirty-five thousand transgender student-athletes in high school, which would mean a mere 0.44 percent of high school athletes are transgender.

Given the minuscule number of trans athletes, the swath of legislative efforts and hateful campaigns targeting youth and high school students is absurd. As pointed out by Erin Reed, an American journalist and advocate for transgender rights whose writings appear in her Substack newsletter

Erin in the Morning, it seems unfathomable that just a few years ago, gender diverse people could easily access puberty blockers and hormone therapy in every state with little pushback. Now that has all changed with legislative efforts blocking these basic forms of healthcare and conservative politicians calling for the elimination of transgender people explicitly or implicitly. Reed describes how these efforts are rampant and only gaining steam in the US, setting the tone and emboldening efforts by right-wing politicians and activists around the world. "This was a coordinated strategy from the right to use sports and bathrooms to usher in a new era of anti-trans oppression. It was never about sports; it was never about bathrooms: elimination was always the end goal," Reed writes.[15] Bans against trans women and girls in sports have now become one of the most successful anti-LGBTQ+ policies being pursued in the US.

Moral panics promote the idea that marginalized, and often powerless, individuals and groups pose a threat to society so large and so severe that they must be halted by any means necessary. Trans people, considered deviant, have long been the target of such efforts, but have now become a deeply entrenched obsession of the political right around the world with hundreds of anti-LGBTQ+ bills and pieces of legislations being pursued and implemented. Hugely popular and controversial podcaster Joe Rogan, for example, has told his audience of millions upon millions that transgender people are a sign of "civilizations collapsing."[16] Not climate change, not artificial intelligence, but trans people, who comprise a very small percentage of the entire population. American right-wing commentator Matt Walsh has called "gender ideology" one of the "greatest evils in human history."[17] Far-right Republican congresswoman Marjorie Taylor Greene said in 2022 that "some of the most dangerous people in America are trans-terrorist."[18] And conservative site *Daily Wire* contributor Michael Knowles told the Conservative Political Action Conference in 2023 that "for the good of society . . . transgenderism must be eradicated from public life entirely."[19]

Historically, panics and mass hysteria have ensued over many things including satanic worship, video games, Judy Blume books, and rap music. In the mid-twentieth century during the Cold War, the "Lavender Scare" saw the persecution of gay people in the US under President Dwight Eisenhower, who in 1953 signed an executive order calling for the investigation and removal of gay men and women from the federal government workforce.[20] Upward of ten thousand people who were gay, or just suspected of being gay, lost their jobs or were subjected to invasive interrogations about their personal sex lives. The belief was that queer workers were a national security threat because they were vulnerable to extortion and blackmail and falsely considered to be weaker in moral character than heterosexual people. As historian David K. Johnson points out in his 2004 book on the topic, *The Lavender Scare*, the gay backlash was partly a response to the increased visibility of queer people in public and in pop culture at that time, and it was easy to conflate them with Communists. Johnson describes this wave of repression as "a classic case of scapegoating."[21] The 1980s and 1990s saw the rise of the Satanic Panic across North America. Also known as the Satanic Ritual Abuse or "recovered memory" scandal, in which children were encouraged by law enforcement and social workers to recall instances of childhood sexual abuse at the hands of caregivers that never actually happened, psychotherapists, feminists, and educators on the left joined together with conservative Christian groups to stoke fears of an epidemic of satanic worship and sexual predation that was later shown to be wildly exaggerated.[22] It resulted in more than twelve thousand unfounded cases opened by police into parents, teachers, daycare workers, and so forth. The foundation of the Satanic Panic is believed to be rooted in the backlash to advances in women's rights, specifically the increases in women entering the workforce; homophobia against daycare workers; and "end-of-millennium" anxieties. There was a fear that women going back to work and putting their children into daycare would disrupt or dismantle the nuclear family and traditional social values. It was never really about Satan worshipers. Remnants of the Satanic Panic can still be felt today. Just look at QAnon followers and Republican Party influencers who peddle conspiracy theories about the ritualistic abuse of children by Democratic leaders and affiliates. Some of their outrageous claims include that Satan is responsible for so-called moral aberrations like abortion and LGBTQ+ people.

With respect to trans people, we see predictable panic behaviors and fearmongering around trans women using bathrooms that align with their gender identity. With what were known as the "penis panics" or "washroom wars," which we delve into in later chapters and discuss how they're rooted in the same anxiety over segregated washrooms in the 1950s and 1960s, they've always been framed as efforts to protect white cisgender girls and women. But, in reality, those efforts are about maintaining the strict sex and gender binary that serves to buttress the power and privilege held by white heterosexual cisgender men.

More recently, Drag Story Hour events, where storytellers incorporate the art of drag in reading books to children at bookstores, schools, and libraries, have also become the subject of a moral panic. Launched in 2015 in San Francisco by author and activist Michelle Tea, these events seek to promote literacy among children from ages three to eleven, as well as to promote an appreciation for diversity. Panic over Drag Story Hour, and drag performance in general, became more pronounced around 2022, in tandem with mass anti-trans backlash as clusters of counter-rallies occurred across the US, UK, Canada, Australia, and other countries. That year, there were more than 140 documented instances of harassment toward drag performances in the US alone. In May 2023, a group of neo-Nazi protesters outside a drag event in Ohio held up anti-trans flags with threatening slogans including "There will be blood."[23] Throughout 2022 and 2023, numerous states implemented or pursued legislation to ban people in drag from reading to children and performing in general.[24] The narrative pushed by these anti-trans radicals is that Drag Story Hours, led by pedophiles, are harmful to children because they corrupt their innocence and groom them into becoming queer. But what this panic boils down to is paranoia over the subversion of traditional heteronormative roles for men and the celebration of freedom to express oneself however they please.

Unless and until these types of moral panics can be quelled, policymakers and conservative leaders will more than likely continue to build their political appeal on the baseless notion that LGBTQ+ people, especially trans people, are a threat to children and families. Why would politicians care so much about this topic? It's simple: if drag queens and LGBTQ+ people are made to be villains, those going after them can present themselves as moral crusaders, as heroes worthy of praise and trust. And votes.

THE ARCHITECTURE OF A MORAL PANIC

The video opens with close-up shots of two young girl wrestlers adorned with protective headgear who are about to spar.[25] "All any athlete wants is a fair shot in competition. To play by the rules," the narrator states as the athletes stare intensely at each other. We then cut to the moments after the match has concluded. The referee holds up the arm of the girl who won as the other girl who lost looks forlorn. The spectators and coaches cheer at the winner's victory. "But what if the rules change," the narrator continues ominously. The girl who lost is then replaced with a towering cisgender man opponent, and the referee holds *his* arm up because *he* is now the winner, displacing the girl who won. She now looks upset, ostensibly because she lost the match to the man. The narrator of the video, which was a 2019 campaign attack ad against Democratic Kentucky governor nominee Andy Beshear, warns that if Beshear wins reelection, there won't be any rules at all when it comes to competitive sports. "Anyone at any time can change teams for any reason," the narrator declares. The video ends with a montage of hysterical tabloid headlines, such as "Trans Athletes Are Making a Travesty of Women's Sports" from the *New York Post*. Beshear ended up defeating the Republican incumbent in the end. But this video, released by the American Principles Project, a conservative think tank that refers to itself as the "NRA for families," heralded the new wave of anti-transgender legislative efforts in the US and elsewhere.[26] This moment picked up where the failure of anti-transgender bathroom bills left off.

Anti-trans legislation and sentiment have continued to grow ever since, in large part fueled by the American Principles Project. That group has latched onto the issue of trans athletes to further drive a wedge between liberals and conservatives. In an interview with CNN in April 2022, the group's president, Terry Schilling, outlined how the "sports issue" was only ever a means to make anti-trans policies, broadly speaking, more palatable to legislators.[27] In other words, the transgender sports debates served as an entry point to attacking the rights of all LGBTQ+ people and must be viewed as part of the larger political project of the right in US politics. "The women's sports issue was really the beginning point in helping expose all this because what it did was it got opponents of the LGBT movement comfortable with talking about transgender issues," said Schilling. (In 2020, Schilling found himself in hot water for his Tweets about LGBTQ-inclusive sex education curriculum, saying he didn't want to have to teach his children about "the sordid world of gay couples.")[28] With trans athletes, Schilling's group and others like it, which typically espouse homophobic views too, have found a surefire way to push for anti-trans policies of all types.

Schilling's approach and worldview seems to align with sentiments held by most Americans. A Gallup poll from June 2023 found that a large majority of Americans, 69 percent, believe that trans athletes should only be allowed to play on teams that match their birth gender. That number rose a startling seven percentage points from the same poll two years earlier in

2021.[29] Alex Kirshner aptly wrote in *Slate* in 2023 that, for the moment, right-wing conservatives have "a winning argument" on this issue.[30] They've managed to convince people that trans girls and women have an unfair advantage in sports competition, something that helps anti-trans activists bolster their overall argument that trans women are not "real" women, and trans men are not "real" men. This argument has also pierced through to cisgender individuals who have transgender people in their lives, a group that is usually more supportive because of their personal connections to the community. "Americans who know . . . a transgender individual have become less supportive of allowing transgender athletes to play on the team of their choice." Currently, 30 percent of those who know a transgender person favor allowing athletes to play on teams that match their current gender identity, *down* from 40 percent in 2021. While supporters and detractors of trans inclusion feel strongly about their stance on this polarizing topic, there is gray area on either side.

The idea of vulnerable women and girls and their need for protection is a frequent fixation of those seeking to curtail human rights, especially when it comes to those of marginalized communities. A common refrain is, "What about the girls?" The bathroom bills sought to protect women and girls from predatory men. But those legislative efforts were exposed as blatant discrimination against transgender people, not to mention impossible to enforce, whereas sexism in sports is baked into sports and is upheld through the segregation of teams and leagues. Men are assumed to be athletically superior to women in all cases. This is the type of argument that people, including progressives, can't seem to find consensus on. Progressives who are the first to say they support transgender people and their human rights are just as likely to call for bans against transgender women in sports. When it comes to transgender women participating in sports, the moral panic surrounding protecting women and girls at all costs prevails. This is an example of progressives finding themselves trapped inside moral panics and, perhaps unwittingly, keeping them alive for the benefit of their right-wing counterparts.

Understanding where moral panics come from and how they are structured is important to identifying and avoiding them. In the 1970s, a group of British academics authored the seminal book *Policing the Crisis: Mugging, the State and Law and Order*, about the supposed rise of a new type of crime in Britain at the time: mugging. The authors expose how the phenomenon of mugging was fueled and, in some respects, created by the very institutions that were trying to crack down on it, namely the police. In this context, as in the case of many other moral panics, Black men were singled out to allow the state and law enforcement to boast about how well they were maintaining public safety. The myth of Black male criminality led to an expansion in arrests, and law enforcement and the state presented that rise in arrests as proof of effective public safety policy. As Stanley Cohen shows throughout his scholarship, there is a symbiotic and incestuous relationship between news media and state and law enforcement officials. They need each other for relevancy and currency. The state apparatus needs the media to distribute its narrative to the public, and the media thrives off sensational and dramatic stories and rhetoric in order to garner an audience. At the root of this relationship is money and power. Cohen provides us with three key common denominators among moral panics.[31] Recognizing these three pillars is helpful to deciphering and dismantling what is happening and continues to happen in the moral panic over trans people and athletes:

1. *First*: Mass media—and by extension, social media—maintains focused attention on the behavior of people or groups of people.
2. *Second*: There is a gulf between the concern over the given situation or group of people and the real threat posed. The perceived threat usually outweighs the actual threat.
3. *Third*: Though the subject of the moral panic may become less of a focus over time, the hysteria that ensues nevertheless results in long-lasting laws that are vindictive and serve to bolster the agenda of the carceral state. The result is often an irreparable shift to society.

When it comes to moral panics about transgender people specifically, what we are seeing today is not new. But it's been among the most extreme, dangerous, far-reaching, and successful moral panic in US history, and it's showing no signs of slowing down. Trans women, in particular, face vitriol and demonization, which is linked to misogyny. Scapegoating trans people, as with the myriad other targets of moral panics, is easier than dealing with the real existential threats to society. With life expectancy plummeting in developed nations, birth rates declining, climate emergencies worsening, interest rates rising, healthcare systems collapsing, and wealth inequality becoming more pronounced by the day, it's easy to see how seductive it is to redirect people's attention elsewhere. At the same time, much of the anti-trans backlash is a response to increased trans visibility and efforts to boost and affirm trans rights. There's also been strong dissent against medical programs that provide trans and gender diverse youth access to puberty blockers.

In times of social and economic upheaval, it's almost a cliché for systems of power to blame and scapegoat visible minorities and those with less or no power. Moral panics, generally, result in regressive laws and policy changes coupled with punitive measures. Civil rights and freedoms are targeted and sometimes even demolished. "Anti-gender movements are not just reactionary but *fascist* trends, the kind that support increasingly authoritarian governments," esteemed American philosopher and sociologist Judith Butler wrote in *The Guardian* in 2021.[32] "They are typical of fascist movements that twist rationality to suit hyper-nationalist aims." In 2021, Arkansas became the first state to enact a ban on gender-affirming healthcare for minors.[33] A court judge eventually blocked it, but that didn't stop Republican legislators from reinstating it in 2023 with a proposal that would make it easier for people to file malpractice lawsuits against doctors who provide such care to minors, including hormone therapy and puberty blockers, for up to thirty years after the person turns eighteen. The statute of limitations for rape charges in Arkansas is six years (with some exceptions).[34] If Republican legislators were genuinely interested in protecting children, they'd have a longer statute of limitation for rape charges. Arkansas's anti-trans proposal is now being considered by other states. Proponents of these efforts say it's all being done in the name of protecting children. In fact, it's putting their lives and well-being at risk.

THE ROLE OF THE MEDIA IN MANUFACTURING PANICS

In terms of the media coverage of transgender people and athletes, the media has been culpable of perpetuating stigma and false narratives about LGBTQ+ people. This is especially the case for right-leaning outlets and tabloids around the world. In the early aughts, particularly in the British tabloids, trans people, especially trans women, were blamed for corrupting children, carrying out violence against cisgender women, and even threatening free speech. These stories often conflated or distorted the truth and were riddled with inaccuracies. The coverage mirrored similar stigmatizing and warped coverage of and headlines about gay men throughout the 1960s and 1970s. "Homo Nest Raided, Queen Bees Are Stinging Mad," the *New York Daily News* declared in response to the Stonewall riots in New York City in 1969.[35]

More recently, Fox News has been leading the charge against trans people (and, really, all marginalized people), dedicating countless hours and resources to anti-trans segments and articles that are misinformed, hysterical, and harmful. The news outlet has become synonymous with transphobia and is well known for its breathless coverage of trans issues. By torquing the reality of what trans people are facing and calling for, these news anchors and reporters use their platforms to make up their own narratives that fit their conservative agenda. Over the course of less than a month in 2022, Fox News broadcast nearly two hundred anti-trans segments, including one about Transgender Day of Visibility in which former host Tucker Carlson claimed that most trans children have been "led to where they are by adult predators."[36]

Scholarship is emerging about the ways social media platforms have become instruments of moral panics. Social media algorithms favor clickbait content that's likely to generate intense emotion and outrage among users. It also prioritizes and rewards virality rather than education or information in the public interest. Information and content on social media flow exponentially quicker than it does in traditional news media. It also flows within echo chambers. "By allowing users to remain cloistered within their preferred tribes and visions of reality, digital platforms encourage misrecognition and distort understanding of social issues, making the acceptance of bloated rhetoric more likely," wrote James P. Walsh, a professor in criminology and social sciences at the University of Ontario Institute of Technology, in a 2020 academic journal.[37]

Leading up to and during the state legislative sessions in the US in 2021, trans athletes became a prime vehicle through which right-wing political actors perpetuated moral panic. Anna Baeth, research director at Athlete Ally, and Anna Goorevich, a University of Minnesota researcher, delve into this in their chapter in the 2022 academic book *Justice for Trans Athletes*. They examined more than 1,200 news articles about trans athletes to reveal how they became subjects of the moral panic trap. The authors also cite Cohen's definition of a moral panic, which occurs when a group of people are deemed "a threat to societal values and interests; [the moral panic's] nature is presented in a . . . stereotypical fashion by the mass media; the moral barricades are manned by . . . right-thinking people. . . . Sometimes the object of the panic is quite novel and at other times, it is something which has been in existence long enough, but suddenly appears in the limelight."[38] The authors conclude that "conservative politicians are leveraging trans athletes to frame themselves as protectors of a higher moral agenda, despite the politicians' legacy of apathy towards women and trans people in sport." Further, they contend that this moral panic, like ones of the past, will not result in the protection of cisgender women; rather, it will replicate and bolster the prevailing systems of power that have hindered the potential for gender equity in sports.

The rampant anti-trans coverage in right-wing outlets and tabloids has sadly permeated mainstream and typically progressive news institutions as well. There have been many disappointing instances where these esteemed outlets have fallen prey to the anti-trans agenda. In doing so, these outlets, along with their right-wing counterparts, continue to stoke the moral panic so that politicians, especially conservatives, may be viewed as moral saviors defending women's sports and therefore worthy of their position of power and reelection. TransLash Media, a Black, trans-led nonprofit news organization, recently studied more than ten thousand words of front-page coverage on transgender issues in the *New York Times*.[39] Story headlines include "They Paused Puberty, but Is There a Cost?" and "Report Reveals Sharp Rise in Transgender Young People in the U.S." The group found that these and other front-page stories were "trans-skeptical" and helped spread disinformation about young trans people. Instead of approaching trans people and their stories as a human rights issue, news outlets including the *Times* are increasingly treating the issue as debatable and infusing their coverage with pseudoscience.

GLAAD, an LGBTQ+ advocacy group, slammed the *New York Times* in April 2023 for what it described as inaccurate and harmful coverage of the trans community.[40] It went even further to claim that the paper's coverage has been weaponized against trans people. "Prominent front-page coverage has frequently missed the big picture of the trans community, choosing instead to hyper-scrutinize essential and mainstream medical care, undermining its support among readers who know next to nothing about this care, while laundering extremist talking points as legitimate concern," GLAAD stated in an extensive press release by trans writer and journalist Serena Sonoma.[41] "*The Times*' reporting is being weaponized against the trans community and is therefore actively contributing to an ongoing climate of discrimination and violence." Sonoma laid out how the Missouri attorney general, Andrew Bailey, cited a *Times* piece titled "The Battle over Gender Therapy" to justify an "emergency" state ban on gender-affirming care for all trans people—from children to adults.[42]

Although it often feels like media coverage goes two steps forward and one step back when it comes to trans issues, in recent years there is now more scrutiny of problematic stories, and it seems that the general public is becoming increasingly aware of misleading coverage. There's been a great effort among some journalists and broadcasters to inform the public and to look at peer-reviewed evidence amid inflammatory statements coming from state leaders and other public figures. More recently, a great deal of valuable and in-depth investigative and explanatory journalism has helped fight harmful policies and debunk and demystify misinformation and disinformation, such as the reporting of ESPN's Katie Barnes, *Vox*'s Aja Romano, and freelance reporter Katelyn Burns, to name just a few journalists.

Social media has also served as a direct and prominent outlet for trans individuals (both athletes and non-athletes), scientists, family members, and allies who wish to dispel harmful tropes. One of the most-respected voices in this space is former Division I NCAA swimmer Schuyler Bailar, a Harvard student who was the first trans man to compete on an NCAA men's team. With a combined following of over six hundred thousand on his Instagram and TikTok accounts, he uses his platform to myth-bust problematic articles and advocate for the LGBTQ+ community.[43] A huge portion of the content he publishes is devoted to fact-checking bigotry and misinformation in real time. However, amid the deepening cultural divide, it's sometimes easy for progressives to remain ensconced in their echo chambers, speaking only to each other and failing to break down the seemingly impenetrable wall between them and the anti-trans naysayers.

When discrimination against people is allowed in one area of life, it opens the door for it to happen everywhere. We're seeing it now as anti-trans paranoia has already begun to seep beyond the realms of sports and medicine and into, of all places, school theater. In the fall of 2023, a school district in the conservative town of Sherman, Texas, an hour north of Dallas, made international headlines after its high school production of the musical *Oklahoma!* was halted after a trans student was cast in a leading role that didn't align with their assigned gender at birth.[44] School administrators let parents know that the school would only cast students in roles that aligned with their assigned gender at birth. Not only did several trans and nonbinary students lose their parts in the play, but cisgender girls cast in roles for boys and men also lost the parts for which they'd been cast. The situation escalated further when a teacher who opposed the administration's decision was escorted out of the school by the principal. It was a rare case of schools clamping down on gender roles in theater, but within a few days, the administration reversed course, restoring all the cast members back to their original roles. Still, it likely caused some trauma and damage among the student body. Although the reversal was seen as a victory for the gender diverse students and LGBTQ+ advocates who fought for it, the whole debacle revealed the broader impacts of transphobic discourse and panic within sports.

And beyond school theater, the panic around trans participation has also spilled into other activities around the world. For one, the International Chess Organization (Fédération Internationale des Échecs, or FIDE), the Swiss-based governing body for the board game, announced in the fall of 2023 new playing restrictions for both trans men and trans women.[45] The federation said it would bar trans women from participating in women's chess altogether until "further analysis" could be conducted, something that could take up to two years.[46] Chess, which requires no physical acumen whatsoever except finger movements, is banning trans people from playing on the chess teams that align with their gender identity. The organization is essentially shouting from the rooftops that it believes men are smarter than women, and codifying that belief. And it gets worse. Players who previously won in women's categories and later medically transitioned to affirm their gender identity as men would also be stripped of those titles, per the rules. Trans women, similarly, would also be stripped of their previously won titles. No, this isn't from an article in *The Onion*, this is real life. "The new regulations will make trans chess players all over the world face a horrible dilemma: transition or quit chess," professional French chess player Yosha Iglesias wrote on X, formerly known as Twitter.[47] Iglesias has also said that neither she, the only openly trans player ranked as a master by FIDE at the time, nor any other trans player she was aware of had been consulted on the matter. Granted, there is already an open category in competitive chess where men and women, trans or cisgender, can play together, but the new policy sparked a discussion over why chess is segregated at all. There appears to be no consensus on this matter in the way that there is a larger consensus with respect to physical sports, but some have speculated that it's because of the large discrepancy between the number of men players and women players, with only 14.6 percent of chess players in the US being women as of 2020.[48] According to the chess news site ChessBase, the women's category in chess exists to encourage increased participation among women, not because women inherently perform at a lower level in the game.[49] Thus, the typical arguments against transgender women competing don't hold water, as it's implausible to claim that transgender women have an unfair advantage. It appears that the trans moral panic has been co-opted by chess organizers.

In other activities where perceived advantages between men and women are not an issue, the list of trans bans and restrictions is growing. In November 2023, trans women were banned from the England Ladies angling team—fishing—after three members of the team resigned for refusing to compete alongside a trans woman teammate (they remain banned as of this writing).[50] Concerns have also been raised as to whether trans women have an advantage in darts competitions. The troubling thing about these types of bans and controversies—which can't hide behind science and biology—is that they signal the true motivations behind excluding trans athletes: transphobia, bigotry, and fear of the unknown.

FURTHER IMPACTS FOR FAMILIES AND BEYOND

The moral panic around transgender and nonbinary children has concrete and irreversible impacts not only for trans people themselves, but also for their families and communities. In states such as Texas and Alabama, where being trans or a caregiver to trans children is borderline criminalized, families are fleeing their homes to live in places where they won't face the potential wrath of the state or where they will be able to access gender-affirming care without fear. Moral panics also tacitly and explicitly encourage bullying and exclusion of transgender children, while also fueling unhinged conspiracy theories that lead to real-life violence.

In 2022, false posts claiming that Boston Children's Hospital performed genital surgeries on minor children went viral on TikTok and other social media platforms.[51] These false claims were picked up and promoted by a slew of right-wing media outlets and figures, including blogger Matt Walsh, mentioned earlier, who claimed "gender ideology" was the greatest threat to humanity.[52] The panic and fury over these false claims fueled targeted harassment of the doctors and child patients at the hospital and led to one woman being charged with threatening to bomb the hospital. And it wasn't just the Boston hospital that was targeted; the posts spurred similar threats toward other children's hospitals across the US. "What starts with a post or a tweet quickly spirals into bomb threats, harassing phone calls, death threats and more, and the pace of it has been relentless," said Human Rights Campaign senior VP Jay Brown in a statement.[53] "This is having a chilling effect on lifesaving and evidence-based care that improves mental health outcomes and leads to a better quality of life for those who receive it."

The politicians and special interest groups fueling the backlash to trans rights and trans inclusion seem to find it easier to focus on portraying LGBTQ+ people as villains than it is to deal with actual forms of abuse and inequality. "Demonizing a minority has never really protected anyone's safety, though it has often helped boost the power of political opportunists," wrote Toronto-based sex educator Kai Cheng Thom in a column for the *Globe and Mail* in 2023. "Instead of fighting one another for scraps, we need to acknowledge that the real monster isn't trans people—it's our inability to address the root causes of our societal ills."[54] When moral panics occur, the true victims are those who have been targeted, in this case trans and nonbinary people and athletes. And yet, there are a few notable people whose resilience shows us that, even when the whole world seems to be against them, it's possible for gender diverse athletes to succeed and even change these environments for the better.

CHAPTER 2

A BRIEF HISTORY OF GENDER DIVERSE ATHLETES

Since the turn of the twentieth century, sports have come to be seen as a tool for fashioning and promoting heteronormative attributes associated with cisgender men that were perceived to be under threat. In the view of many Americans, organized sport was also turning young men away from becoming weak, soft, or gay—a paranoia that remained pervasive until at least the 1990s. Later, as pro sports led to lucrative corporate sponsorships and endorsements, queer elite and professional athletes had to remain in the closet and were under immense pressure to uphold the traditional roles of men and women and the gender binary of masculinity and femininity. As queer people fought and still fight today for their right to play sports while being their authentic selves, trans people are in their own unique battle for their lives and their place in sports.

Organized sports served to preserve the gender binary based on not only who was *included*, but also who was *excluded*. Women were forbidden from participating in sports or physical activities deemed excessive, lest they become more masculine and therefore unattractive to men. In a 1938 article in *Maclean's* magazine, the writer described one sprinter, believed to be the American Olympian Helen Stephens, as a "big, lanky, flat-chested muscular girl with as much sex appeal as grandmother's old sewing machine."[1] This type of sentiment strove to maintain the existing social order of the time, which was achieved when women embraced hyperfemininity and kept to the domestic realm in service of men. As the twentieth century continued, women pushed the boundaries for inclusion, a prominent example of which was the implementation of Title IX, the 1972 landmark gender-equity legislation that banned sex discrimination in federally funded education programs in the US.[2] Still, it has been a slow-moving journey toward equality, and women are still not even able to play all sports, let alone be treated equally in them. Consider that the first women's Olympic marathon did not take place until 1984;[3] the women's triple jump, not until 1996;[4] and both the pole vault[5] and the 20 kilometers race walk, not until 2000.[6] Women never had their own race-walking event, though in the 2024 Summer Olympics, the first-ever mixed team relay took place, replacing the men's individual event.[7]

And while women continued to push for inclusion throughout the twentieth century, they were also affected by the homophobia that's deeply baked into sports institutions. Many women who participated in or excelled at sports were deemed to be gay, whether or not they actually were. And the label brought with it intense stigma and discrimination. As authors Eric Anderson, Rory Magrath, and Rachael Bullingham point out in their book *Out in Sport*, the treatment of professional tennis players Martina Navratilova and Billie Jean King serves as a reminder of how hostile sport and media could be toward gay women.[8] After they came out in 1981, each player's income took major hits owing to rampant homophobia, as major sponsors wanted nothing to do with gay athletes. In particular, the public ordeal of Navratilova coming out was so negative that rather than inspiring others to come out, it likely ensured more elite athletes remained closeted, according to research.[9] By the 1990s and early 2000s, gay women and gay men were generally accepted under certain conditions and in certain places around the world, though the gender binary and pressures to uphold stereotypical forms of masculinity and femininity remained intact. By the new millennium, sport had also conditionally accepted gay men as long as they either participated in feminized sports (like ice dancing) or remained silent in masculinized sports (like ice hockey) through the unwritten policy of "Don't Ask, Don't Tell."

As more and more prominent athletes began to come out as gay, such as the NFL's Michael Sam and US women's national soccer team captain Abby Wambach, they helped promote inclusivity within not only their sport but sports overall, and, slowly, broader society and culture. But men's sports, both historically and presently, remain generally less open and accepting of LGBTQ+ people compared to women's sports. The reason why is rooted in the very nature of the creation of women's sports and the mere existence of women athletes. Organized sports were never meant for women, meaning that women athletes always had to defy expectations and buck against what society deemed as acceptable. Men's leagues, on the other hand, have remained much more fixed and intertwined with their hypermasculine, heteronormative origins. As we left the twentieth century and entered the twenty-first century, implicit and explicit homophobia remained ingrained in the world of men's professional sports, with it often dubbed "the last closet" for its lack of LGBTQ+ representation.[10] There were very few or zero openly gay athletes in the top five professional men's sport leagues: baseball, soccer, basketball, football, and ice hockey.

As queer players continue to fight for respect and equality, transgender athletes at all levels represent the next frontier in the broadening of inclusion and acceptance within sports and beyond. The presence and struggles of trans athletes have also helped further lay the groundwork to question gender segregation and traditional heteronormative roles across all sports. Understanding the experiences of trans athletes, from team sports to individual sports, and what they face and continue to face today is crucial in dismantling our biases and envisioning a better way forward for the sports world. There are many athletes to help illustrate the inflection points along the way, but in this chapter we have chosen five whose stories add unique dimensions to this issue and set the stage for future discussions about fairness in sports, hormones, and media coverage of these issues. Learning about their struggles and successes may, we hope, foster much-needed empathy.

RENÉE RICHARDS: THE VIEW FROM MEN'S AND WOMEN'S TENNIS

American tennis player Renée Richards was the first openly transgender athlete of record, for which she attracted national attention to trans athletes and laid the groundwork for their inclusion.[11] For the first forty years of her life, Richards lived as a man and an ophthalmologist with a wife and kids, something she details in her two autobiographies, *Second Serve* and *No Way Renée*.[12] Richards also played competitive tennis, ranking 6th out of the top 20 players over thirty-five years old on the men's side. After physically transitioning and changing her name to Renée, the French word for "reborn," she moved from New York to California, where she tried to lead a private life in her new identity. This desire for privacy was thwarted when she was "outed" publicly by local journalist Richard Carlson (father of former Fox News anchor Tucker Carlson) during a tennis tournament in 1976, capturing national headlines. Richards was catapulted into overnight fame and notoriety. "And what had I done to merit this interest?" asks Richards in *No Way Renée*. "Simply put, I had undergone a male-to-female sex-change operation and then had the temerity to play in an amateur women's tennis tournament."[13]

Her story became an international sensation, and she began receiving letters from people around the world encouraging her to continue playing just as she was. Richards went back and forth deciding whether to keep playing competitively, until she came across remarks from sports commentators and journalists who said that she would never make it or be able to play in the US Open as a woman; nor could she join the Women's Tennis Association, the main organizing body for women's professional tennis. Even though Richards had no plans to do either of these things, being told that she *couldn't* lit that competitive fire within her and made her want to prove everyone wrong. "I made that decision to fight for my right to do it, mostly because I'd been told that I wouldn't have been allowed to do it," Richards told NPR years later.[14]

After Richards was outed, three major tennis federations proceeded to impose requirements forcing all women participants to verify their sex through chromosomal testing, something that Richards refused to do when she applied to play in the US Open on the women's side in 1976. She sued the United States Tennis Association, which oversees the US Open, saying she was being discriminated against. The USTA, for its part, stated she needed to be barred because she had an athletic advantage over cisgender women. Richards reluctantly took the chromosome test, and the results were ambiguous. In the meantime, her court battle against the USTA ended up before the New York State Supreme Court, which ultimately sided with her in 1977. "This person is now female," stated the judge, who added that the chromosomal testing requirement was "grossly unfair, discriminatory and inequitable."[15] The ruling allowed Richards to play in the US Open, where she ended up losing to Virginia Wade—throwing some cold water on the notion that she would automatically beat any cisgender woman—but made it to the doubles finals.

Richards went on to play doubles with tennis legend and gay rights icon Billie Jean King and, after Richards retired, went on to coach tennis champ Martina Navratilova, mentioned earlier, to two Wimbledon titles. However, Richards did not go on to lead the battle for trans athletes, nor even trans rights writ large. She has rebuffed the aims of the trans movement, believing firmly that gender is binary, and is uncomfortable with her status as a trans pioneer. Further, she has said she believes that going through a testosterone-driven puberty provided her with inherent and irreversible competitive advantages over her cisgender counterparts: "I know if I'd had surgery at the age of 22, and then at 24 went on the [tennis] tour, no genetic woman in the world would have been able to come close to me," Richards said in 2012.[16] Interestingly, Navratilova, whom Richards once coached, was dropped as an ambassador for Athlete Ally in 2019, and condemned as being transphobic by many human rights groups, after she published an op-ed in the *Sunday Times* saying that it was "insane" that trans athletes who "decide" to become women had achieved wins and titles that "were beyond their capabilities as men."[17]

LAUREL HUBBARD: FIRST OPENLY TRANS OLYMPIAN

While Richards was vocal and welcomed the media attention during her own fight for inclusion, some trans women want nothing more than to quietly participate in their sport. That was the stance of New Zealand powerlifter Laurel Hubbard. Hubbard's story is one of both triumph and tragedy, and speaks to the ways in which trans athletes, like Richards, sometimes become hesitant or reluctant faces for the cause. Even as a child, Hubbard felt conflicted about her body and with what it meant to be masculine. She initially gravitated towards weightlifting because it was seen as a stereotypical endeavor associated with cisgender men. "I thought perhaps if I tried something that was so masculine, perhaps that's what I would become," Hubbard told New Zealand public broadcasting outlet RNZ in 2017.[18] "Sadly, that wasn't the case." Still, Hubbard discovered joy in the act of lifting weights and found it thrilling when she could complete an intense lift correctly. Hubbard's rise to weightlifting prominence began when she set the New Zealand men's national junior record in 1998, at the age of twenty, with a 300 kilograms (600 pounds) total in the +105 kilograms class, with a snatch of 135 kilograms and a clean and jerk of 170 kilograms.[19] (The snatch is an exercise in which a barbell is raised from the ground to above one's head in a single motion, whereas the clean and jerk, a two-part lift, involves lifting the barbell from the ground to just above the shoulders and then thrusting it upward above the head.)

Hubbard stopped weightlifting after she turned twenty-three years old because "it just became too much to bear" as she was struggling to cope with her gender identity.[20] She was overwhelmed with the pressures she faced in trying to fit into a world that, as she described, "perhaps wasn't really set up for people like myself."[21] She resumed competing in 2012, at age of thirty-five, when she began medically transitioning through hormone suppression treatment. Five years after that, in 2017, Hubbard had come out as trans and garnered national attention in New Zealand after she set a record in Oceania on the women's side at the 2017 North Island Games and won gold at the Australian championships. Amid her wins, she faced a barrage of criticism from her competitors and members of the weightlifting community, as well as merciless attacks online for being a trans woman. Iuniarra Sipaia, a silver medalist from Samoa, told reporters that despite having undergone a physical transition, Hubbard's "emotions, strength and everything is still a male. So, I felt that it was unfair because we all know a woman's strength is nowhere near a male's strength no matter how hard we train."[22] This would not be the last time that Hubbard's identity and participation would be subjected to intense scrutiny.

Hubbard shot to international fame, becoming known outside her small country, after she went on to win two silver medals at the 2017 World Weightlifting Championships in Anaheim, California, making her the first New Zealander to ever win silver at the worlds. In the wake of the wins, she continued being subjected to an onslaught of online attacks. Shortly after her silver win, Hubbard stuck her neck out and engaged with the news media. For Hubbard, she always would have preferred to just lift weights and be left alone. She never saw her transgender identity as a tool for some public awareness campaign or as part of some broader agenda. While her fellow competitors got to lift weights in relative peace and have that be taken at face value, when Hubbard did it, it became imbued with larger significance. She was forced, unlike them, to justify or explain who she is. "I am who I am. I'm not here to change the world," Hubbard said after the championship.[23] "I just want to be me and just do what I do." Every day, she tried her best to block out any negativity, which added even more weight onto her shoulders. "All I can really do is focus and lift." Hubbard also expressed grace toward the cruelty of her naysayers and critics. "People believe what they believe and when they're, I suppose, shown something which is new and different to what they know, it's instinctive to be defensive," she reflected.[24] "It's not really my job to change what they think, what they feel, or what they believe. But I just hope that they look at the bigger picture, rather than just trusting whatever their gut might have told them."[25]

One reporter who was interviewing her pointed out the science behind trans athletes and that Hubbard, by all accounts, met those criteria in place by the International Olympic Committee at the time, which was that trans women needed to be on hormone replacement therapy for at least one year in order to compete on the women's side. Her testosterone levels met the IOC thresholds for women at the time. And Hubbard pointed out that she, in 2017, had met the previous IOC guidelines set in 2003, which were much stricter in requiring that trans women athletes needed to have undergone gender-confirmation surgery followed by at least two years of hormone therapy. "I am not competing under a recent rules change, I'm competing under rules which have been in place now for 14 years," Hubbard said.[26]

Fast-forward to June 2021 when the New Zealand Olympic Committee announced its weightlifting team for the upcoming Summer Olympics in Tokyo, which had been postponed from 2020 to 2021 due to the COVID-19 pandemic. Hubbard would compete in the +87kg women's category. Her announcement made waves because, at the age of forty-three and a decade older than any other athlete competing against her in the event, she would be the fourth oldest weightlifter to compete at the Olympics. But that was dramatically overshadowed by the fact that Hubbard is a trans woman, and her announcement as the first openly trans athlete to compete in an individual event at the Summer Olympics was met with international outcry and denouncement. During the event itself, Hubbard struggled to lift 275 pounds, as she bowed out after being unable to make a clean lift in the snatch section of the two-part event. Her official result ended up being classified as "did not finish."[27] In her second of three attempts, Hubbard appeared to have successfully lifted the barbell, but the judges swiftly ruled that she had not held the bar steady enough above her head. Every single person who beat Hubbard at that event was a cisgender woman.[28]

After her time competing on the Olympic stage, Hubbard spoke to journalists in an intimate press conference, sitting on a wooden bench in a gray workout shirt and mustard-yellow cap.[29] "I'm not going to pretend that this is the easiest point in my sporting career, but it is what it is," she said in response to a reporter asking her, simply, how she was doing.[30] "It's so easy for people to forget that athletes are human, that we suffer from the pressure, from the expectation, and we feel the disappointment when things don't go according to plan." After the press conference, Hubbard disappeared. She headed back to New Zealand and hasn't been heard from since. What her experiences highlight is that not all trans athletes want to have the spotlight on them, let alone be a face for the cause. Might Hubbard's scores have been better had she not been hindered by all the noise? We will never know.

QUINN: FIRST TRANS AND NONBINARY OLYMPIC MEDALIST

While Laurel Hubbard was participating in the Tokyo Olympics, there was also a young nonbinary athlete named Quinn who was making history on the soccer pitch. It was a momentous year for transgender and nonbinary visibility at the Olympics, and helped show the world that inclusion was not only possible but could be a beacon of hope for all athletes in a time when the state of trans inclusion was and still is quite bleak. Quinn is a twenty-six-year-old midfielder from Toronto who is part of the Canadian National Women's Soccer Team. At Tokyo, Quinn, who goes by one name and uses they/them pronouns, became the first openly trans and nonbinary person to win a gold medal—or any medal—at the Olympic Games when Canada won against Sweden. "I don't know how to feel," Quinn wrote on Instagram following the gold medal win.[31] "I feel sad knowing there were Olympians before me, unable to live their truth because of the world. I feel optimistic for change. . . . Mostly, I feel aware of the realities. Trans girls being banned from sports."[32]

Quinn is far from the only trans or nonbinary athlete who has been forced to think about the impact of their visibility. But Quinn's experience is distinct because they are playing in the division that aligns with their sex assigned at birth. There are no blood or hormone tests required, no examinations or invasive questioning to undergo to justify or permit their participation. Every other athlete discussed in this chapter identifies as transgender and has made a transition to a different gender category. But what happens when an athlete transitions socially in a way that doesn't have to do with hormones? That's where Quinn comes in, and their story informs the conversation about how we can be more inclusive of gender diverse athletes who can't or don't want to undergo hormone therapy during their sports career.

Before playing soccer, Quinn tried out a bunch of different sports, then swam and skied competitively. They also tried track and field, but when competing at school events they would inexplicably be overcome with what they now understand to be panic attacks—shortness of breath and paralysis. Quinn thinks they experienced this anxiety because track and field is an individual, not a team, sport. They thrive in team environments when they are surrounded by supportive peers, and feel insecure when alone on the field or in competition. Quinn was drawn to soccer after watching a bunch of little league games with their parents as a young kid. "The second I got to play, I was just addicted," Quinn told us on a Zoom call in 2023.[33] At just fifteen years old, Quinn made the Canadian National Women's team. While playing their sport with mostly supportive teammates was an incredible experience, Quinn also learned that, as someone who didn't identify as a woman, figuring out their gender identity in a binary world wasn't without its challenges. For Quinn, playing soccer and getting into the "zone" was one of the only times when those struggles took the back burner. "That's definitely one of my favorite experiences," Quinn continued. "To operate anywhere I feel most comfortable with my body. It's such an interesting contrast, because you have times where it can be so difficult. And then . . . you strip it down to the most basic experience of sport, which is just you exploring how your body can move and operate and excel in certain ways." On September 10, 2020, Quinn took to Instagram to officially come out and take away the burden of playing their sport as someone they are not. "Coming out is HARD (and kinda [b.s.])," Quinn wrote in their coming-out post alongside a photo of them leaning on a paddleboard.[34] "I know for me it's something I'll be doing over again for the rest of my life." From then on, Quinn started to feel more comfortable as a nonbinary athlete. "Taking those steps, coming out publicly and understanding . . . I could change the language [about] how people saw me and how people communicated with me and about me," Quinn told us.[35] "And getting top surgery [double mastectomy] was huge for me. That made me feel like sports was an option in terms of how I felt playing in women's sports." Quinn was reclaiming their identity and reclaiming the sport in a way that made sense for them.

In the public understanding of trans athletes, many people assume there is only one way that trans athletes can and want to transition while playing sports, which is to transition physically and eventually change the gender division in which they compete. There are nuances within the trans community that are also reflected in the sports world but aren't necessarily talked about or reported on because it's not as controversial and therefore not worthy of attention. There are several reasons why a nonbinary athlete or a trans athlete would stay on the team that aligns with their sex assigned at birth and *not* make the switch to the other side. Since coming out, Quinn has always played on the women's side and has not sought to switch to the men's side, even though there are aspects of playing in the women's division that are triggering to Quinn—for instance, the jerseys that taper in at the waist in a traditionally feminine way, and the shorts that are a lot shorter than those in the men's kit. Another hurdle is the gender-based names for leagues. In Quinn's case, the league they currently play in is the National Women's Soccer League (NWSL)—they play for the Reign, a team based in Seattle, Washington—so whenever they refer to the league they play in they're forced to use a label that doesn't align with their gender identity.

While Quinn has been able to make themself feel comfortable and succeed at this elite level, the vast majority of nonbinary athletes, especially youth, are continuing to struggle with the immense barriers and discrimination that prevent them from entering, let alone thrive in, team sports at all. A November 2023 study from Simon Fraser University in British Columbia delved into this issue and found that 11 percent of nonbinary youth in Canada currently participate in team sports—an abysmally small percentage considering that 67 percent of the country's youth from ages three to seventeen participate in one or more organized sports and activities, according to a survey published in the same year.[36] In studying youth from fifteen to twenty-nine years old across Canada, including 2,513 nonbinary youth (the largest study of its kind to date), the researchers found that 66 percent of nonbinary youth in Canada who have avoided joining an organized team sport have done so because they would have had to play on a binary-gendered team—either men's or women's. And four out of five of the youth surveyed said they avoided joining a team because of the locker room layouts. The researchers provided a number of possible solutions to address these issues, including allowing nonbinary athletes to play on the gendered team of their choosing, for school environments to pursue co-ed teams, and to have gym classes divided up by competitiveness instead of gender.

Quinn's journey is important because it shows the need for discussions about cisgender and transgender athletes to move away from the finite gender binary of man or woman, male or female. Stories like Quinn's and Harrison's demonstrate that your identity isn't determined by your physical appearance, and can also inspire trans and nonbinary athletes to join and find happiness in sports, even if they don't fit into the typical gender norms or follow mainstream expectations of the typical trans athlete's journey. A one-size-fits-all approach to trans participation simply isn't viable, and by pushing those flimsy boundaries, Quinn is carving a path and doing what they need to do to be the best athlete they can be while living an authentic life.

PATRICIO MANUEL: FIRST TRANS PRO BOXER

So far, we've explored the individual sport path through the perspectives of trans women and nonbinary athletes. Now let's pivot to a trans man's perspective through the eyes of Patricio Manuel, the world's first openly trans professional boxer. His journey from fighting on the women's side to fighting on the men's reveals the flip side of gender norms and the often-harmful stereotypes pushed onto athletes. While Manuel doesn't know exactly what led him to boxing, he thinks the impulse might have been somewhere deep within his DNA because, as he explains, he's African American on his father's side and Irish American on his mother's side. "Both of these cultures have a lot of fistic ties," Manuel, who's now in his late thirties, told us in the summer of 2023.[37] For Manuel, there's something to be said about oppressed groups literally fighting for their place in the world, and that struggle calls to him. In middle school and high school, while attending an all-girls school in California, Manuel played softball on the women's side but had started disassociating and struggling with mental health owing to his gender dysphoria. He eventually quit softball and gravitated toward martial arts and boxing. At the end of 2001, his grandmother took him to his first boxing lesson with a coach in Los Angeles. The coach looked at Manuel and said, "Oh, I hope she's here to box, she looks tough."[38] Manuel remembers puffing up when he heard that. At that moment, he fell in love with the sport and it remained that way. "The discipline, the realness," he said, naming the reasons why he enjoys boxing so much. "There's so much authenticity in boxing and also the individualism that I wasn't getting in softball."[39]

It took years of hard work—literal blood, sweat, and tears—but he started excelling. Manuel describes one of his early trainers at the time as being very "old school," taking a sink-or-swim approach of throwing rookie boxers like Manuel straight into the ring. "They threw me in with this one young boxer, and he just beat the piss out of me," Manuel recalled.[40] Throughout this time, Manuel was also gaining muscle and losing weight, so his body was organically starting to take the stronger, more masculine physique he dreamed of, though he didn't have the knowledge or language to express that at the time. Manuel just noticed he was feeling physically and mentally better. And the thing about boxing is that when you spar, it's mixed gender. Cisgender men fighters spar with women and vice versa. People are there to work with each other as individuals, regardless of gender, something that made it easier for Manuel to focus on his identity as simply a boxer, full stop.

Although Manuel's experiences with boxing, especially in those formative years, were supportive and positive, he acknowledges that there's rampant homophobia and transphobia throughout the sport and the community around it. This homophobia is targeted more toward people assigned male at birth who are queer or trans and diverge from the stereotypical hypermasculine culture of boxing. As for gay or bisexual women and trans men, Manuel says there's a little more space and acceptance, but feels that his experience of being respected and embraced could be an exception. "My style is very masculine and who I am today is a straight trans man; it resonates really well with them [cisgender men in boxing]."[41]

While Manuel was feeling more aligned with himself, it would still be a while before he considered socially and physically transitioning. He became so busy with training at the elite level that he really didn't have time to stop and think about it. Manuel went on to become a five-time US national amateur champion on the women's side in his matches between 2006 and 2012. In 2012, he competed in the women's US Olympic trials for the London Olympics, the first time that women would be eligible to compete in boxing. It was a huge moment for him—he could make history as one of the first women boxers to make it to the Olympics. But then it all came crashing down when he suffered a shoulder injury during the trials in Spokane, Washington, and was forced to withdraw altogether. "I hit rock bottom," Manuel said. "I had to realize that I had to start looking at myself as a person first and foremost. And I think that was really the first time as an adult I had looked at myself as beyond being a boxer and beyond being an athlete."[42] Manuel realized that he had prioritized being an athlete over being himself, and that his whole identity, as with many other athletes, had become inextricably linked with his role as a competitive athlete.

The following year, as he was healing, he also began transitioning, though at first he struggled to access hormone therapy in California. The whole thing was frightening. "I just didn't want to be able to not compete. That was it. I love this sport and it was the thing that made me who I am and I wasn't ready to give it up." As a trans man, Manuel was worried about facing rejection and exclusion. In 2013, he began medically transitioning with hormone therapy and stopped boxing in the women's league. He worked to abide by the IOC guidelines for testosterone that were in effect at that time. Manuel satisfied those requirements by 2015, when the IOC announced new, less stringent requirements for trans athletes as a result of the intervention of another trans athlete, whom we will discuss next. The guidelines stipulated that trans men who were assigned female at birth, like Manuel, were allowed to compete in the men's division *without any restrictions whatsoever.*[43]

By 2016, Manuel was approved by USA Boxing, the sport's highest national governing body in the US, to fight in the amateurs on the men's side. It was the first time that the organization implemented this trans policy, which had existed only in writing to that point. The existence of this trans policy, and the fact that a trans man was competing against cisgender men in one of the most violent sports, is momentous, setting a precedence that is knocking out gender norms and the notion that a cisgender man, in any situation, will always dominate someone who was assigned female at birth. As of mid-2024, Manuel has gone 3–1—undefeated in all but one of his matches—since his professional debut in 2018 at the Oscar De La Hoya–founded Golden Boy Promotions event in Indio, California. Manuel, who was thirty-three at the time, scored a four-round unanimous decision victory over his opponent, super-featherweight Hugo Aguilar, who found out about Manuel's transition two days before the match. Manuel became the first trans boxer to fight in and win a professional boxing match in the US. In a highly masculine environment, news of Manuel's transition could have easily been met with disrespect and misunderstanding. But his opponent proved this wrong. "For me, it's very respectable," Aguilar told reporters. "It doesn't change anything for me. In the ring, he wants to win, and I want to win too."[44]

Not all boxers have the same mentality as Aguilar, however, when it comes to respect for their opponents. After Manuel's historic win, it took five years for him to find another fight and a boxer willing to step in the ring with him. In September 2019, Manuel became the face of the Everlast boxing brand, which would have been a great opportunity for any fighter looking to gain notoriety and fight against a well-known boxer like Manuel. Nonetheless, there were numerous cases where fights were booked but then opponents mysteriously pulled out just before the scheduled match, leading one to wonder if Manuel's gender identity had something to do with it. The very idea of potentially losing to someone that is not a cisgender man can be emasculating for an individual whose identity rests on machismo.

While Manuel shows us that any competitive athlete, including trans boxers, can compete in a division that aligns with their gender identity, the World Boxing Council (WBC) has continued to push for an entirely separate division for transgender athletes. In this proposed division, boxers would be allowed to compete only against opponents whose assigned gender at birth matches theirs. The president of the WBC, Mauricio Sulaimán, stated that in the newly proposed trans-specific division, "women to man or man to woman transgender change will never be allowed to fight a different gender by birth," meaning that only trans men could compete against trans men and trans women could only compete against trans women.[45] Sulaimán said in a livestream filled with transphobia in 2020 that being transgender is "not accepted" because there's "a difference between a man and a woman" and "there's no in between." For Manuel, the new trans-specific division would mean that he could not compete against cisgender men, as he had been for years before this announcement. Manuel and other boxers slammed the idea of the creation of a segregated division for trans boxers, saying that the WBC was ignoring his story and success winning fights against cisgender men. "It's inherently dehumanizing," Manuel told reporters about the proposed new division. "When I walk into the gym, I'm treated no differently than any other man in all aspects of training."[46]

At the beginning of 2024, USA Boxing announced a new policy for transgender athletes. The shockingly regressive policy requires trans boxers to undergo full genital-affirming surgery and has a four-year hormone testing requirement for both trans men and trans women to be able to compete against their cisgender counterparts. The policy is seemingly doing away with the trans-specific category pushed for previously by Sulaimán, but now makes boxing one of the most restrictive sports for trans people. Genital reassignment surgeries are invasive, they don't affect athletic ability one way or another, and they "jeopardize athletes' dignity and autonomy," according to Athlete Ally.[47] This move is yet another example of how sports institutions are becoming increasingly ignorant of approaches rooted in human rights and basic science—and how these entities are susceptible to the strength of the far-right media machine.

CHRIS MOSIER: RACING FOR TRANS INCLUSION AT THE OLYMPICS

Chris Mosier, a Team USA competitor in the duathlon, represents the power of visibility and the importance of seeing successful trans athletes. In the summer before Harrison came out publicly through an ESPN article, he first saw Mosier when he was featured in *ESPN The Magazine*'s annual Body Issue in 2016. An examination and celebration of athletes and their bodies, the Body Issue features high-profile athletes from all different sports and genders engaging in their sport or training while naked. The edition featuring Mosier was the first Body Issue to include a trans athlete. "I think the reason I felt so inspired to do it is that I'm finally at a place where I feel very comfortable with my body," Mosier says in the article, whose photos depict him running and biking in a lush green forest, top surgery scars and all.[48] He proved to the world that being both an elite athlete and trans was possible and beautiful.

But it took years for Mosier to get to this point after enduring relentless criticism for his body, dating back to 2009, when he was racing in the women's category. Mosier felt the most out of place at the starting line, with all eyes on him, standing among women when he didn't look like the rest of his competitors. His androgynous appearance and short hair garnered negative attention and shame from spectators and the broader racing community. He even had a police officer ask him during the Fifth Avenue Mile road race in 2009 if he was competing in the wrong gender category. Before he was a duathlete, his main race was the triathlon (which consists of running, biking, and swimming while a duathlon consists of just biking and running). One of the main reasons Mosier made the switch from the triathlon to the duathlon was the very gendered swimsuit that clearly signaled that his gender identity and expression didn't match how he was born. Beyond the racing events, this same stigma followed him into the training facilities and the various swimming pools he used. There were even times when women asked him to leave while he was changing in the women's locker room.

When this became too much in 2010, Mosier decided to physically transition, change his name, and switch to competing in the men's side. "Until recently I still was holding on to that idea of finishing in a very high place in my [women's] category," Mosier told the *New York Times* in the lead-up to the race.[49] "Now I don't expect to finish as high. I just want to enjoy being comfortable in the race." In his first race competing in the men's category in the New York City Triathlon, he did better than even he expected, placing

58 out of 384 for men between the ages of thirty to thirty-four, and 233 out of more than 3,140 participants.[50] That placed him in the top 7 percent.

In 2015, Mosier continued his upward trajectory by earning a spot on the Team USA sprint duathlon men's team in the 2016 World Championship, which made him the first openly trans athlete to join a US national team that did *not* align with their assigned gender at birth. At the time, Mosier was unsure of his eligibility to compete at the Duathlon World Championship in Spain due to IOC policy regarding the participation of trans athletes. In 2015, Mosier challenged the IOC policy that required trans athletes to have undergone gender-confirmation surgery, along with other requirements. He successfully advocated for the surgery requirement to be dropped, making him eligible to participate in that race and future races. "Changing other policies means there can be young people out there who can fall in love with sport at a very young age and not have to compromise their identity as a person or their identity as an athlete in order to participate in those sports," Mosier told ESPN in 2016.[51] In 2020, he became the first openly trans athlete to compete on the team that aligned with their gender identity in the Olympic trials for the US national team, competing not in the duathlon but in the 50-kilometer race walking event, though he couldn't finish due to an injury.[52]

Mosier exemplifies the power that one person can have in bringing about change for athletes across many sports around the world. The changes he helped bring about at the international level have trickled down to national and local sport governing bodies and have helped reshape broader public opinion about trans athletes and trans people. There's still so much work to be done, but without Mosier, we would likely still be decades behind in terms of progress. Many more athletes would be barred from participation in elite sports because of discriminatory and arbitrary rules.

Trans athletes have real, fulsome lives, but in public discourse, they are often relegated to the chemicals in their bodies. Mosier pushed these policies beyond their hyperfocus on the genitals and hormones of athletes, both cisgender and transgender, in favor of privacy, dignity, and more bodily autonomy. But all this progression can only go so far if the structural inequalities in sports aren't also tackled. Our systems and attitudes need to be overhauled, and our attention needs to become laser-focused on the failures of the sports administrations and systems. If we fail to do so, these entities will continue to worsen, leaving behind more youth, both cisgender and transgender.

CHAPTER 3

FAIRNESS FALLACY

I t was Harrison's senior year playing with the Black Bears women's ice hockey team at the University of Maine, and they were about to take on one of their biggest rivals, the Boston University Terriers. One of Boston's players at that time was Marie-Philip Poulin, who had just returned from a gold-medal Olympic win for Team Canada.[1] She scored the winning goal in overtime against the Americans. She's the best of the best, known as the Sidney Crosby of women's hockey, and before any game, Harrison's team was constantly reminded by coaching staff and other players to watch out for her prowess. Poulin stands four inches taller than Harrison and had at least forty-five pounds on him. And yet, height and weight disparities aside, Harrison's sole task for that game was to shadow her and thwart her every move. Was it unfair for Harrison to be pitted against Poulin, who was larger and far more skilled? Absolutely not. It was a challenge, to be sure, but that's what sports are about. When playing against the superior Boston players, the only outcry from the Black Bears regarding fairness on the ice was in regard to suspect calls by the refs, lopsided penalties, and missed clock stoppage—never players like Poulin. Not once in Harrison's sixteen-year hockey career had players like Poulin been seen as having an unfair advantage. Every other player, regardless of rank, was instead urged to elevate their own game to try to match players like Poulin or beat them to the best of their ability. Fairness was not discussed in terms of size or skill level, as it has increasingly become in discourse for the exclusion or restriction of trans people in sports today.

The fairness conversation, when viewed through the lens of women's sports and women athletes, misleads people into thinking that physicality is the only thing that makes it fair, that women aren't capable, and their bodies need to be protected and policed at all costs. This framing ignores the deeply rooted systematic inequalities in sports. If fairness were instead explored through men's sports, we wouldn't be focused on physicality and strength in the same way, because men are assumed and *expected* to be able to protect themselves. In some sports, such as ice hockey, boxing, and rugby, violence and injury are even expected and championed. Fairness instead would be looked at through the lens of access—access to financial resources, training, legacy, what have you. Why shouldn't this be the same for the women's side? Let's break this down.

The ideals of "fairness" and a "level playing field" are frequently invoked as a reason to keep trans athletes, particularly women athletes, out of competitive sports. Concerns about a level playing field can refer to doping, cheating, and match-fixing, all things that people seek to eradicate in order to uphold respect for the game, the athletes, the spectators, and the corporate interests involved. We cannot allow trans people (read: women) to play in leagues that match their gender identity, the argument goes, because it will give them an unfair advantage or put cisgender athletes at a disadvantage. Many policies and laws that are geared to exclude trans people from sports have the word "fair" or some iteration of it in the title and/or text of the law. Many US states, from Florida to New Jersey, have implemented or are pursuing some version of a "Fairness in Women's Sports Act."[2] On the other side of the world, the Australian government has used the same rhetoric in its own version through proposed legislation such as the "Save Women's Sports" bill.[3] Yet again, the concept of fairness is obscured, and the onus is placed onto women athletes and sports to solve it. But sports have never been fair at all, for reasons that mainly have nothing to do with gender, biology, or hormones. In reality, it is socioeconomic status, race, and sometimes sheer luck that helps determine the success of an athlete, wherever they live or compete.

When it comes to the discussion about trans women in sports, the term "competitive advantage" is often brought up as a means to keep them out or to overstate their abilities. The presumption is that they automatically embody the utmost athletic prowess. However, considering that the transgender community is one of the most disenfranchised groups in society, very few trans people, let alone athletes, have access to the resources required to become an elite athlete, and it shows in the dearth of trans athletes in competitive sports. Stating that a particular thing about an athlete, such as their hormone levels, is the primary ingredient for success is one of the most misguided conceptions that exists about athletes and sports. Many factors are at play when it comes to whether an athlete makes it or not. The illusion of inherent fairness in competitive sports is just a pipe dream, and the reality that all athletes are on level playing fields is simply not true. The truth is that athletic greatness really comes down to access. Access to the best resources such as equipment, coaching, nutrition are paramount—not one's biological makeup. In the same way that moral panics divert the public's attention from the root causes of social ills and the matters that are truly important, the "fairness in sports" slogan is a way for organized sports to divert attention away from the haves and have-nots in the athletic community, regardless of gender identity.

FINANCIAL BARRIERS

Money and financial capital are the most obvious barriers to achieving fairness, and the downsides of capitalism in sports are most felt among youth. Gender identity is irrelevant in this structural inequality. Financial access can facilitate or hinder an athlete's ability to fully reach their potential and make it into the upper echelons of sport. For the most part, even in high-income countries, it is the existing structures and their economic barriers to participating in organized sports that makes things inherently unfair. Experts have been warning for years about the rising costs associated with recreational sports. A 2017 cover story for *Time* magazine traced how children's recreational leagues in the US alone became a $15 billion industry, and the industry continues to grow.[4] In Canada, it's become an industry worth 9 billion Canadian dollars, according to research that surveys the field.[5] The average family in the US pays nearly $1,000 per year for one child's primary sport, according to a 2022 survey about youth sports by the Aspen Institute.[6] Nearly 60 percent of families surveyed said they were facing financial strain from their children's sports participation. Many families said they were reducing the number of seasons, leagues, and sports their children could play given this reality.

Not surprisingly, there's also a racial disparity in terms of who is spending money on sports for their children. The same Aspen Institute survey also found that Black families, who earn an average of $28,000 less than the median white family, were less likely to spend money on sports than their white or Hispanic peers.[7] For young girls, the numbers become even bleaker. Girls of color and girls of lower socioeconomic status are more likely to enter sports at an older age, participate at far lower rates than their white peers (especially boys), and drop out of sports earlier.[8] A Centers for Disease Control study found that in 2020, 70 percent of children from families with incomes higher than $105,000 participated in sports.[9] However, the rate of participation plummets to around 30 percent for families that are at or below the poverty line. This growing disparity among youth has been called a "physical divide."[10] This all comes amid general concerns across the globe about rising costs of living. More than half of all Americans, for example, are considering taking on extra jobs just to make ends meet. Sports, seen as additional or even luxury activities, might be the first on the chopping block for household budgets.

More expensive sports like ice hockey and figure skating have been criticized for excluding marginalized communities, as those who can afford it are mainly white, wealthy athletes. At the low end, the cost of competing in figure skating is about 10,000 Canadian dollars a year, according to Skate Canada, with some costs even running as high as $30,000 per year. Even the rapper Snoop Dogg has pointed to the overwhelming whiteness of hockey, telling CBC News in 2023, in the midst of his failed attempt to bid on the Ottawa Senators NHL team, "I've been watching hockey for about 25 years now and I watch more and more kids that look like me play the game, but I'm not seeing it being offered to the kids over here in America. . . . The kids need to know that there is an option to play hockey if you look like me."[11]

A New York Times feature in 2020 examined the rising cost of youth hockey and how the next generation of players is being affected as a result.[12] The story chronicled the journeys of families struggling with the costs, some having to choose which of their children could play the prohibitively expensive sport and others doing fundraising through barbecues and other events. "The cost is extremely high and it's not really manageable for most working-class families to afford to put their kids in hockey," New Jersey Devils forward Wayne Simmonds told the Times.[13] Just how expensive are we talking? One sports research organization found that the average Canadian family spends US$1,300 per year on hockey equipment, tournaments, and registration fees. This is likely just a fraction of the total cost to play and excel at hockey, because this figure doesn't include all the extra fees that parents and guardians have to pay to help their kids get ahead, such as private training and coaches, hockey camps, gas money for traveling, babysitting costs for other siblings, and weight training. For parents who are hoping their children will end up in the elite ranks such as the NCAA, the NHL, and the PWHL, some are even sending them to schools with specialized hockey programs such as The Hill Academy and the Canadian International Hockey Academy, which count Sidney Crosby as an alumnus, and where tuition costs run as high as US$40,000 a year.[14] How can the average person or family compete when these types of resources are available for only those who can afford it?

League officials are making some incremental moves to bring increased transparency about these problems and pursue solutions to get more minority athletes playing and being part of hockey leagues. At the end of 2022, the NHL released its first-ever report on diversity and inclusion, which showed that 84 percent of NHL employees and teams are white.[15] The report was a two-year endeavor spurred by the 2020 murder of George Floyd, a Black man, by a Minneapolis police officer. Though many NHL teams and players issued statements condemning racial injustice in the wake of Floyd's murder, the league faced a wave of criticism for not being active on racial issues in the public sphere in general. Data for that year showed that less than 5 percent of the players in the NHL were Black or people of color.[16] Kim Davis, the league's executive vice president of social impact, growth, and legislative affairs, said there's work to be done to make the NHL more appealing to applicants from underrepresented groups—and to appeal to a broader fanbase.[17]

So, what does this all have to do with trans participation in sports? Well, when we think about trans women and their competitive advantage, we mostly think about their bodies as the source. But what if we look at advantage through the access lens? Going back to the case of Renée Richards, the trans woman who played elite tennis, the US Tennis Association sought to exclude her from the US Open over fears that she wielded an athletic advantage over her cisgender women competitors as a trans woman. However, not one word was mentioned about the other, provable socioeconomic and structural advantages that Richards already had. This includes the privilege of playing tennis as a youth at an exclusive prep school, going on to compete at Yale University, and moving into a lucrative career in medicine that allowed her access to resources to facilitate her training that most other people would only dream of. If a trans athlete, particularly a woman, does well, the main consideration in evaluating their success is the extent to which they went through puberty. This is clearly only the tip of the iceberg when it comes to what makes an athlete great. A major reason why Richards was able to compete and be a great tennis player was not her sex assigned at birth; it was more likely her white privilege, which was bolstered by her access to superior resources and training. It's a type of advantage that is far more ubiquitous among elite tennis players. It's a lot easier to target someone's gender identity than it is to discuss more complex issues regarding privilege and oppression.

"THE MATTHEW EFFECT": HOW BIRTH MONTH RELATES TO SUCCESS

The systemic inequalities in sports sometimes come down to the simplest and most obvious issues. What if someone told you that the month in which an athlete is born also plays a crucial role? We're not talking about horoscopes, but there is a sort of cosmic luck that comes into play for kids born earlier in the year. This phenomenon was discovered and researched by Canadian psychologist Roger Barnsley, who first explored what is known as "relative age theory" in ice hockey in the 1980s. Canadian journalist and author Malcolm Gladwell summarizes Barnsley's research well in his 2008 book *Outliers*, where he shows how our typical explanations for success—that is, hard work and determination—are suspect or even wrong. Gladwell writes, "Success in hockey is based on *individual merit*—and both of those words are important. Players are judged on their own performance, not on anyone else's, and based on their ability, not on some other arbitrary fact. Or are they?"[18] Gladwell poses this before delving into Barnsley's illuminating research on the relative age effect, also known as the "birthdate effect" or the "Matthew effect." (The latter term typically refers to something or someone that accumulates a social or economic advantage. Gladwell quotes the Book of Matthew 25:29 at the start of the book's first chapter: "For unto everyone that hath shall be given, and he shall have abundance. But from him that hath not shall be taken away even that which he hath.") Barnsley, along with his wife and colleague, A. H. Thompson, first gathered statistics on every player in the Ontario Junior Hockey League (OJHL), the top junior league in Canada where the majority of the players go on to play in the NHL.

Through their research they discovered that January was the month in which most of these elite players were born. The second most were born in February and the third, unsurprisingly, in March, and so on. According to the study, there were five times more players born in January than there were players born in November in the entire OJHL. Struck by the league's age data, Barnsley and Thompson turned their attention to other elite hockey leagues of all different age ranges, from all-star teams composed of eleven- to thirteen-year-olds, all the way up to players in the NHL. The results they gleaned were shockingly consistent with those from the OJHL: 40 percent of the players were born between January and March, 30 percent between April and June, 20 percent between July and September, and 10 percent between October and December. "In all my years in psychology," Barnsley states in the chapter, "I have never run into an effect this large. . . . You don't even need to do any statistical analysis. You just look at it."[19]

The cause of this phenomenon is so glaringly obvious that it calls into question the framework for breaking up all sports by the age of the participants. In Canada, the eligibility cutoff for age-class hockey is January 1, which thus lumps all athletes born in the same year into one category.[20] The younger the players are, especially preadolescent players aged eight to twelve, the more the twelve-month gap matters in terms of their physical and mental development. In a country like Canada where many children are essentially socialized to play professional hockey from the day they put on skates, players are picked out as potential elites at young ages. Coaches start to select players to make up rep-level teams ("rep" stands for "representation," and "rep-level" designates the highest caliber of athletes for that age range in each association), and, of course, they are going to select the biggest, most physically coordinated players. These players are the ones who have benefited from those crucial extra months of maturity and growth. From that point on, those who have slight physical advantages because of their birth month have access to better coaches, more ice time, and more games than the players who happened to be born later in the year. These benefits compound year over year, making the players who are born earlier better over time. The surge in attention and resources they are more likely to receive is not necessarily because they are better athletes, but rather is a side effect of being born earlier.

Hockey isn't the only sport where this happens. It occurs in European soccer as well, as the continent has a rep program structure similar to that of hockey in Canada. In England, the eligibility date is September 1.[21] During the 1990s, in the Football Association's Premier League, there were 288 players born between September and November and only 136 players born between June and August. In international soccer, the cutoff date used to be August 1, and in one tournament, 135 players were born three months after August 1 and only 22 were born in May, June, and July.[22] The arbitrary framework in which sports are broken up by cutoff dates has skewed sports so heavily that fairness, again, is called into question.

How can it be fair for a child born in a later month to be at such a disadvantage? And why are we focusing on targeting transgender athletes, who make up less than 1 percent of the athletic population at recreational levels, when there are systemic factors such as age cutoff dates affecting the way some sports are structured? One way forward would be to end the practice of selecting kids so early for elite teams, before each athlete has had time for their bodies to develop. If youth were all playing at the same level, developing together in those crucial early years, it would allow late bloomers to catch up to the others. We would then have a more realistic and inclusive sense of which athletes have the capability to excel. Recreational sports leagues could be encouraged to consider having more than just a single cutoff date per year per sport. Setting up multiple divisions for young children per age range, broken up by a specific number of months—for example, quarterly or every six months—could be a way to truly level the playing field.

LGBTQ+ PEOPLE ACCESSING SPORT

When it comes to access to resources, LGBTQ+ individuals, especially trans and nonbinary people, are more likely to be in financially precarious situations than cisgender people. And if they are racialized, that compounds their precarity even more. Statistics Canada published its first census results on the gender diversity of the Canadian population in 2022. The findings revealed that gender diverse people had a higher rate of poverty than cisgender individuals.[23] Trans women had a higher poverty rate than cisgender women (12 percent and 7.9 percent, respectively), and trans men also had a higher poverty rate than cisgender men (12.9 percent and 8.2 percent), while nonbinary individuals had the highest rate, at 20.6 percent. More than one in five nonbinary people live in poverty, the researchers said. A similar study of LGBTQ+ people in the US published in 2023 found that 23 percent of LGBTQ+ people in the US lived in poverty that year, up from 17 percent in 2021, and LGBTQ+ people of color had higher poverty rates than their cisgender counterparts.[24] These statistics indicate that LGBTQ+ athletes are already behind in terms of having the financial means to excel at their sport. As scholars Ali Durham Greey and Helen Jefferson Lenskyj note in the introduction to their 2022 edited collection, *Justice for Trans Athletes*: "If trans women and girls are excluded from sport for the competitive advantage that they allegedly have over cisgender women and girls . . . then it would be logical to assume that it would be fair to exclude other athletes with physical or social advantages."[25]

An example of the struggles faced by transgender athletes, especially trans youth athletes, is that they, like most youth, primarily rely on their parents to pay for their equipment, the cost of enrollment or participation, and transportation to events, games, and tryouts. More so than cisgender children, LGBTQ+ youth are at risk of not being accepted by their parents and caregivers and may not have financial support or any type of support from them. They may be forced to find their own way to make ends meet when it comes to their training. If they are under sixteen years old, they will be kept from participating because it is virtually impossible for them to raise their own funds to play on their local sports team. Exacerbating this problem is the fact that even if an athlete is legally allowed to work, there are many situations where they may not be able to get or keep a job because of transphobia or other types of prejudice. A 2018 study in the UK found that one in three employers were "less likely" to hire a trans person, and nearly half reported they were "unsure" whether they would hire a trans person.[26]

THE PARENTAL ADVANTAGE

What about when athletes benefit not only from structural advantages into which they're born, but also their family members? It's not uncommon for parents and caregivers to put their children into the same sports they played and pass on their knowledge and skill sets to help them excel, but this custom is most impactful and relevant among elite and professional sports dynasties. Once again, such advantages are praised and beloved. Take a look at brothers and NFL stars Peyton and Eli Manning, whose father, Archie Manning, played in the NFL for thirteen seasons and likely inspired both of them to follow in his footsteps as a quarterback. Then there's NBA basketball legend Steph Curry, who is the son of Dell Curry, a member of the Charlotte Hornets, among other teams. Of course, there are tennis stars and sisters Serena and Venus Williams, who were blessed with a mother and father who became their tennis coaches. Lastly, there's the boxing royalty father-daughter duo of Muhammad Ali and Laila Ali. It's not a stretch to assume that Muhammad literally showed Laila the ropes in becoming an undefeated champion with twenty-one knockouts.

Researchers have proven a link between young people's success in sports and the athleticism of their parents. In 2019, Stuart Wilson, a postdoctoral researcher in human kinetics at Queen's University in Ontario, analyzed data involving 229 athletes from Australia to Canada, in what was believed to be the first study of its kind.[27] Those athletes were grouped into categories based on whether they were "elite" (had competed at international levels), "pre-elite" (junior or senior national team participation), or "non-elite" (lower levels of competition). Wilson then compared these athletes' participation with their parents' history of participation in sports and their overall achievements and expertise. He found that athletes in the elite category were three times more likely to have parents who participated in competitive sports than the pre-elite athletes and were twice as likely as non-elite athletes to have parents with such an athletic history. For Wilson, the findings showed that the parents' experience of playing sports made them better equipped to support their own child's journey in athletics.[28]

Particularly at the youth levels, the exclusion of trans athletes is not an evidence-based solution to address inequalities in sports participation, nor do credible experts in this area pursue it to achieve true equality and fairness. Further, it's important to view fairness as a continuum, and also to ask ourselves whether achievement in sports is ultimately about the ends—winning—or the journey to get there. Karissa Niehoff, the CEO of the National Federation of State High School Associations in the US, wrote a 2018 ESPN article about trans athletes and the approach she has taken to this issue in her home state of Connecticut. Neihoff said, aptly, that her association doesn't look at fairness in terms of winning and losing. "It's more about opportunity and access. We want to be fair there first."[29]

Today, there are various solutions and initiatives around the world dedicated to this issue of fairness that provide a foundation on which to build and expand. Private organizations, banks, and sports leagues of all types have acknowledged that deserving kids are often left on the sidelines as a result of high registration fees and other associated costs that pose participation barriers. And although there are some opportunities through subsidization, free equipment, and donations through scholarships and grants, many kids still fall through the cracks. While admirable, these measures are simply not enough to offset the deeply entrenched disparity that is rooted in capitalism. Addressing structural inequities in general is complex, and well beyond the scope of this book. Tackling structural inequities in young people's access to sports is a seemingly more manageable endeavor, but it is still nonetheless complicated and will take time, effort, and political will. Researchers and experts seem to agree, however, that the solution lies in schools and ensuring that youth sports are deeply interwoven into the public school system. Society should consider access to sports through schools as important a priority as free school lunch and breakfast programs. Most people, of course, do not view sports and the provision of food as the same in terms of meeting a child's needs, but when the focus on sports shifts from winning to health and physical activity, it becomes clear how both these things can play a role in student enrichment.

One country that seems to have figured out the key to keeping youth sports participation high is Norway, where a whopping 93 percent of youth participate in sports,[30] compared with around 50 percent or less in North America.[31] At the root of its sports regime is the national Children's Rights in Sport declaration, introduced in 1987 and updated in 2007, which outlines the ideal athletic experience that every child should have.[32] It touches on safety and the importance of sports to form friendships. Clubs or organizations that violate the rules risk losing funding. In Norway, the overall cost of entry into sports is low, and travel teams don't form until youth hit their teenage years. Interestingly, and perhaps controversially, coaches and administrators also don't start picking out the most talented and skilled athletes until they hit their teens, when they are further in their development. Just look at the 2018 Winter Olympics in Pyeongchang, South Korea, to see the impact of the Norwegian way: the country that garnered thirty-nine medals, the most medals won. (For comparison, the US came in fourth in total medals, with twenty-three.)[33] It's an impressive feat for a country of just 5.5 million people—much less populous than the US, with 336 million, and Canada, with nearly 39 million.[34]

Total and complete fairness will be difficult to achieve, but if the solutions to increased access to sports lie in subsidies for youth and in schools, then it behooves governments and advocates to question and decry efforts that exclude trans youth in the name of "fairness" and because of a misunderstood hormone called testosterone. All athletes and sports regulatory bodies would benefit from freeing themselves of the tunnel vision accompanying the current debate over hormones, and from recognizing that physical performance, whether or not we are athletes, does not hinge on one thing, and certainly not on one or two chemicals.

CHAPTER 4

THE HORMONES QUESTION

Joanna Harper began running at a young age while growing up in the small town of Parry Sound, Ontario, about three hours north of Toronto. Harper fell in love with distance running because she could beat her father at it. She went on to run in high school and college at the University of Western Ontario, where she studied physics and became a nationally ranked runner. In late summer of 2004, at the age of forty-seven, Harper came out publicly as a trans woman and started undergoing hormone therapy that reduced her testosterone levels. Very quickly, Harper noticed an impact on her running abilities—that she was slower and less powerful. Her decline in pace happened within a matter of weeks, and not gradually, something that took Harper by surprise. Her time in the 10,000-meter race dropped to at least five minutes slower than her previous personal best before her medical transition. "It just blew me away," Harper later told *Science*. As a medical physicist by training, Harper's scientific interest was piqued, and she began to document her journey with hormone suppression and how it affected her as an athlete.[1]

Harper would go on to publish the first peer-reviewed article on the performance of transgender athletes before, during, and after hormone therapy. That study, published in the *Journal of Sporting Cultures and Identities* in 2015, contained a bombshell revelation: trans women on hormone suppression treatment did not perform better than their cisgender women competitors in various races than they had against their cisgender men competitors prior to their physical transition.[2] Basically, the trans athletes' level of competitiveness was the same against cisgender women as it was when they previously competed against cisgender men. It should be noted that this study was based on a small sample of only eight trans women runners in middle age, including Harper herself, but it nonetheless provided useful data upon which she and others would be able to build. The year her study was published, Harper became the first transgender person to advise the International Olympic Committee on issues regarding gender and sport. And she would continue her own research, leading the way for others as well, into the relationship between hormones and athleticism. But now, a decade since Harper's research first came out, far too little research has been conducted on this topic, and there are still so many questions that need answers. Even as the volume of research increases, there ought to be a streamlined and consistent approach as to how this research is understood and incorporated into policies.

As transgender and nonbinary communities, including high-profile athletes, have become more visible in recent years, so too has the scrutiny and policing of trans bodies. And it seems like everyone, from researchers to armchair experts, has their own, sometimes contradictory, opinions on appropriate hormone levels for athletes. Guidelines surrounding transgender athletes have been called "sport's unsolvable problem" by Ross Tucker, a South African exercise physiologist who was involved in the creation of World Rugby's transgender eligibility policy, which prohibits trans women from participating.[3] Certain hormone levels that are too high or too low can make or break entire careers—for athletes of all gender identities. Take the case of two-time Olympic gold medalist runner Caster Semenya, who was born with naturally high testosterone levels due to what is known as her difference in sexual development, or DSD, a condition that occurs when a person is born with reproductive anatomy that doesn't fully align with the gender binary. Semenya, whose case we will explore later in greater detail, declined to compete at the 2021 Tokyo Olympics in protest of the rules put forward by her sport's governing body, which required Semenya and other athletes with similarly high testosterone levels to medically suppress those levels in order to compete.[4] Matters have been further complicated by the recent medical and ethical queries that have been raised as to whether any and all women should have to lower their testosterone levels if they don't fall within the arbitrarily acceptable range. Contrary to popular belief, scientific evidence does not suggest whether, or to what degree, hormone levels consistently grant competitive advantage. So instead of asking how much testosterone is in an athlete's body, the real question to answer is: How might a better understanding of the science behind hormone therapy make for more inclusive and evidence-based policies that support rather than exclude some of the most vulnerable and marginalized people who just want to be able to play the sports they love?

To start, let's explore what exactly our hormones are and what they do. Simply put, hormones are the chemicals that manage various functions throughout our bodies. Scientists have identified more than fifty types of hormones, and different glands produce hormones that are then released into the bloodstream, where they are picked up by receptor cells in different tissues.[5] Hormones do things like help control our metabolism (which helps us function), energy and mood levels, growth and development, reproduction, and physiological responses to stress, injuries, and other environmental factors. Because the main reason for talking about these hormones here is that they are the focus of the debate regarding trans and nonbinary athletes in sports, we will focus here on the three types of sex hormones—none of which are strictly feminine or masculine.

People assigned female at birth (AFAB) typically have two ovaries that produce estrogen, progesterone, and testosterone. People assigned male at birth (AMAB) typically have two testes that produce testosterone. Although AFABs typically have higher levels of estrogen than AMABs, folks assigned male at birth do produce a type of estrogen called estradiol, which is crucial to sexual function, including the production of sperm. The terminology that we will use throughout the rest of the chapter will be very body-specific, and it's important to note the sensitive nature of this type of terminology, especially when it comes to sexual reproductive parts and functions that are typically gendered by society and culture. Trans, cisgender, nonbinary, or intersex people should not be reduced to simply the type of body they have or how it functions. It's also important to note that the language that we are using to describe identities and bodies is ever-changing and evolving.

Transgender and nonbinary athletes are often thought about in terms of the hormones they have in their bodies and what will or will not allow them to compete and excel in sports. However, there are very human aspects to this debate that reach beyond the confines of sport. Most, if not all, trans policies in place for sports do not consider that the prescription hormones taken by some trans and nonbinary athletes allow them to be happy and functional members of society. Indeed, the reasons why trans and nonbinary athletes take hormones in the first place have nothing to do with sports at all, let alone their performance in the athletic realm. While it's not always the case, many transgender people choose to undergo hormone therapy as part of their physical transition process to help them better align their body with their gender identity. In recent years, the number of trans people seeking hormone therapy has risen and the age at which people seek it has been dropping.[6] Some researchers attribute the rise in trans people seeking hormone therapy to increased acceptance and de-stigmatization of trans people in general, owing in large part to empathetic news coverage and social media, which has empowered trans people to share their perspectives and experiences. Hormone therapy can be done on its own or in tandem with various physical surgeries such as top surgery (double mastectomy), phalloplasty, and vaginoplasty. There are many ways for a transgender person to physically and socially transition, and these are just a few examples. There's no correct or incorrect approach. Right now, for the purposes of our research, we're focusing on people who choose to undergo hormone therapy as part of their transition.

A 2022 study led by the Stanford University School of Medicine that drew on the largest-ever survey of US transgender adults—more than twenty-seven thousand respondents—found that trans people who began hormone treatment as teens were less likely to have suicidal thoughts or engage in problematic substance use than those who began hormone therapy as adults.[7] The study also found improved mental health among trans people who underwent hormone therapy at any age than those who wanted to undergo the treatment but never did. That evidence was confirmed and expanded on in another study published in 2023 in the *New England Journal of Medicine* that examined 315 transgender youth between the ages of twelve and twenty over the course of two years while they were being treated with hormone therapy.[8] It's a groundbreaking study, as this type of research, especially for youth, is few and far between. The researchers here measured the incidence of negative feelings and emotions like depression and anxiety, as well as positive emotions such as satisfaction and mind-body alignment. On average, the study concluded, participants noted increased positive emotions compared with their emotional state before beginning hormones. Understanding these effects is "crucial, given the documented mental health disparities observed in this population, particularly in the context of increasing politicization of gender-affirming medical care," the study authors write.[9]

Nonbinary people and transgender men who choose to undergo hormone therapy will often undergo a testosterone regimen to help masculinize their facial features. Testosterone prompts the body to undergo some aspects of the puberty experienced by cisgender men. For some, it can halt the menstrual cycle and decrease estrogen creation within their ovaries. Other physical impacts can include facial and body hair growth, an increase in muscle mass, and the thickening of vocal cords, producing a deeper voice. Conversely, for nonbinary people and trans women, feminizing hormone therapy induces the body to undergo the puberty experienced by cisgender women. Their hormone therapy may involve taking medicine that blocks the effects of testosterone and includes taking estrogen, which can induce breast development, slow hair loss, reduce facial and body hair growth, increase body fat, and reduce muscle mass. Regardless of gender identity, all of this is done primarily to gain comfort in one's body.

The argument that trans people, particularly trans women, physically transition as a means to dominate women's sports overlooks a crucial detail: life outside of sports. Physically transitioning is something not done on a whim and alters most aspects of life. On top of all the irreversible physical changes that hormones do to an individual's body, there is also the potential for the individual to face social stigma and be ostracized from family and loved ones. Coming out as transgender can be an extremely vulnerable experience. People's reactions can range from indifference to disdain, verbal abuse, and even physical violence. Trans people do not endure all this emotional turmoil unless physically transitioning is absolutely crucial for their survival. The goal for most transgender and nonbinary people beginning this journey is hopefully to feel like their true selves and achieve some level of confidence and harmony with who they are and how they appear to themselves and society—not to excel at sports.

Now that we have discussed the impacts of hormone therapy for transgender people who have already experienced puberty, let's look at things earlier in human development, i.e., before pubescence. Prior to puberty, it makes little sense to segregate children in sports based on gender, as there is little to no difference between testosterone concentrations related to athletic performance between cisgender girls and boys prior to puberty.[10] We see this through data and research on sex differences in youth who participate in competitive swimming. For example, research published in the open access journal *PLOS ONE* in 2019 showed that the top five swimmers on the girls' side demonstrated faster swimming velocities compared to the top five swimmers on the boys' side, and the girls who ranked 10th to

50th place demonstrated similarly faster swimming velocities than their boy counterparts up until ten years of age. "We conclude that prior to the performance-enhancing effects of puberty, the best girls outperform the best boys at spring and endurance swimming events," the researchers wrote.[11] "Our findings are in direct opposition to universal findings in elite adult athletes that boys are faster than girls." For Schuyler Bailar, the Harvard University swimmer and the first transgender athlete to compete on an NCAA Division I men's team, this swimming case study, and others, opens the door to better understanding the impacts of hormones and the way we're conditioned to think about sports in general. Bailar also pointed us to recent swimming times for swimmers age ten and under[12] and age twelve and un-der[13] in which the girls' qualifying times were often the same or faster than the boys'. The fact that the girls' qualifying times are faster in this context points to the fact that girls are, generally, socialized to have a higher level of focus by paying attention, which translates to better athletic performance. "They actually swim better, but it's true for other sports, too," Bailar told us. "So the whole 'boys are faster than girls' is complete B.S. before puberty; and even after puberty, it's marginal at the beginning."[14]

Another piece of research that supports the conclusion that testosterone does not automatically equate to dominant athletic performance was a study released in *Human Kinetics* in 2016 of fifty-two teenaged Olympic weightlift-ers. The levels of testosterone, cortisol, and dehydroepiandrosterone-sulfate (a hormone that helps produce both testosterone and estrogen) in twenty-six boys and twenty-six girls were monitored across two elite weightlifting compe-titions.[15] According to professors Katrina Karkazis and Rebecca Jordan-Young in their invaluable book, *Testosterone: An Unauthorized Biography*, this study suggests that lean body mass has a complicated relationship with testosterone. Though the research concluded that the sex differences that emerge during puberty were observable (with the boys being on average larger than the girls), the researchers counterintuitively found there was a *negative* relationship be-tween testosterone levels and athletic performance among the teens competing in the girls' weightlifting category. In other words, teens competing on the girls' side with lower testosterone could, in fact, lift *more* weight. Among the athletes competing on the boys' side of similar size in the study, there was no significant relationship between their hormone levels and their performance during the competition.[16] Once again, the relationship between testosterone, performance, and advantage is not clear-cut.

Although there is often very little, if any, hormone-related difference in athletic performance between prepubescent girls and prepubescent boys, testosterone exposure during puberty may result in hormone-related differences in height, pelvic bone structure, and leg bones in the lower limbs that can and do provide an athletic advantage to folks after they have gone through a testosterone-driven puberty.[17] These physiological aspects do not change later in life, post-puberty, even if the person chooses to undergo hormone therapy. So, if a trans woman takes testosterone blockers, for example, it is true that she will still retain those physiological developments that came about during her testosterone exposure during puberty. Similarly, trans men who take testosterone after going through puberty will not develop hormone-related physiological differences such as those relating to height and pelvic bone structure.

The changes during puberty are irreversible, but there is very little science on the direct correlation that these changes have in terms of athletic performance when it comes to transgender adults. It's also important to acknowledge that the experiences and effects of puberty look different for everyone, regardless of gender identity, and therefore varies among trans women as well. The idea that all trans women are automatically going to be exponentially taller, heavier, and stronger than their cisgender women peers is just not accurate. For example, just because a cisgender man goes through a testosterone-driven puberty does not mean they are necessarily six feet tall (as much as they might wish they were). There's wide height variation among the general population, across different parts of the world, that seems to be overlooked in the discussions about trans participation.

As already mentioned, there's a significant lack of robust and current scientific data on the relationship between hormones and athletic performance, including the extent to which testosterone and testosterone blockers can help or hinder an athlete's overall endurance, speed, strength, agility, and other traits important to sports. On this point we can turn again to professors Karkazis and Jordan-Young in *Testosterone: An Unauthorized Biography*, who, citing a behavioral endocrinologist, explain that while testosterone is important and fascinating, it's far too simplistic to say that it is the single most important determinant of athleticism. "The idea that raised testosterone in any human being leads to better athletic performance is shaky," Karkazis and Jordan-Young write.[18] This is so, they argue, because there isn't one singular master trait that accounts for or explains athletic performance in different athletes. As evidence, they cite a 2008 paper that confirmed testosterone can increase muscle mass and power, as well as maximal voluntary strength, but it doesn't seem to necessarily build a better athlete overall.

Athletic performance does not require the same skills or capacities for all sports. Just because you're a good basketball player does not mean you'll be a good tennis player. In a similar vein, athletes who excel at their given sport might not excel in a variation of that sport. Perhaps the best illustration of the latter point is Usain Bolt, the Jamaican sprinter considered to be the fastest human on earth. Now retired, Bolt holds the world record in the 100-meter and 200-meter sprints, and the 4x100-meter relay. Bolt has repeatedly said that while he's the best at these short sprint events, he does not run the 800-meter sprint because he's quite slow at it. He's tried it before and trained hard for it, but it's just not his forte. "A woman could beat me," he told a reporter in 2013. The reporter tried to rebuff the notion and thought that Bolt must be joking. "You're going to get in trouble for that," the reporter chided. But Bolt doubled down: "It's true, though, they could!"[19] And he is correct. Karkazis and Jordan-Young note that in 2018 alone, 498 women ran faster than Bolt's best time in the 800-meter sprint, which is 2:07. This includes nearly a hundred teenage girls who beat his time. "Sex isn't always the most sensible way to divide athletes, even within a particular sport like running," the authors continue.[20] "The idea that there is one core ingredient in the magic sauce for every conceivable sport is frankly absurd." While this conclusion should seem like basic common sense, for some reason, any fraction of nuance gets lost or ignored by anti-trans lawmakers and activists. Given the wide variety and significant differences among and between sports, why would a blanket, catch-all policy be appropriate or sound? Especially one based on a single hormone.

THE TROUBLES IN OHIO

In June 2022, Republicans in the Ohio House of Representatives passed a bill to prohibit trans girls from playing on girls' sports teams—from kindergarten to college. The bill specified that any athlete playing on the girls' side who was suspected of being a trans girl would be forced to verify their gender. Opponents of the bill questioned the process through which a child's gender would be verified. (During the course of the legislative debates, it was eventually revealed there was only one known trans varsity athlete in all of Ohio high school sports.) The bill would require a physician to physically examine schoolchildren's hormone levels or genetics, or perform an examination of "internal and external reproductive anatomy"—a full pelvic exam—in the event of a dispute over the gender of an athlete participating in women's sports.[21] Full pelvic exams, especially for this type of purpose, is not standard practice in pediatrics. The stigma around having one's gender identity called into question, let alone having to be subjected to invasive actions, is incongruous with efforts to promote the safety of children.

The verbiage of the Ohio bill was understandably met with great scrutiny, especially the "physical examination" requirement.[22] The lawmakers heard testimony from young trans athletes and their families who pleaded with state senators to vote against it, saying that under such a law, they would be forced to move away to another state to protect the lives and dignity of the young athletes. Those who testified included Ember Zelch, a trans girl who was eighteen years old at the time the bill was being discussed.[23] While in high school, Zelch was a catcher on various high school softball teams. Though she was about to head off to college, she testified before the committee numerous times to fight efforts to ban trans girls from sports. From 2015 to 2023, an eight-year span, only twenty-four trans girls received official approval from the Ohio High School Athletic Association to participate on the sports teams that aligned with their gender identity. Before the new proposed ban, the state required that a trans woman athlete needs to either be on hormone therapy for one year or have a physician's note outlining how she is not at a physiological advantage compared to her cisgender peers. In 2023, Zelch, who started hormone therapy in her freshman year of high school, was one of just six trans girls granted such approval. Zelch's case is interesting because, as her mother, Minna Zelch, testified in Columbus with her permission, she has actually tested as having *less* testosterone than the average cisgender girl. The typical testosterone range for people assigned male at birth is between 300 to 1200 ng/dl (nanograms per deciliter). For people assigned female at birth, it's typically between 20 and 75 ng/dl. Zelch's mother told the committee that according to a recent blood draw, hers was 12 ng/dl—far lower than her cisgender peers. So, what is the panic surrounding people like Zelch based on? The efforts of Zelch and others were effective in removing the genital inspection provision, but it was subsequently replaced by birth certificate verifications. Ultimately, the bill, having failed to get a majority vote in the state senate, was killed at the end of 2022. The saga continued, however, with a new iteration of the bill dubbed the "Save Women's Sports Act"—a copy-and-paste of dozens of other bills like it—that was successfully passed in June 2023. It did not include a genital inspection provision.[24]

We need to be wary of any statements and laws that claim to be certain and declarative when it comes to the hormone question. Blanket bans against trans athletes are not supported by science, and they typically manipulate and cherry-pick the data that *does* exist to fit problematic solutions built on fear, laziness, and a moral panic rooted in transphobia and misogyny. We hear so much about new bans against trans athletes, yet so rarely is the actual scientific research, or lack thereof, on the matter discussed. One study being used to justify bans of this kind is a 2020 study of transgender adults in the US Air Force.[25] It provides limited but, surprisingly, very useful data (for reasons we'll explain) on the impacts of both testosterone and testosterone blockers on athletic performance in three military fitness tests: the 1.5-mile run, push-ups, and sit-ups. The research subjects were twenty-nine trans men and forty-six trans women all under the age of thirty who started hormone therapy as part of their transition while serving in the Air Force. Researchers looked at how the individuals' hormone regimens affected their fitness test results, and how they affected their physiological compositions as well. This study is great because it's based on fitness scores that span over ten years—from 2004 and 2014—and it's one of the only studies of its kind with such extensive longitudinal data. The results showed that prior to taking hormones, the trans women were able to do 31 percent more push-ups and 15 percent more sit-ups, and were able to complete the 1.5-mile test 21 percent faster than their cisgender women counterparts. After two years on hormones, there was no longer any difference in the results for push-ups and sit-ups between the trans women and the cisgender women. The gap between their 1.5-mile run results closed, going from 31 percent to 12 percent—meaning the trans women were still able to run faster than their cisgender counterparts, but their run times decreased by 19 percent. The study concludes that more than twelve months of testosterone suppression may be needed to "ensure that transgender women do not have an unfair competitive advantage when participating in elite level athletic competition."[26] However, at no point do the researchers call for any sort of ban for trans women athletes. In fact, the study helps support the position that there ought to be inclusion that is evidence-based.

The result for the 1.5-mile run has been strategically weaponized by anti-trans policymakers and government officials to support their broad bans and perpetuate the false narrative that trans women are dominating women's sports. One Republican Kansas senator, Roger Marshall, cited the US Air Force study—only this study and only the 1.5-mile run result—in a 2021 op-ed for Fox News.[27] In that piece, he criticized President Biden's executive order that allows student-athletes to play on the sports team that aligns with their gender identity. While Marshall correctly summarizes one aspect of the study, he fails to mention the results of the other tests. He also conveniently ignores the caveats made by the study's authors, including that more research is needed on these issues and that the participants' external athletic routines were not considered as part of their findings. In addition, Marshall fails to mention that the study also lacks a control group of trans women who did not go through a hormone regimen, an essential feature of peer-reviewed scholarship. Further, it's worth pointing out that the sample size is minuscule and involves only people in one branch of the military. The website PolitiFact, run by the Poynter Institute, asked the study's co-author, Dr. Timothy Roberts, the director of the adolescent medicine training program at Children's Mercy Kansas City, about Marshall's characterization of his research. "For strength or technique-based competitions, Sen. Marshall is misrepresenting our research," Dr. Roberts told the outlet.[28] Dr. Roberts also said that the running results need context. While the average trans woman in the study is still faster than the average cisgender woman after two years on hormones, the trans woman is still slower than the top 9 percent of cisgender women runners. "Advantage? Yes," he continued. "[Will trans women] destroy women's sports? No."[29]

HORMONE THERAPY AND TRANS MEN IN WOMEN'S SPORTS

The controversies and debates regarding trans inclusion and hormones in sports typically revolve around trans women, while the sacrifices and experiences of trans men are often left out of the conversation. For trans men athletes, a physical transition through hormone therapy usually is possible only if they participate in the men's category or gain a medical exemption. In elite sports, where hormones and other banned substances are strictly regulated, some trans men and nonbinary people are forced to either leave their sport prematurely or put their personal life on pause to continue being an athlete at their current level.

Some trans men and nonbinary people may opt for receiving low doses of testosterone to help them experience a slower physical transition—to have a slight deepening of their voice, a slight masculinization of their body and facial features over time. These small variations in hormones in one's body may not have a large impact on their athletic performance, but it could have a huge personal impact on that individual's comfort in their everyday life. It may also allow them to continue playing the sport they love while feeling more comfortable with their bodies.

We saw this type of experience with professional soccer player Parker Dunn, a twenty-three-year-old trans man from England who played in the FA Women's National League South for the London Bees Football Club until 2024. Parker, who as of mid-2024 hasn't yet begun physically transitioning, told us over Zoom about how it's hard for him to hear his own voice and that it makes him feel small in social settings, not wanting to speak out loud. Harrison remembers that at the time he was openly trans but not yet taking testosterone, it was difficult to not have a lower voice. His higher, prepubescent voice was something that he always felt was an automatic giveaway, a "tell" for people that he wasn't a cisgender man. When Harrison would use his "pre-T" voice to talk to people, he found that they would become confused and not know whether he was a man or a woman or another gender.

As of this writing, Dunn has yet to physically transition with testosterone because he plays in the women's division, where the current rules around testosterone use are vague and uncertain. Although testosterone use is technically allowed in the women's division, it is highly restrictive and allowed only in small doses. Dunn, a defender, is in a similar position that Harrison was in his hockey career and is trying to make himself feel as comfortable as possible until he can begin the physical transition that will necessitate his retirement from women's soccer. He's desperate to start taking testosterone to help lower his voice, not to achieve any sort of athletic advantage. "I just want my voice to drop and then I could forget about all the other things," Dunn explained to us.[30] But that must be put on hold for now until he can get some sort of guarantee that the rules will remain in place and can be followed with relative ease. "What I worry about is the FAA [Football Athletic Association] saying that 'you can go on testosterone for a little while your voice can drop,' and then they turn around a year later and they're like,

'Any athletes who have taken "T" can no longer ever play,'" he continued. "So, for me at the moment, it's all off the table." Dunn's fear that the policies could change on a whim without the FAA providing adequate lead-up time or doing proper research is warranted, as we've seen the NCAA and other sports entities make sudden policy changes and go back and forth on their own inclusion policies.

Once trans athletes begin their hormone therapy, they may find themselves stuck in limbo. It can be a time full of chaos, shame, anger, and confusion. For trans men playing on the women's side of their sport, even considering the idea of hormone therapy as part of their transition process puts their future in their current sport in jeopardy. Because of anti-doping protocols in many leagues, taking testosterone disqualifies you. Some trans men may decide to delay their physical transition to stay in their sport, but this can lead to potential mental health risks because they can't live as their authentic selves outside of sport. As highlighted through Harrison's journey in the introduction, what caused him the most turmoil while playing in the NWHL with respect to his gender identity had more to do with how he was viewed by others outside of the sports world than within it. However, switching from the women's league to the men's is not always an option for athletes regardless of whether hormone therapy is permitted. And the competitive status that that athlete has on the women's side does not necessarily translate to the men's side.

Trans women athletes are also faced with their own set of challenges when it comes to hormones. There are more restrictions and enforced delays—for instance, trans women in the NCAA need to be on hormone therapy for one year before they can compete on the women's side. This waiting period can, as with trans men, lead to potential mental health risks as well as the athlete quitting and walking away from their sport prematurely. "There's a gray area that gets lost because people see it in (black and white)—you're born a man or a woman. It's a life or death issue for (transitioning) transgender women who have a sport as their sanctuary through dark times," Juniper "June" Eastwood, the first transgender Division I cross-country runner, told *USA Today* in 2021. "It becomes, quit the sport that's saved you or keep competing but be open to scorn."[31]

While many critics mainly focus on the physical changes and performance of trans women in research studies, the athletic performance of trans men is often overlooked and, in most cases, downplayed. The 2020 US Air

Force study opens up a larger conversation and calls into question the argument that anyone who has gone through a testosterone-driven puberty will be an overall better athlete than someone who hasn't. (We'll get into this in later chapters, but this oversight and the overall framing of trans men not being a physical threat to their cisgender men counterparts is rooted in deeper societal forces such as misogyny and sexism.) The main finding for trans men in the Air Force study, according to most of the media coverage, is that after a year of hormone replacement therapy, there was no longer a difference in performance between the trans men and the cisgender men. In actuality, trans men outperformed cis men consistently in one of the three fitness tests analyzed: sit-ups. Delving deeper into this research and the way it was discussed led to an epiphany for Harrison about how the human mind can get in the way of understanding reality when it's been conditioned to believe a certain narrative perpetuated by society.

The narrative that Harrison believed up until then was that for the most part, a body assigned female at birth is supposed to be weaker than a body assigned male. No matter what. Although Harrison is no longer training as a professional athlete, he continues a rigorous fitness routine and participates in co-ed CrossFit classes. During these sessions in Toronto, the workouts are curated by a coach, and suggested weights for each exercise are broken into two groups: a lower weight for the members on the women's side of the class and a higher weight for the members on the men's side. Believing that his body was inherently weaker than most of the cisgender men in the class, who are generally heavier and taller than him, he usually went by the lower weight suggestion. After reading the study discussed above, he remembered that he was almost five years on testosterone and, according to the data, his body was four years past the point of being on par with his cisgender men counterparts in terms of strength. His mentality shifted on what his body was capable of, and he was pleased to discover that he could actually lift more than in past sessions. When performing a clean and jerk, with much less weight than Laurel Hubbard would lift, he went from lifting 115 pounds to 140 pounds over the course of a few weeks. Any fellow gym rat knows it's virtually impossible to increase one's strength by that much in such a short time. Harrison discovered that it was a *mental* block that affected the amount he was able to lift and not his physical capabilities. It was mind-blowing, and he's made a conscious effort to increase his weight amounts and physical exertion beyond what he assumes is possible. These days, he often outperforms the other men in his class.

The athletic mindset or psychology is something that researchers are constantly investigating. What makes an elite athlete elite? What makes one athlete better than the other when they have the same physical capabilities? It's the mindset. There's a reason why athletes are revered in areas beyond the sport arena. They are brought into places like Fortune 500 companies and Ivy League schools to share what makes them focused, determined, a team player, a champion. The power of the mind isn't something that can be easily quantified and studied. It's more elusive and subjective than what many typically assume. But there is something to be said about how the narratives we tell ourselves shape our actions, our beliefs about ourselves, and our capabilities. It might sound cheesy, but there's a lot of power in the established wisdom that when you believe you can't do something, you can't, and when you believe you *can* do something, you can. When someone is assigned female at birth and is constantly told what their body can't do and who they can and can't be stronger, faster, and generally better than, their mind can be trained to believe it. We will never know the number of cisgender women athletes who have not truly reached their athletic potential because of this problematic and toxic mentality.

Trans men are also held back by this same narrative. Shortly after Harrison came out as trans, he was very active on social media and people constantly commented on his various posts and videos. This is a comment pulled from a YouTube post about Harrison's discussion of trans athletes in sports:

> It's not that people don't feel threatened by trans men competing in male sport. It's more that people really don't mind at all primarily because they wouldn't really be able to compete successfully in the first place. There's the odd exception like the trans male boxer Pat [Patricio] Manuel who won a match (admittedly the fight was limited to only four rounds against a fellah who'd never won anything) but essentially no trans man, whether pre- or post-op, has any chance whatsoever of participating at a competitive level in male physical sport although of course they are more than welcome to try.[32]

This is just one of the countless number of comments with this rhetoric and, believe it or not, this is one of the nicer messages. This comment is from

2021 and, since then, Patricio Manuel, the boxer being scrutinized and whom we discussed in chapter 2, has had two more professional boxing bouts in which he beat his cisgender men opponents handily. There are many trans men athletes who have successfully competed against and beat cisgender men opponents in their chosen sport. A couple other great examples include Schuyler Bailar, the Harvard swimmer mentioned earlier, who by the end of his collegiate career excelled in the men's division across the NCAA in his best events, ranking in the top 13 and 15 percent of swimmers in the 100-yard butterfly and 100-yard breaststroke, respectively.[33]

These anonymous keyboard warriors all sound the same, spouting the tired and false refrain that trans women are dominant and trans men are weaker when they compete against athletes that align with their gender identity. What the commenter quoted above didn't acknowledge—and most likely couldn't be bothered to easily look up on Google—is that Manuel is a decorated boxer on the women's side as well. The reality for most sports fans is they immediately discount all of Manuel's incredibly prestigious titles and athletic achievements simply because the word "women" is put before them. Manuel is an incredibly gifted athlete who, no matter what division he competes in, will excel because he does not subscribe to the narrative that how he was born dictates what he can achieve. He trains hard and fights hard, and respects his opponents no matter their gender identity. Moreover, he is a formidable physical force among cisgender men; in one particular bout, he stood five inches taller and nearly four pounds heavier than his opponent.

Although understanding the existing science and myths about hormones is important to being a well-informed participant and ally in the discussions about trans inclusion in sports, a narrow focus on testosterone and hormones can be a distraction from arguably more important issues. When maintaining such a singular focus on something, it's easy to ignore the more complex issues, such as race and class, that have a deeper impact on sports and sports performance, as we've already discussed. Karkazis and Jordan-Young refer to fixations on testosterone as "T talk." "In an alchemy between folklore and science, T talk validates familiar cultural beliefs as scientific, and scientific accounts get a free pass on some of the details and consistency that they would otherwise need to provide," they write.[34] In other words, testosterone has become such a loaded term that it can now be used as a shield against true debate or questions about testosterone and its impacts on trans athletes.

If a sports regulatory body invokes testosterone levels as a reason why it needs to impose gender verification testing or other regulations, its motives are taken at face value and rarely questioned.

Joanna Harper, the trans athlete and researcher mentioned earlier, says that the science regarding hormones, particularly testosterone, is still in its infancy and there likely won't be definitive consensus on the science for at least twenty more years. She commends sports regulatory bodies such as the International Olympic Committee for admitting that they don't have all the answers and won't make policy decisions on the basis of shaky evidence. The IOC has essentially taken the position that until we have better data, trans exclusion is not the answer. "What I would say is that until we know for sure, sport's governing bodies should do the best they can with the data that exists, with the knowledge that we have today, with the understanding that any policy they create now should be subject to change once we get more data," Harper told reporters.[35] "That I think is a more reasonable approach than either saying there shouldn't be any restrictions on trans women or we shouldn't let trans women in until we know for certain."

CHAPTER 5

PANIC AT THE OLYMPICS

In the 1930s, it was still very much an unusual sight to see a woman athlete, let alone an elite one. At the 1936 Berlin Olympics, in the same stadium where runner Caster Semenya would go on to win her first world title more than seventy years later in 2009, rumors swirled that 100-meter runners Polish-American Stella Walsh and her rival, American Helen Stephens, were men—the speculation was based solely on their appearance. These fears came about at this time that was marked by an overall paranoia about "male intruders" entering women's spaces, sports specifically. Regulators and spectators were constantly on the prowl for men who were masquerading as women in order to fraudulently compete in women's sports. One example of actual fraud at the 1936 Olympics was German high jumper Dora Ratjen, who purported to be a woman but was later discovered to identify as a man. It should be noted, however, that even though Ratjen was outed for being deceptive, and did not even identify as a woman, he ended up placing fourth overall behind three cisgender competitors.[1] (Ratjen's performance against the cisgender women challenges the idea that any man can outrun or beat a woman athlete, no matter their training.)

As a child growing up in Cleveland, Ohio, Stella Walsh excelled at many sports, including baseball, and even played on the boys' team. Prior to the 1936 Olympics, Walsh stood out from her peers for her shyness and the fact that she didn't like using the same changing room as the other women. While this doesn't prove anything about her gender, she was nonetheless isolated and seen as "other." Helen Stephens, for her part, turned heads because she was nearly six feet tall, noticeably muscular, and had a deep voice.

After Stephens clinched the gold medal, the Olympics committee ordered a manual inspection of her genitals, concluding that she was, as she had always claimed, a woman. German authorities had to issue a statement to the media declaring that Stephens had passed a "sex check." The following year, she successfully sued an American magazine called *Look* for $5,500 after it ran a piece with the headline "Is This a Man or a Woman?" After retiring from sports, Walsh stepped away from the spotlight to live her life under the radar. But after she was tragically killed in a robbery in 1980, an autopsy of her body found that she had no uterus and an underdeveloped penis, something that prompted a barrage of negative and harmful publicity, including the constant refrain that "Stella was a fella." Walsh was posthumously accused of cheating throughout her competitive sporting career, though she abided by all the rules that were in place at the time.[2] Even in death, Walsh could not escape society's obsession with feminine ideals and the cruelty that comes with upholding them. To this day, in the discussions about the inclusion of gender diverse athletes in track and field and beyond, such obsessions with feminine ideals remain pervasive.

When the modern Olympics relaunched in the late nineteenth century, its founder, Baron Pierre de Coubertin, declared that he was wholeheartedly against including women in any competitions. De Coubertin said that women's participation in sports was "impractical, uninteresting, ungainly, and, I do not hesitate to add, improper."[3] Other choice statements by de Coubertin on the issue highlight his unabashed belief that bodies assigned female at birth are inherently inferior to those of people assigned men at birth. "No matter how toughened a sportswoman may be, her organism is not cut out to sustain certain shocks," de Coubertin wrote in 1910. "Her nerves rule her muscles, nature wanted it that way."[4] General public opinion also bucked against the mere idea of women athletes, particularly in competitions that promoted strength over more artistic qualities.

For centuries, sport was for men only and was the place where masculinity was cultivated and proven. But as more women began to enter sports in general, and elite competitive sports in particular, administrators and regulators at the early modern Olympics became obsessed with maintaining and upholding the segregation of men and women athletes at all costs. To do that, women were, for decades, forced to prove their gender. This was frequently done through "gender verification exams" at the Olympics and by other international sports regulators. These procedures and practices, though they have evolved over time, have helped shape perceptions about athletic inclusion and gender broadly speaking. No other entities have so forcefully and consistently tried to figure out who counts as a woman than the International Olympic Committee (IOC) and other organizations including the IAAF (International Association of Athletics Federations, now known as World Athletics). Today, what we can glean from this history is that efforts to make sports fair, however well-intentioned, can morph into misguided and harmful practices that end up negatively affecting all athletes, and women athletes in particular—the very people purported to be at the center of efforts to promote gender equality.

The treatment of women athletes participating in the Olympics, and especially intersex women, has an unsavory history that is illuminating for our current debates about what makes an athlete and who gets to be acknowledged as a woman. Understanding this history and the impact of institutional overreach regarding athletes' bodies has become even more crucial today as antiquated and violating "gender verification exams" are on the rise again, most alarmingly for transgender youth, with states like Ohio discussing genital inspections for any student-athlete who is merely suspected of being trans.[5]

NAKED PARADES

By the 1960s, women's participation in the Olympics and other elite levels of sport began to surge, with the number of woman-only events increasing to include most sports. Throughout this surge, gender verification procedures and exams remained commonplace and accepted at international sport championships and events, known colloquially as "naked parades" or "nude parades."[6] All women participants also had to undergo gynecological exams at the 1966 Commonwealth Games in Kingston, Jamaica, before they were allowed to compete. Reports indicate that athletes participating on the women's side were asked to line up outside an examining room without being warned about what they would be asked to endure, which was later described as akin to groping. That same year, at the IAAF European Track and Field Championships held in Budapest, 243 women athletes had to fully disrobe to be inspected by doctors to verify their gender. No abnormalities were reported.[7]

The following year, in 1967, athletes on the women's side had to submit to gynecological exams at the Pan American Games in Winnipeg, Manitoba.

Maren Seidler, an American shot putter who was only sixteen years old at the time, recalls the trauma of having to experience the exam, describing it as "hideous." Even though she was not afraid of not passing the test, she "just felt that it was humiliating," she said.[8] The Polish Olympic Committee president at the time, Wlodzimierz Reczek, agreed with this sentiment and wrote a scathing letter to the IOC that year describing the gender verification tests as unnecessary. "Repeated gynecological examinations of the young girl athletes, even several times in the course of one year, make an unpleasant environment around those athletes and are a form of discrimination," he wrote. "There are no generally accepted criteria of sex for women athletes and the light-minded arbitrariness in the interpretation of the results of examinations may harm the examined persons."[9] This is something that athletes on the men's side have never had to contend with.

The "nude parades" and physical examinations were eventually replaced with molecular cell–based tests. These tests, which would not require women athletes to disrobe and be humiliated that way, were seen as a more clinical and respectful way to carry out gender verification. But they were not without their faults and problems. Besides being scientifically dubious, to say the least, they were also based in a panic over rooting out women athletes with even just the mere appearance of falling outside the rigid, and socially constructed, gender binary. Athletes participating on the women's side who passed these tests and were deemed to be women, full stop, were bestowed with laminated cards that served as "certificates of femininity" that they had to keep on them at all times in case of on-the-spot inspections from authorities.[10] Even if women did not have biological characteristics associated with people assigned male at birth, these tests prevented athletes who had chromosomal markers considered non-normative from participating. For example, Polish sprinter Ewa Klobukowska was disqualified from participating for failing a sex test in 1967 that reportedly revealed she had an "extra chromosome" and "male-like characteristics."[11] These lab-based chromosome tests changed the notion of womanhood for sports broadly speaking.

What's even more disheartening is that these testing methods were proven faulty in short order.[12] They also resulted in the stigmatization and ostracization of people assigned female at birth with "androgen insensitivity." This fixation on testing for abnormalities and physical characteristics that render women outside the norm of their cisgender women counterparts has resulted in many women being rejected from competing at the Olympics.

There are other countless women who chose to disqualify themselves or not enter competition to avoid the prospect of undergoing such testing. As with all other gender verification tests, athletes on the men's side were never subjected to them. And if they *had* been subjected to these sorts of chromosomal tests, it's possible some of their results would have shown an extra X chromosome, meaning they could have been assigned female and not male.

By 1996, at the Centennial Olympic Games in Atlanta, Georgia, there was a groundswell of opposition to the laboratory-based sex determination and verification testing. Led by women's sports groups, including the Women's Sports Foundation and the IOC's World Conference on Women and Sport, this opposition argued that testing based on chromosome analysis is not only highly discriminatory but also irrelevant and costly. This pushback sparked a sequence of positive changes to problematic policies. In 1999, the IOC conditionally rescinded its thirty-year-old requirement for on-site gender screening of all women entered in women-only events at the Olympics, with the policy going into place the following year in Sydney, Australia. Experts at the time called for the requirement to be permanently rescinded, and also urged for the education of athletes, sports governors, medical delegates, and sports physicians regarding the recognition of biological nuances in discussions about and decisions related to sex organs and physiological criteria.[13] While cisgender women were the first to fight for their right to participate with dignity, gender diverse and intersex athletes would be the next to rip apart invasive and arbitrary testing.

To address the ethical concerns with these types of tests, the IOC Athletes' Commission ended mandatory gender testing at the 2000 Olympic Games in Sydney on a trial basis. Both the IOC and IAAF proceeded with gender-verification tests only when an athlete appeared suspect—still a vague criterion, but at least more limited than before. The implications of a testing regimen carried out on a case-by-case basis opens up the potential, as we've already seen throughout history, for athletes (mostly women) to face targeting, discrimination, and humiliation. Putting the notion of womanhood on display and subjected to constant measurement sets a dangerous precedent that has led to an untold number of athletes, with Caster Semenya being the most widely known, being exiled from their sport and maligned by their community. But her story has become crucial and has shaped our understanding about intersex athletes, as well as the broader debates and controversies regarding gender and race in competitive sports.

The early 2000s ushered in a changing landscape regarding the way gender diversity was dealt with at the highest levels of sport. It also saw some of the most pivotal examples of athletes who, while not transgender, began to shatter the gender paradigm and open new pathways for solidarity and shared struggles. There are a few things to clarify when it comes to Caster Semenya, whose story will anchor much of the rest of this chapter. For starters, the thirty-two-year-old South African runner was assigned female at birth and identifies as a woman. She has never identified as intersex and eschews the label, instead preferring to call herself "a different kind of woman."[14] Throughout her career, track authorities have claimed that her condition makes her "biologically male," something that has enraged her. Semenya has a rare intersex condition called 46 XY DSD, which stands for either "difference" or "disorder" of sex development. It's a condition where the person has one X chromosome and one Y chromosome in each cell, something that's typically found in people assigned male at birth (people assigned female at birth have XX chromosomes), but the person with DSD is born with sex organs that are ambiguous. In Semenya's case, her 46 XY DSD condition leads her body to naturally produce higher levels of testosterone than the average cisgender woman.[15] As a result of this condition with which she was born, Semenya would be treated like an athlete that was illegally doping, a blatant violation of fair play, even though her above-average testosterone levels occurred naturally, without any external intervention or choice on her part.

Semenya became known internationally in 2009 at the age of eighteen, when she competed at the World Track and Field Championships in Berlin in the 800-meter race, at the same stadium where Stella Walsh came in first in the 1936 Olympics. Even before she hit the track, Semenya's gender identity drew suspicions over what sources described to the British tabloid the *Daily Mail* as her "astoundingly quick" abilities.[16] In other words, Semenya appeared too physically masculine—too excellent of an athlete—and South Africa's athletics regulators were urged to test her, to scrutinize her physicality and her biology. Semenya's coach, Michael Seme, told South African media outlet News24 that he understood why people would ask questions about Semenya "because she looks like a man. It's a natural reaction and it's only human to be curious," he said. "But I can give you the telephone numbers of her roommates in Berlin. They have already seen she has nothing to hide." Semenya's identity as a woman would be put on trial in front of the world, and the jury was a cohort composed mostly of white men from the Western medical establishment. Countless people commented online and on South African news sites, accusing the investigation into Semenya as being racially motivated. "Our Caster is a woman," one person wrote. "These European people cannot handle the fact that an African can actually be a champion in something and will always try to bring us down."[17]

Semenya says that a couple weeks before the race in Berlin, she had the impression she was about to undergo some routine drug testing, but then learned she would be forced to undergo a cascade of invasive tests by the IAAF/World Athletics—by an endocrinologist, a gynecologist, and a psychologist, involving both external and internal examinations—to supposedly determine whether she was indeed eligible to race on the women's side. It was Semenya's first-ever gynecological exam, in a foreign country and in her second language, no less. Semenya's race event took place while the results of the tests were still pending, meaning she was still eligible to compete with this cloud of uncertainty hanging over her head. She ended up winning gold. Later, Semenya found out, to her surprise, that she was born with a difference in sex development, specifically that she was born without a uterus and had undescended gonads. "To be honest, I didn't care then, and I don't care now what the medical findings are," Semenya writes in her 2023 memoir *The Race to Be Myself*. "I was born a girl and raised as a girl. That was and is the end of the argument for me."[18]

In an astounding display of ethical bankruptcy, those test results were leaked to the media, allowing hordes of people to comb through and analyze Semenya's personal health information. Her basic human rights, dignity, and privacy had been egregiously violated in the name of saving and preserving women's sports. It opened the floodgates to degrading news coverage and remarks from her fellow runners. "Could This Women's World Champ Be a Man?" reads a *Time* magazine headline.[19] Australia's *Daily Telegraph* proclaimed that Semenya was a "hermaphrodite," a harmful and antiquated term that has been denounced by medical experts. Italian runner Elisa Cusma, one of Semenya's competitors at the time, said: "These kinds of people should not run with us. . . . For me, she is not a woman. She is a man."[20] The IAAF threatened to ban Semenya from competition unless she underwent surgery to remove the undescended gonads. She refused and threatened to sue, instead conceding to taking estrogen to lower her testosterone levels to 10 nanomoles per liter of blood or less. The estrogen hormone therapy, which she refers to as "poison," wreaked havoc on her body and made her lethargic.[21] Still, Semenya kept succeeding at running, desiring only to make it to the next Olympics. She achieved that goal but was still subjected to further ridicule and disdain. At the London Olympics in 2012, the Russian runner Mariya Savinova, another one of Semenya's competitors, told reporters there was no way Semenya was a woman. "Just look at her," Savinova said.[22] Amid all the uproar, Semenya was nevertheless determined to power through it and do what she does best: run.

In London 2012, Semenya carried the flag for South Africa at the Olympics opening ceremony. These games proved highly dramatic and revealing for both Semenya and Savinova. In the 800-meter race, Semenya came in second place. Savinova, a woman whose gender was not under scrutiny, came in first, finishing 1.04 seconds ahead of Semenya. In the running world, that's a meaningful difference. But three years later in 2015, in an ironic twist of fate, Savinova was stripped of her gold medal after she and four other Russian athletes were disqualified and banned from the Olympics over doping violations. In 2017, the Court of Arbitration for Sport, located in Switzerland, backdated the disqualification to 2010, which meant the 800-meter gold medal from London 2012 would now be awarded to Semenya. But she would continue to be forced to defend her place on women's teams, and her battles against international authorities were only just getting started.[23]

A few years later, a developing gender identity case involving Dutee Chand, a young Indian sprinter, would bring about new changes and controversies. Like Semenya, Chand's physical appearance and the way she ran drew outrage and panic from regulators, this time because of an anonymous tip from a fellow competitor. Neither Chand nor Semenya could have predicted how their stories would intertwine and chip away at the core beliefs of one of the most powerful sports administrations in the world. In 2013, Chand made history when she became the first Indian athlete to make the finals in the 100-meter dash at the World Championships. That same year, she garnered titles at the Indian national senior athletics championships. In 2014, she won gold at the Asian Junior Athletics Championships in the 200-meter and 4x400-meter relays, putting her on the path to more greatness on the world stage and possibly the Olympics. After her 2014 win, Chand was brought in to test for hyperandrogenism—a condition in which the body produces excess amounts of testosterone—when sports regulators deemed her muscles to be too pronounced and her stride "too impressive."[24] Like Semenya, she had believed these were routine drug tests, but they were actually chromosomal testing and gynecological examinations to supposedly confirm her gender. Also, like Semenya, Chand was subjected to mortifying procedures including photographing and measuring her genitalia, as well as blood and urine tests. "I was made to understand that something wasn't right in my body, and that it might keep me from playing sports," Chand told reporters.[25] Her tests, too, were leaked to the public without her consent.

As a result of testing positive for hyperandrogenism, Chand was unceremoniously deemed ineligible to compete on behalf of India at the Commonwealth Games. She was also booted from the Indian roster for the 2014 Asian Games. These entities were upholding the 2011 guidelines put in place by the IAAF that imposed testosterone restrictions for women with hyperandrogenism.[26] At the time, the IOC had similar criteria in effect. Chand was told that in order to participate, she had to undergo various medical interventions such as hormone therapy, blockers, and surgery. She refused. "It's like in some societies, they used to cut off the hand of people caught stealing," Chand told the *New York Times*. "I feel like this is the same kind of primitive, unethical rule. It goes too far."[27] Even in her home country of India, where stereotypical gender norms are highly revered, popular media outlets backed Chand, who is openly queer, and decried her mistreatment. Chand, wrote columnist Manu Joseph in the *Hindustan Times*, has defied the odds by sprinting alongside "women who were much larger than her, women from affluent nations, who ate foods as children that she had never seen, received healthcare that she was not fortunate to receive, and were trained in ways that were beyond her means until late in her life."[28] Joseph added that Chand's competitors, by virtue of being born in high-income countries, had "unfair advantages" compared to her. Chand's testosterone levels, by contrast, "are her being."

Chand sought to fight the 2011 guidelines and took her appeal to the Court of Arbitration for Sport. She claimed that her condition of hyperandrogenism should not preclude her from participating. In 2015, the court ruled in Chand's favor and gave the IAAF two years to sufficiently show that testosterone is linked to athletic performance. It was a huge moment that would have ripples effects beyond Chand and, eventually, for Semenya. In questioning the validity of linking testosterone with athletic superiority, the ruling also is important for transgender athletes and helped set the stage for future international policies. "While the evidence indicates that higher levels of naturally occurring testosterone may increase athletic performance," the court wrote in its decision, "the panel is not satisfied that the degree of that advantage is more significant than the advantage derived from the numerous other variables which the parties acknowledge also affect women's athletic performance: for example, nutrition, access to specialist training facilities and coaching, and other genetic and biological variations."[29]

At this point, it seemed like things were progressing in the right direction. But in the wake of this ruling, the IAAF was on a mission to meet that two-year deadline to show inherent links between testosterone and athletic performance. While this research was being carried out, both Chand and Semenya were allowed to participate in the 2016 Olympics in Rio de Janeiro, and Semenya was allowed to stop taking estrogen in the lead-up to it. Chand participated in the 100-meter event but did not make it to the semifinals. Semenya won gold in the 800-meter event at 1:55.28. Burundi's Francine Niyonsaba came in second place at 1:56.49.[30]

Fast-forward to April 2018, when the IAAF was now ready to reveal the findings of its two-year testosterone fact-finding mission, and a new hyperandrogenism policy. This time, it went further than the position it had before Chand challenged the policy. The new policy declared that all athletes competing on the women's side had to meet a testosterone threshold that was *half* the previously accepted testosterone levels, going from 10 nanomoles per liter of blood to 5 nanomoles per liter. Further, the rules targeted only the 400-meter, 800-meter, and 1,500-meter races, all of which Semenya would likely enter. Chand's 100-meter category was noticeably not on the list, leaving her unscathed and able to continue participating in her preferred event. Although Semenya and Chand do share many similarities in the way they have been unjustly treated by their sport because of natural occurrences in their bodies, they do *not* share the same condition. Chand was diagnosed with hyperandrogenism, while Semenya has intersex condition. "Hyperandrogenism" refers to when someone's body produces high levels of hormones, whereas "intersex" is a broad term that describes people born with reproductive anatomy that fall outside that of the stereotypical gender binary.[31]

Semenya said she would not abide by the new IAAF criteria. Now, it was Semenya's turn to take the IAAF to task and to court. Again, though she hasn't publicly said she's intersex, this case was another tacit acknowledgment of it. Through her lawyer, Semenya called the rules "an affront to the spirit of the sport." But the court did not side with her, ruling that discriminating against women with her condition was necessary to achieving and maintaining integrity in the events targeted by the guidelines. Semenya tried to appeal but lost again. She lashed out against the IAAF's decision and its recommendation that she take oral contraceptives as a way to reduce her testosterone levels to put her in compliance. She told reporters that she had been forced earlier in her career to take contraceptives and that they had debilitating effects on her mental and physical well-being. She vowed to never allow it to happen again. "The IAAF used me in the past as a human guinea pig to experiment with how the medication they required me to take would affect my testosterone levels," Semenya said. "Even though the hormonal drugs made me feel constantly sick, the IAAF now wants to enforce even stricter thresholds with unknown health consequences. I will not allow the IAAF to use me and my body again."[32] Semenya also expressed concern for her fellow women athletes who would feel compelled to comply. "This cannot be allowed to happen," she asserted.[33]

Because she rejected the IAAF ruling, Semenya was barred from defending her gold in 2021 at the Tokyo Olympics. Critics of the IAAF's pursuit of enforced hormones for intersex athletes included the Organisation Intersex International, which argued it was problematic to require women to take artificial hormones in order to compete. Hida Viloria, the group's spokesperson, said that it "seems contrary to the very ethos of athletic competition, which punishes the use of steroids and instead encourages making the most of one's natural talents."[34] The findings of the hyperandrogenism report released by the IAAF to support its even stricter testosterone requirements, which Semenya rejected, were released in the *British Medical Journal*. During the Tokyo Olympics in 2021, the journal issued a correction stating that there was no conclusive scientific evidence to support a causal link between testosterone and athletic achievement. So the data that the IAAF used to support its report and corresponding policy was unsound and therefore bunk. For Semenya, that error meant she was unnecessarily denied the chance to compete at the Olympics. For an athlete with such a finite window to compete at this level—each Olympic Games happens only every four years—it's devastating to think about. She was deprived of the right to end her Olympics on her own terms. She was being punished and shunned for the body with which she was born.

To keep doing the thing she loved, Semenya chose (or was given no other choice) to participate in the 2022 World Athletics Championships, held in

Eugene, Oregon, her first international competition since 2017.[35] She chose to run the 5,000-meter race instead of her specialty 800-meter race, because she refused to submit to the IAAF regulations that required her to undergo treatments to reduce her testosterone levels. In the end, Semenya didn't make it to the finals and came in 13th place overall. In July 2023, she won a landmark legal decision for sports when the European Court of Human Rights ruled that she had been discriminated against by the IAAF/World Athletics testosterone requirement. However, the court didn't strike down the rules, and World Athletics stated they would remain in place, meaning that, barring any changes, Semenya will continue to be banned from her sport and unable to compete in the 800-meter race at any Olympics. Though the ruling doesn't explain, we can infer that what prevented the court from striking down the rules was a lack of courage and not wanting to confront World Athletics. The court nonetheless cast doubt on the validity and implications of the hormone regulations, stating that there's a "lack of evidence" that Semenya's higher testosterone levels give her an athletic advantage. That statement strikes right at the heart of the purpose of the World Athletics regulations, which have always been positioned, like so many other rules like them, as existing to protect women's sports. "Caster has never given up her fight to be allowed to compete and run free," Semenya's lawyers said in a statement. "This important personal win for her is also a wider victory for elite athletes around the world. It means that sporting governance bodies around the world must finally recognize that human rights law and norms apply to the athletes they regulate."[36]

It should be noted, again, that there are no testosterone limits or restrictions whatsoever for athletes on the men's side. So, if a cisgender man has naturally higher testosterone levels, it doesn't matter. Semenya has said that her biology should be praised the same way Michael Phelps's arms are, Michael Jordan's vertical jump height is, or Usain Bolt's wider-than-average stride is. Nobody is suggesting any measures be taken—certainly not impositions entailing invasive medical procedures or drugs—to address Phelps's, Jordan's, or Bolt's advantages. As Vanessa Heggie, a historian of modern science and medicine at the University of Birmingham, notes in the peer-reviewed science journal *Endeavour*, women who excel at sports will generally come across as more "masculine" in terms of their stronger physique, compared with women who aren't athletic. What sex and gender testing does is set an "upper limit" or a ceiling on women's sporting performance. It sets a threshold for being *too* good, and any woman who crosses that threshold is deemed too masculine and becomes targeted for investigation. "For men there is no equivalent upper *physiological* limit," Higgins continues. "No kind of genetic, or hormonal, or physiological advantage is tested for, even if these would give a 'super masculine' athlete a distinct advantage over the merely very athletic 'normal' male."[37] There are obvious racial undertones at play here as well. As a Black woman from the developing world, Semenya automatically must face yet another layer of discrimination. So too does Chand as a Brown woman from India. If Semenya or Chand had been straight, cisgender white women dominating track arenas, it is almost certain that their bodies would have not been attacked and subjected to this level of scrutiny. They would likely have been praised for their skills and superior athleticism.

Semenya's case begs us to reconsider what we know about the gender binary and the ways in which the regulatory frameworks of sports entities are sufficient and insufficient when confronted with the untidy realities of the gender spectrum that have always existed among athletes. "With these suspicion-based criteria still in place, aesthetic judgments of femininity remain important facets of gender verification. The failures of testing highlight the explicit desire—and inability—to preserve the divide between Woman and Man through science," writes researcher Kathryn Henne in the *Journal of Women in Culture and Society*.[38] Testosterone-based tests and requirements also prop up a binary of trans girls who are deemed to be "non-threatening," those who transitioned before a testosterone-driven puberty began, and "threatening" trans girls, those who transitioned later in life. Yet again, this status quo leaves it up to those in power, mostly cisgender men, to determine what makes or does not make a woman.

Each step in the gender verification systems and regimes of international elite sports not only has failed to determine what womanhood means but also has failed to determine what's unfair in competition. It's worth highlighting again that Semenya is not transgender. And intersex people and transgender people are, clearly, not to be conflated. However, the tension between what is fair in organized sports and the basic human rights of the participants is on full display in Semenya's and Chand's controversies, the same tension that is at the heart of the debate over transgender athletes. "The science of gender isn't set in stone," Semenya writes in her memoir. "Maybe the hormonal makeup of my body does give me an advantage. Then, so what? It's mine."[39]

Semenya and Chand's battles expose the paradoxes and contradictions in the notion of "fair play" when it comes to the discrimination they've faced because of their biological makeup and can also be extended to trans and nonbinary athletes who are struggling with the same hurdles. Chand has explicitly supported the inclusion of trans women athletes. "To be honest, I don't see such athletes [trans women] getting any unfair advantage during competitions," Chand said in 2022 after FINA, the world governing body for swimming, voted to ban trans women athletes from competing in women's competitions if they had gone through male puberty. "They have already faced a lot of societal pressure and humiliation reaching where they are today. No need to make things difficult for them. Accept it as God's gift because what's happening in an individual human body shouldn't concern others. These athletes want to grow up like this, so let it be."[40]

Even though the idea of fair play is understood to uphold the "natural" gifts of athletes, the gender-verification mandates and scrutiny faced by Semenya and Chand show that these ideals are harmful and perpetuate stigma and misinformation when it comes to gender diversity. When harmful rhetoric about competitive advantage swirls around, stigmatized individuals are treated differently by their peers. The people directly affected are those closest to the actual competition—coaches, trainers, and teammates—with women, especially cisgender women, being affected most of all. This was on full display during the 2024 Olympics in Paris, when athletes competing on the women's side in boxing were unwittingly thrown into a worldwide anti-transgender hysteria, even though there were zero transgender women athletes at the Olympics.[41] This controversy exposed, again, how right-wing anti-trans politicians and pundits use misinformation, disinformation, and bigotry to propel their agenda and sow division.

Although boxers Imane Khelif, of Algeria, and Lin Yu-ting, of Taiwan, were assigned female at birth and have always competed on the women's side, they were swiftly accused of being transgender and subjected to a barrage of online hatred and misgendering, including from former US president Donald Trump, Italian premier Giorgia Meloni, and *Harry Potter* author J. K. Rowling. Again, neither athlete is trans. The outcry against Khelif reached a fever pitch after Italian boxer Angela Carini quit her fight against Khelif after 46 seconds, saying she was hit too hard (something that should not be unexpected for an Olympic boxer). "I felt a strong pain in my nose," Carini told reporters, after she walked out of the ring, refusing to shake Khelif's hand.[42] False rumors that Khelif was trans swirled, with many people falsely characterizing her as a "biological male." It's important to note that it's illegal to be transgender in Algeria, so this assertion, although false, could have put Khelif's life in danger. This misinformation was fueled by reporters that Khelif and Lin Yu-ting had been disqualified from a 2023 International Boxing Association (IBA) event because of a failed unspecified gender verification test, the results of which have never been made public.[43]

The IOC banned the Russian-run IBA in 2019, after long criticizing its governance and testing procedures. To fill the regulatory void left by the ban, the IOC took it upon itself to use its own 2016 rules to determine boxers' eligibility based on gender. Khelif and Lin Yu-ting both met those qualifications to participate on the women's side. In the days following the outcry, many news outlets had to correct and apologize for erroneously referring to the athletes as transgender. Carini also apologized, saying, "I apologize to her and to everyone. I was angry because my games had already gone up in smoke. . . . If the IOC said she can fight, I respect that decision."[44] Beyond the fact that this incident was another example of misogyny and transphobia, there were clearly racist overtones at play here, as there are with Semenya and Chand. As long as hatred toward women and those who fall outside the gender binary is allowed to fester, this type of outcry and misguided witch-hunting will continue to take place and cause further harms to women's sports.

CHAPTER 6

THE MYTH OF SAVING WOMEN'S SPORTS

Iszac Henig was in and around pools and bodies of water from a very young age. He can't even pinpoint when he fell in love with the sport because it's always been entrenched in his DNA. Henig grew up in Menlo Park, California, and frequented the ocean and tide pools a short drive away, where he'd spend hours searching for underwater creatures.[1] He started competitive swimming at the ripe age of four. A decade later, after he turned fourteen, Henig, who'd been raised as a girl his whole life, told his mother she had a son. Though Henig's mother accepted this to some extent, Henig started doubting himself, thinking that he must have been wrong. So, throughout high school, he tried to discover womanhood in a way he found comfortable and make sense of himself. He explored his queerness more at the end of high school and into his college years at Yale University, where he competed on the school's Division I women's swimming team. In Henig's sophomore year, when the COVID-19 pandemic hit, he decided to take a year off to reassess his life plan. "That was the time where I really slowed down and let myself question things again and think about things really deeply," he said. It struck him that he had been right all along from the age of fourteen: he was transgender, and he had been his mother's son this whole time.[2]

Chipping away at a lifetime of negative messaging and stereotypes about transness, Henig leaned in and began to feel more genuine and comfortable with himself. He publicly took on a new name along with he/him pronouns and underwent a double mastectomy in 2021. Upon returning to the Yale campus that fall, he had to decide whether he would stay on the women's swimming team or switch to the men's for his final two years of college; he had fast enough times to make it on either. But staying on the women's side meant that he couldn't undergo testosterone therapy owing to the NCAA policy at the time. In the end, Henig delayed hormones and decided to stay with the women's team, where he felt embraced and loved by his teammates.[3] This decision would propel him into what would become one of the biggest controversies involving trans athletes to date, and his story would end up debunking one of the most pervasive myths about women's sports: that trans participation is society's biggest hurdle to winning the fight for gender equality in sports.

Danne Diamond, a three-time Muay Thai US national champion fighter and coach, is a communications consultant with expertise in LGBTQI+ sports policy and the former director of policy and programs at Athlete Ally, a New York–based group that supports LGBTQ+ athletes, coaches, and fans. Diamond told us that the myth that people assigned male at birth are always better athletes is steeped in sexism, and it's inaccurate. "It suggests that if a woman is too good at a particular sport, that she somehow competes her way out of the women's category because there's no way that a woman can be a particular level of elite athlete," Diamond told us.[4] "The idea of trans girls and women competing against cisgender women athletes tends to trigger emotional responses, playing on stereotypes about gender and biology. It's a myth that needs to be dismantled at the root in order for us to achieve equity in sports and in society generally."

There are countless examples illustrating that cisgender men are not, in fact, athletically superior to women. An obvious example is that very few cisgender men could beat Serena Williams at tennis. It's also doubtful that many cisgender men would want to pick a fight with pro wrestler Ronda Rousey. Yet, the idea that trans women pose an existential threat to all women's sports and all women athletes has become rampant and is being successfully used to pass harmful laws and policies to keep trans women out of competitive sports. But these crusades that masquerade as efforts to save women's sports are misguided and are causing unprecedented harm to women's sports, while also reinforcing problematic stereotypes and tropes that serve to render women as second-class citizens and athletes. As blanket bans against trans people at all levels of sport and age groups are becoming more routine, it's never been more important to dismantle these myths and provide a clear framework on how we really can, and must, save women's sports.

Again, the anxiety around the presence of trans women in women's sports leagues is rooted in the misconception that trans women athletes are at an advantage compared to their cisgender counterparts. In reality, trans women are at a disadvantage in relation to cisgender women in some categories of athletic ability. In April 2024, the results of a groundbreaking, and contentious, study funded by the International Olympic Committee were released in the *British Journal of Sports Medicine* that showed that transgender women athletes are at a relative *disadvantage* in many key areas of athletics compared to their cisgender women counterparts. The study involved thirty-five transgender athletes—twenty-three trans women and twelve trans men—who had undergone at least one year of gender-affirming hormone replacement therapy. The study also tested nineteen cisgender men and twenty-one cisgender women for the purpose of comparison. While the trans women athletes displayed better handgrip strength, they also had lower cardiovascular fitness and jumping abilities compared to the cisgender women. Though the study authors warned against coming to broad, sweeping conclusions based solely on this research, which involves a very small sample size, they also warned against blanket bans against transgender athletes. "Trans women are not biological men," Yannis Pitsiladis, one of the study's authors and a member of the IOC's medical and scientific commission, told reporters.[5] The study was published ahead of the 2024 Paris Olympics, where swimming, track and field, and cycling had barred trans women from participating on the women's side. This study builds on the limited body of existing research on trans athletes and proves that more is needed. And meeting the need for further research means that more trans athletes need to be able to participate in sports, not be banned from them.

The overall misconception and hysteria regarding trans women participating in sports stems from a lack of understanding of how trans healthcare and sports policies work, and the misogynistic viewpoint that boys are necessarily strong and girls are necessarily delicate. Tennis giant and outspoken gay rights advocate Martina Navratilova found herself in hot water in 2019 after she wrote an op-ed in the *Times of London* asserting that it was "insane" and "cheating" to allow trans women to participate in women's sports. For Navratilova, any man could "decide to be female" by taking hormones and then dominating in the sport in question.[6] This is a classic hypothetical and an irrational fear of something that just isn't based in reality. Even if these views are framed as protecting women's sports, we can't ignore that they largely come from a disregard and hatred toward trans lives and a refusal to see trans women as women and trans men as men.

The latter can be said about former president Donald Trump, who has capitalized on and fostered the growing anti-trans sentiment among his base. A large part of the 2024 Republican presidential campaign strategy was attacking transgender and gender diverse people—athletes in particular. The hateful rhetoric and misinformation were successful in mobilizing the Republican base and helped trounce the Democrats. At a rally in early 2022, Trump vowed to his supporters that he would ban trans athletes if reelected in 2024: "We will ban men from participating in women's sports," he declared.[7] Here, Trump was reacting to the successes of swimmer Lia Thomas, the trans woman who had just broken the NCAA Division I record in the 200-yard freestyle at the Zippy Invitational in Akron, Ohio. Anti-trans activists responded to Thomas's subsequent national championship win with mass outcry and renewed efforts to clamp down on trans women athletes. The editor of *Swimming World* compared Thomas to the "doping-fueled athletes of East Germany" who participated in the Olympics of the past.[8] Thomas, her coach, and her teammates were subjected to death threats and insults online and in real life, just because she was allowed to swim alongside women. Thomas became a household name, and her win served as a tipping point in the debates swirling around trans athletes and trans rights. To put her win into perspective, Thomas was not only the first openly trans NCAA athlete to win the national swimming championship, but also the first trans athlete to *ever* win a championship in any sport in the entire NCAA.[9] Her win came a whole decade after the creation of the NCAA's trans policy in 2011, and trans women athletes had been competing that entire time. Trans women weren't and aren't dominating college sports . . . cisgender women are.

Thomas's detractors argued that she was stealing potential wins from other swimmers in the women's league. "We must protect women's sports. At all costs. What Thomas has done, beating biological women to win a Division I national championship, is anathema to what sports represents and the spirit of competition," said Caitlyn Jenner, US Olympic gold medalist and high-profile trans woman, in response to Thomas's win. Jenner, though trans herself, has been leading the charge against the inclusion of trans women in elite sports. "I have said from day one I don't want biological boys to be competing against women, especially in school," Jenner said.[10] Jenner and Trump, along with countless others, frequently state that "men" should be kept out of women's sports. In other words, they're calling trans women "men," which is not only highly disrespectful, but plainly false. But it's a great scare tactic, and unfortunately it seems to be working.

This idea that men are coming onto women's teams for their own personal athletic gain, simply to win championships, is incorrect. Nor is it even feasible. Most elite leagues require trans women to have undergone some type of hormone therapy as well as show that they have lived in their trans identity for a significant amount of time. For some leagues, like in the case of the now-defunct Premier Hockey Federation (formerly the National Women's Hockey League), that period was a minimum of two years.[11] It's hard to fathom that any cisgender man would go to such lengths simply to excel at elite women's sports, which are often overlooked and demeaned. Further, depending on the sport, very few women's leagues allow individuals to make a decent living; the accolades and status gained from being an elite athlete are rarely as recognized on the same level as men's sports. Lastly, trans people are subjected to disproportionate stigma and prejudice in most societies. Why would cisgender men put themselves through that just to "place higher" (which is not even guaranteed) in the women's category? They wouldn't and they don't. Thomas, for her part, was a top-level swimmer on the men's side at the University of Pennsylvania. She was frequently securing the highest placings, including number one in the 2019 Ivy League Championships, and was well on her way to qualifying for the NCAA men's championships and even the 2020 Olympic trials.[12] It seems unfathomable that any athlete would put this kind of trajectory at risk, unless there was a serious reason to do so.

In an interview with *Good Morning America*, Thomas stated perfectly the real reason why she and other trans people physically transition: "Trans people don't transition for athletics; we transition to be happy, and authentic, and our true selves."[13] In a quote that appeared in fellow Ivy League swimmer Schuyler Bailar's 2023 book *He/She/They*, Thomas went into her motivations further, telling him that she started taking hormone suppressors in May 2019 without thinking at all about sports or athletics. At this point, she was depressed, something that her teammates noticed and was a cause for concern. She was missing classes and not sleeping properly to the point where she could barely get out of bed. "I was trying not to die at that point," Thomas told

Bailar. "I was doing what I needed to do to live—and that was transitioning, that was HRT [hormone replacement therapy], that was trans healthcare, and that was the choice I felt I had." Thomas went on hormones knowing full well, and despite the fact, that it could end her swimming career.[14]

During her hormone suppression treatment, Thomas continued to swim on the men's side for the 2019–20 season, in accordance with the NCAA's transgender policy at the time. That NCAA policy allowed trans women like Thomas to continue participating on men's teams if they chose to. Under the policy, trans women who are on hormone suppressors (such as spironolactone, or "spiro," and cyproterone acetate) have to be on them for at least one year to be eligible to participate on the women's side. While on the hormones, Thomas finally began to feel better emotionally, and says that the relief she experienced was monumental. She also came out as transgender to her coaches and teammates on the men's side who she still competed alongside during the initial stages of her transition. At a 1,000-yard freestyle race against the Columbia University men's swimming team in 2019, she bravely rocked a women's swimsuit. During that season, her physicality changed drastically, as her muscle mass was reduced along with her strength, all of which contributed to a reduction in her swimming speed. Compared with her performance in the 500-yard freestyle, in which she ranked number one in 2019 prior to taking hormones, her best time dropped by a whopping 15 seconds.[15] Any competitive advantage she may have held before medically transitioning was adequately mitigated. These nuances of Thomas's story have been completely lost in the chatter, as people are hyper-focused on her single championship win, which provides the ideal fodder for anti-trans advocates, and even fellow cisgender women swimmers.

Anna Baeth, Athlete Ally's research director, points out that not only are trans women *not* a threat to the sanctity and fairness of women's sports, but this paranoia is actually a distraction from the biggest threat of all: the sports system itself. "Sports replicate systems of oppression," Baeth said.[16] "The question for me is not 'are trans athletes a threat?' It's 'who is sports threatening the most and how do we combat that?'" In 2021, an anonymous cisgender woman swimmer from Niagara University told the *Daily Mail* that it would be "impossible" for a cisgender woman swimmer to ever beat Thomas. "It was hard going into a race knowing there was no way I was going to get first," the swimmer told the British tabloid.[17] However, this fear about this supposedly "impossible" result was disproved when many cisgender women did in fact beat Thomas in subsequent races. Erica Sullivan, a US Olympic swimmer who won silver in the 1,500-meter freestyle event at the 2020 Tokyo Olympics and came in third place in the 2022 NCAA championship against Thomas in the 500-yard freestyle, has a starkly different outlook on the issue than the aforementioned anonymous swimmer. Sullivan recounted on Bailar's podcast *Dear Schuyler* in 2023 how she feels when people ask her about the prospect of losing to Thomas in a race. "I'd be pissed," she said. "But not because Lia's trans. It's because I don't want to lose."[18] Sullivan, a highly competitive athlete—an Olympian, no less—only cares about how she can beat or at least take on the swimmer in the next lane over. If you are an elite athlete, there are zero excuses for your outcome, and focusing solely on yourself—in this case, literally staying in your own lane—is all that matters. You either perform to the best of your ability, or you don't. Sullivan believes that she came in third place not because she was racing against a trans person. She came in third because she got beat out by two other swimmers. This, rather than Jenner's notion of the "spirit of competition," is the true spirit of competition in its purest form.

This vaguely described "spirit of competition" was not compromised or lost in Thomas's case. Thomas had been on hormone suppression for more than two years by the time she joined the women's side, nearly three times longer than the minimum standard set by the NCAA's trans policy. While not fully conclusive, a growing body of research indicates that one year of hormone therapy is sufficient for trans women's testosterone levels to reach the same range as their cisgender teammates and competitors. Thomas's athletic record further confirms this. After she joined the women's swimming team in 2021 (the 2020–21 season was canceled due to the COVID-19 pandemic), she ranked 46th among women's swimmers nationally and 36th among college swimmers on the women's side. At the NCAA national championship in March 2022, where Thomas won the 500-yard freestyle, she did not break any records. She also finished last in one of her other races. Katie Ledecky, from Stanford University, holds the NCAA record with a time of 4:24.06, almost 10 whole seconds faster than Thomas's time of 4:33.24.[19] Recall the story of Iszac Henig, the trans man swimmer at Yale who opened this chapter. Here's where he becomes an important part of truly understanding the case of Thomas. What's been conveniently overlooked is the fact that Henig, a trans man who swam on the women's side at that time and had not yet undergone any hormone therapy, ended up beating Thomas by more than three seconds in the 100-yard event. Thomas came in sixth place overall.[20] This is another example of pundits avoiding a proper analysis of the data—cherry-picking some results and ignoring others—to suit their transphobic narrative and panic. (For the 2022–23 season, Henig's senior year, he switched to the men's side after starting testosterone treatment in March of 2022.)

Still, the moral panic over Thomas's championship win led to a blanket ban against trans women swimmers by FINA (Fédération Internationale de Natation), the international governing body for water sports competitions recognized by the Olympics. Sports that came under the ban included diving, water polo, artistic swimming, high diving, and open water swimming.[21] The new FINA policy, which received support from more than 70 percent of participating countries, severely restricts trans participation in elite women's events, limiting it to athletes who have transitioned before undergoing a testosterone-driven puberty by age twelve. This is a narrow-minded and unrealistic policy, as trans people rarely medically transition before hitting puberty, and regardless, many US states prohibit teens from accessing gender-affirming healthcare altogether.[22] FINA's is the most sweeping ban on trans women in sports we have seen to date. As part of this move, FINA (which has since been renamed World Aquatics) also became the first sport to set up an "open category" to allow trans athletes to compete in a separate class at the elite level, potentially creating a dangerous precedent in which trans people only compete among themselves. As history has shown us, we know that separate is never equal, whether it comes to gender, race, or class.

Following FINA's lead, myriad athletic organizations worldwide have since announced that they are reassessing their own trans policies. It's a huge step backward for gender equality and inclusion. Former Australian swimmer Maddie Groves, who quit the Olympic trials in 2021 over what she described as a toxic culture within her country's swimming community, slammed FINA's policy change, tweeting: "There are already gender diverse people in swimming and I'm guessing they're not feeling very accepted [right now]. Shame on everyone that supported this discriminatory and unscientific decision."[23] FINA's policy means that no trans woman who didn't happen to be on hormone blockers before they hit puberty will be able to compete in water sports at the Olympics, scuttling Lia Thomas's ambition to one day do so. Trans athletes, including trans women, have been allowed to participate in sports on teams that reflect their gender identity at the Olympics since 2003.[24] In the twenty-one years since, there have been no trans women who have won an Olympic gold medal—or any medals at all. Thomas's story has become a crucial case study for why we need to stay vigilant and actively debunk the myths perpetuated by people like Jenner and Trump. Thomas's situation has been misunderstood and exploited by bad-faith actors who ignore and gloss over pivotal facts. What Thomas's story reveals is that the trans athletic policies that were in place at the time of her win, while not perfect, were effective and prove that any biological competitive advantage she may have had over her teammates and competitors was properly mitigated.

In February 2023, one of Thomas's swimming records in the 1,650-yard freestyle was beaten by her former teammate, University of Penn swimmer Anna Kalandadze, a cisgender woman, who achieved an Ivy League record time of 15:53.88.[25] Kalandadze achieved this time less than an entire season after Thomas achieved her own time of 15:59.71 in the same category. Keep in mind that the record for the 1,650-yard event in the NCAA is still held by Katie Ledecky, who in 2017 shook the swimming world with an astonishing 15:03.31. The naysayers who decried Thomas's participation on the women's team have been noticeably mute on Kalandadze's milestone, not to mention Ledecky's record, which is more than 50 seconds faster than Thomas's time. If we are talking about who is dominating women's collegiate swimming, it's Katie Ledecky. Not Lia Thomas.

Still, Thomas's story and the FINA reaction to it has set the stage for similar problematic approaches undertaken by other international sports regulatory organizations. In February 2023, World Athletics, the international governing body for track and field and other running competitions, announced a policy similar to FINA's: trans women who have undergone a testosterone-driven puberty can no longer compete in women's events at international competitions. Further, in order to compete as a woman, participants must show that they do not exceed testosterone levels of 2.5 nanomoles per liter for at least two years. This total is almost two times lower than previous regulations. All of this is being done in the name of "integrity of female competition," something that was not in question for the duration of World Athletics' previous policy. As we illustrated earlier when we delved into the science regarding athletic performance, scientists agree that this decision is not based on proper evidence. "We actually don't know if there's a biological advantage for trans women over cisgender women because the science is not clear," Australian endocrinologist Ada Cheung, who leads the Trans Health Research program, told the *Sydney Morning Herald*.[26] "FINA's report is really based on a group of people's opinion, it's not a gold standard.

No research has really been done into trans women swimmers or any elite athletes that are transgender. The jury is out." Katrina Karkazis, bioethicist and co-author of *Testosterone: An Unauthorized Biography*, echoed that sentiment, telling CBC News that "FINA has not revealed what evidence they reviewed nor who reviewed it, but many oft-cited studies conclude that there is not yet enough scientific evidence to support specific policies about transgender or intersex athletes. This is not surprising as this is a very nascent area of research."[27] To that end, another negative implication of FINA's move is that it could negatively affect future research on trans athletes and people with differences in sexual development. In the eventuality of trans athletes, an already minuscule population, decreasing in number, so too will the number of potential study participants.

There are going to be some athletes naturally better than others, regardless of their gender identity, and this variation is not considered in the public discourse and outcry about trans women participating in sports. When one transgender athlete has success in their sport (and in these situations, this athlete is most often a trans woman), the response for some reason is to hold the entire community of trans women athletes to the same athletic standards, when this is never the case for cisgender athletes. For example, Serena Williams's domination of women's tennis with her powerful serve did not mean that all women tennis players would have the same serve speed. Once again, Williams is an example of someone whose athletic superiority is celebrated, and no rules or policies are arbitrarily developed to respond to her superiority and "protect" her opponents and peers. As with the athletic ability of any group of individuals, there are many variations in skill level, accessibility, and other factors.

Trans women—like, for example, professional ice hockey player Jessica Platt—have been participating in women's sports for decades without uproar and bombshell policy changes, because they aren't, generally, shattering records and dominating. A look at Platt's stats for the three years that she played professionally in the Canadian Women's Hockey League (at the time the only professional women's hockey league in North America) reveals that she scored two goals and had one assist for a total of three points in forty-nine games. She also had 14 penalty minutes over the three seasons, and for two of these seasons, 0 penalty minutes.[28] Now, points do not always reflect how good a player is, and penalty minutes do not always reflect a player's physical dominance. But, going by the numbers, there's nothing to suggest that she compromised the sanctity of the sport for cisgender women, as most of the naysayers would assume, based on her puberty experience. Platt's athletic story, examined alongside Thomas's, highlights the variation in athletic ability among trans women.

In 2019, *Outsports* published a profile of four trans women athletes who train hard but almost never win. Like most people, they compete for the love of the sport, not because of the need to win, and certainly not with an aim to compete at the Olympics. These women expressed frustration at the public's prioritization of the voices of super elite athletes who don't represent them, something that results in them having to justify their very existence in their sport. "A lot of people don't realize how hard it is to athletically train when you're on hormones," said Tara Seplavy, an American racing cyclist, who started her medical transition in 2018. Seplavy said that she, like most trans women who participate in sports, is good enough to compete, but often not fast or strong enough to necessarily win, despite what the dramatic headlines might suggest. "As my coach said, I'm anti-doping. I'm putting chemicals in my body that detract from athletic performance."[29]

Around the same time as Lia Thomas's 2022 win in the 500-yard free-style, a similar controversy was breaking out within British cycling. That March, cycling's international governing body, UCI (Swiss-based Union Cycliste Internationale), blocked Welsh transgender cyclist Emily Bridges from competing in the British National Omnium Championships in Derby just days before the competition, in response to other riders threatening to boycott the event if Bridges was allowed to ride. An open letter signed by a group of elite cyclists on the women's side, including retired Olympians and researchers, called for UCI to "rescind" its trans policy because this was a "crisis situation" and the "very fragile" future of women's sports was in jeopardy. Bridges was twenty years old and had come out as a trans woman in October 2020. She finished 43rd out of 45th in the elite men's criterium at the Loughborough Cycling Festival in 2021, and that September placed second to last in the Welsh National Championship road race. She then won a men's points race at the men's British Universities Championships a month before—something that fueled the outcry she was facing in the lead-up to participating alongside women in the Omnium Championships. Although Bridges had medically transitioned with hormone suppression, she had met British Cycling's trans policy that required women riders to have testosterone levels below five nanomoles per liter for twelve months prior to competition.

Still, the UCI did not grant her the ability to switch, and because of the outcry over her prospective participation, British Cycling suspended its trans policy altogether pending a review to "find a better answer." This meant that Bridges could also not compete in the Commonwealth Games that summer. (The new policy has yet to be announced as of this writing.) Speaking to reporters after she was blocked from the Omnium event, Bridges said that the claims of unfair advantage carry no weight given that hormone replacement has such a massive effect on trans women's bodies. "The aerobic performance difference is gone after about four months," she told *DIVA* magazine.[30] "There are studies going on for trans women in sport. I'm doing one and the performance drop-off that I've seen is massive. I don't have any advantage over my competitors, and I've got data to back that up."[31]

Bridges's remarks were overshadowed by former British prime minister Boris Johnson's take on the situation. "I don't think biological males should be competing in female sporting events," Johnson said. (In later chapters, we will break down the ways that the use of the phrases "biological males" and "biological females" when referring to trans women and trans men is not only problematic but a strategic and detrimental obfuscation of the truth.) Bridges was already the object of a firestorm of criticism, harassment, and hatred in real life and online, and Johnson's statement made it worse. It reached a point where Bridges started receiving threats of physical violence, forcing her to fear for her safety when leaving her home. "They were real concerns, and it was real fear that I had after the comments were made, and it was scary. I was scared," Bridges told *The Guardian*.[32] In November of 2022, an ITV documentary titled *Race to Be Me* about Bridges's story was released. In it, Bridges says that she's been racing in small-scale events in the women's category. "Despite all this, I'm still here," she says in the film. "This has been the best year of my life. . . . It's kept cycling alive for me, that inclusive community that I wish road and track cycling was and should strive to be."[33] Debates about trans inclusion in sports are leaving out of the discussion the way that enforcement of these policies inevitably leads to more surveillance of women's bodies, both cisgender and trans. Thomas herself put it well in an interview with *Good Morning America* following her championship win: "I'm not a medical expert, but there's a lot of variation among [cisgender] female athletes," she said. "There's just women who are very tall and very muscular and have more testosterone than another [cisgender] woman. And should that then also disqualify them?"[34]

WOMEN'S SPORTS POLICY WORKING GROUP

To understand an alternative stance, one different from ours and in many ways against the inclusion of transgender athletes, we spoke with Donna Lopiano from the Women's Sports Policy Working Group (WSPWG). The WSPWG is an American group launched in 2021 by two former Olympic swimmers: Donna de Varona, who lobbied for the passage of Title IX in 1972, and Nancy Hogshead-Makar, a law professor and author of a book on Title IX titled *Equal Play*. Lopiano, for her part, is the former chief executive of the Women's Sports Foundation, the nonprofit founded in 1974 by tennis legend and gay rights advocate Billie Jean King. Lopiano might not have been the best representative of the group, which is seemingly more hardline and more opposed to trans inclusion than she is, but she was the person the group made available to us. The group's initial purpose was to provide a "balanced" and "science-based" take on the question of trans inclusion that would simultaneously preserve the sanctity of women's sports and accommodate trans athletes. It sought to be a voice representing the middle, as opposed to either extreme end of the debate. However, a closer look at the group's language and rhetoric is nonetheless easily recognizable as trans exclusionist. It should be noted that all the group's six members as of 2023 are cisgender, and none of them are scientists. (The UK anti-trans organization Fair Play, for its part, is run by a cisgender woman who is a research scientist.) One of the WSPWG's first moves after it launched was to call for federal legislation that would, as Lopiano puts it, "either create a standalone statute authorizing separate-sex competitive sports teams, amends the proposed Equality Act to restore a biological definition of sex and permit separate-sex sports, or amend Title IX to authorize separate biological sex competitive sports participation."[35] For trans athletes who didn't suppress, the group did not suggest that they be altogether excluded (as Fair Play would), but instead put forward the idea that they could be given special accommodations to participate through separate races, podiums, and teams.

The WSPWG has faced a barrage of criticism and accusations of transphobia in the years since it was launched, with the Human Rights Campaign labeling it a "hate group."[36] Founder Nancy Hogshead-Makar has been criticized by LGBTQ+ inclusion advocates for saying there was "nothing fair" about swimmer Lia Thomas's win in the NCAA and that Thomas's "domination of the 'women's sport' category has done nothing to engender greater empathy for inclusive practices throughout society for the trans community."[37] She even went so far as to round up sixteen of Thomas's Penn swimming teammates and convinced them to anonymously send a letter to administrators calling for Thomas to be barred from participating in the Ivy League Championships in February 2022.[38]

Hogshead-Makar is motivated by the mission of "protecting women," as she proclaimed in 2022 alongside the Alliance Defending Freedom at the ICONS (Independent Council on Women's Sports) conference,[39] and has a history of repeatedly spewing dangerous and false claims that trans women are "violent at the same rate as other males."[40] It's worth comparing Hogshead-Maker's stance to that of famed long-distance swimmer Diana Nyad—the first and only person to swim unaided from Cuba to Florida—who was an original supporter of the WSPWG. Nyad was recently outspoken against transgender women, those who in her words have "experienced male puberty," and their participation in elite sports, as she outlined in a 2022 op-ed in the *Washington Post*. Within a year, and as the Netflix biopic *Nyad* was being released, Nyad told *Out* that she had changed her mind on the issue and was remorseful. "The science is far more complex than I thought, and there are clearly more educated experts than I who are creating policy to ensure that elite sports are both fair and inclusive of all women," she said. "I now see how all women are negatively affected by the ways transgender women are targeted by discrimination and abuse in sports and elsewhere."[41]

While Fair Play seems primarily concerned about women's physical safety and preserving "safe" spaces for cisgender women, the WSPWG's main concern seems to be that sports-related opportunities are being taken away from women. That's because the group's ideology is rooted in Title IX. Title IX was originally created to carry over protections for women against discrimination in the workforce, set in Title VII, into educational institutions. From the perspective of the WSPWG, Title IX is a tool to propel women athletes toward achieving the highest feats possible in sport, including placing at the top levels of competition, gaining scholarships, and playing professionally. For the group, it's ultimately about winning or putting women in positions to win. But this is a narrow, and for many, incorrect, perspective that is hyper-focused on capitalistic achievement and the notion that sports are necessarily a means to an end. "The original intent and interpretation of Title IX focused on equal opportunity and this idea that sport is educational, that all students have a civil right that is to be protected," Victoria Jackson, a sports historian and clinical associate professor of history at Arizona State, told *Sports Illustrated* in 2022. "There's nothing about Title IX that's protecting the right to win or to be elite in sport." To top this all off, as of 2023, not a single trans women athlete has ever been granted a scholarship in the NCAA. So, how many opportunities have trans women taken away from cis women in this regard? None.[42]

Before Lopiano and others arrived at their current framing—that trans women are the biggest existential threat for women athletes because they are essentially stealing opportunities from cisgender women—they sought a compromise on the controversy about trans girls in high school athletics, hoping to convince regulators and policymakers to come to a consensus. This occurred in Connecticut, before the filing of a lawsuit in 2020 against the Connecticut Association of Schools in response to the cases of Andraya Yearwood and Terry Miller, two trans girl track athletes. In 2018, Christina Mitchell, one of the mothers of the cisgender girls at the center of the dispute, had contacted Lopiano, who had long worked on women's sports in Title IX issues but never on issues regarding transgender people or athletes. That same year, Chelsea Mitchell had raced against Miller and Yearwood at the State Open, with Miller and Yearwood finishing first and second in the 100-meter race and Mitchell finishing fourth.[43] Lopiano was optimistic that she could help the mother and lawyers join forces on the issue and come to a consensus on the inclusion of trans athletes. "There's not a problem that you can't solve with good policy," Lopiano recalled thinking at the time. "Little did I know that this was the toughest policy issue ever to be faced."[44]

Lopiano and other sports policy experts and legal advocates gathered once a week for about six months to figure out their position on the matter. When they got to the issue of high school athletics, specifically track, members in the group raised concerns that if a trans girl runner advanced to the state track championship, for example, it would take away an opportunity for a cisgender girl. The main solution the group came up with to this scenario was to automatically create an additional slot for a cisgender girl to participate, thus eliminating the contingency of that "stolen" opportunity. In practice, this would simply entail the addition of a track lane for the cisgender girl. "The thing we were trying to juggle is how do you protect the opportunities for biological women to participate in sport, which was the Title IX standard, and welcome transgender athletes into women's sports," Lopiano explained. By this point, the group was confident that this could resolve the concerns shared by the cis athletes, their parents, and other parties. But then, Lopiano brought Christina Mitchell to the table with Lopiano's colleagues, with a plan to collaborate and take their joint solution to the governor of Connecticut, Democrat Ned Lamont, for him to implement an executive order on the matter. Lopiano believed that Christina would be aligned with their efforts that would "create this inclusiveness, yet this separate scoring." That turned out not to be the case.[45]

Mitchell, according to Lopiano, had been on board with them up until they discussed the scenario of the added track lane for the runners in the state championship final. Lopiano's solution to that contingency was that there would be two heats in the championship race. Two heats—or qualifying races—with an equal number of runners. This would address the so-called problem of there not being enough lanes on the track to add another cisgender runner, should a trans girl advance to the finals. "And that's where she shut down," Lopiano lamented.[46] Mitchell's rationale for dismissing the two-heat solution was that it removed the opportunity for a cisgender girl to compete against all the best athletes in a single race, because the existence of separate heats meant there would be a heat she would not be in. After that exchange, Mitchell distanced herself from Lopiano's group and went on to align herself and her daughter Chelsea with the Alliance Defending Freedom (ADF), the right-wing Christian legal defense fund that ultimately spearheaded the lawsuit over Yearwood and Miller. ADF has an unabashedly exclusionary approach that has no space for trans women athletes and has continued to weaponize bias against the two Black transgender athletes to further push its agenda to eliminate the rights—perhaps even the very existence—of trans women.

To demonstrate the supposed travesty of trans women participating in sports and to bring people into their fold, ADF and the WSPWG consistently use the tactic of invoking dramatic sob stories. During our conversation, Lopiano recounted a story she heard secondhand about how on the eve of the NCAA swimming championship involving Lia Thomas, one of the swimmers from an opposing college put down a pile of towels and told her mother that she wanted to "practice." The mother replied, "Practice what?" To which the swimmer responded, "I've got to practice covering myself and getting dressed in my swimsuit because Lia [Thomas] is going to be in our locker room." For Lopiano, this anecdote proved the "sad" reality of including trans women in women's sports. Besides the many dubious aspects of this story, which we have no way of verifying, Lopiano seemingly wanted us to empathize with this cisgender athlete, and her mother, for being uncomfortable.[47]

What is the source of this discomfort? It's rooted in the misguided idea that cisgender women are victims and that trans women embody the worst of the patriarchy. In Lia Thomas's case, the inverse is true: Thomas was the one being ogled at and objectified in the locker room. It was her cisgender peers who were spying on her and leaking information about her to the press; one teammate even anonymously shared Thomas's alleged locker room habits with the *Daily Mail*. Sports journalist Karleigh Chardonnay Webb characterizes the teammates' behavior as akin to being a "peeping tom." And the obsession with Thomas's body betrays a "horrific exoticization of trans people's bodies," according to *Guardian* reporter Johanna Mellis. Thomas's detractors incorrectly perceive her as a male encroaching on a women's space.[48] If they are set in that belief, there is no compromise to be made. Again, if you do not see trans women as women, or aren't willing to, there is not a way forward.

This was not the only anecdote that Lopiano shared. She mentioned how a women's basketball coach, Helen Carroll, in the 1970s dealt with conflict between the straight and gay players on her team.[49] Lopiano said that Carroll made her team sit down and instructed them that they weren't going to leave the locker room until they understood and accepted each other. For Lopiano, the team ended up being stronger because of this initiative that Carroll oversaw. "And she did exactly the right thing," Lopiano said in praise of her. "This is how you handle difference, right?"[50] It's curious that Lopiano was so passionate about the potential for conversation and understanding among teammates of different sexual orientations but mourned the fact that a cisgender athlete felt uncomfortable in the locker room with a trans woman, and that it was solely the fault of the trans woman, with no possibility for consensus or understanding for this situation. Taking a page from Lopiano, imagine if the "scared" swimmer with the towels resolved to follow Carroll's initiative and come together with Thomas to respectfully (and perhaps privately) discuss their experiences in the locker rooms and beyond. This could be a fruitful way to "handle difference."

In these discussions with groups and people that vocally oppose Harrison and his community's access to sports and basic human rights, it's hard not to get defensive, not to mention emotional. The urge to shut down and not listen when someone says something that goes against one's core values is natural. Much like the heated discourse within families when politics comes up over the holidays, it can feel like you're wasting your breath or talking to a brick wall. It's exhausting, it's hurtful, and it's taxing on one's mental health and well-being. Although Harrison was open during the conversation with Lopiano, who seemed to genuinely want to find a way for trans people to be welcomed in sports, it was challenging for him to realize that true integration was never the objective. The true motive was figuring out a way to keep this group of people separate through the false auspices of equality. It serves as a reminder of all the efforts and resources these groups are putting toward such a small and vulnerable group of people, when, as we have discussed, there are so many ongoing and worsening structural inequalities in women's sports. Adding an extra lane on the track or an extra heat here and there will do nothing to address the roots of discrimination and biases, not only for women's sports but for trans people in general. The search for answers gets muddied by witch hunts against trans athletes.

THE REAL BARRIERS IN WOMEN'S SPORTS

Questions about perceived biological and genetic advantages are only ever raised—and obsessively scrutinized—when the discussion is about women athletes. What if we interrogated the discrepancies between men's and women's sports in the same manner as we currently do regarding the participation of trans athletes? The roots of the discrepancies between men's and women's sports are unequal finances, access, and misguided and arbitrary safety concerns.

Let's begin by tackling the preoccupation with maintaining safety in women's sports. Currently, this preoccupation plays out in a way that ends up being detrimental to the success and viability of the sport and the players. This was illustrated in the little-known saga over body checking in hockey at the 1990 Women's World Championship, held in Ottawa. It still is the only international women's ice hockey tournament to have ever allowed full body checking, something that's always been allowed in men's leagues. But body checking was suddenly ruled illegal mid-tournament after some women suffered head injuries. Organizers had concluded that many countries' teams could potentially be injured when playing against the North American and European players, who were deemed stronger than the other countries owing to their world-class training.

The European women's hockey leagues had already allowed body checking at this point, so they also had the advantage of knowing how to hit and respond to hits relatively safely. The 1990 ban led to body checking being prohibited around the world. Since then, players have decried the bans as sexist. "I think it's a double standard. I was watching the Olympics, and I can't think of any other sport where the rules are different for men and women," Amanda Gushue, a player in the Southern Alberta Women's Hockey Association who supports body checking in women's leagues, told the *Calgary Journal*.[51] Though some argue that body checking ought to be banned in women's hockey to protect smaller players from larger ones, the size and height differences are just as stark in men's hockey: the average height for players in the NHL is six foot one, but the league has featured a wide range of heights, ranging from five-foot-four Nathan Gerbe to six-foot-nine Zdeno Chára.[52] But a ban on body checking has never been pursued for men.

Another aspect of the body checking ban is that it made hockey players on the women's side *more* vulnerable to head injuries. Yes, you read that correctly. Since women are not trained at an early age in how to hit and take a hit safely, they aren't expecting contact during games. So when the contact inevitably happens in a sport as high-paced as this one, the severity of the impact is more dangerous, as players are not taught how to properly brace themselves. The NCAA Injury Surveillance System (ISS) reported that women's hockey had the highest rate of concussions of any of the sixteen men's and women's collegiate level sports teams.[53] The fact is that hockey is one of the only sports that has a different set of rules and norms for men and women. Tune into any NHL game and you are likely to see violence in the form of blood and teeth getting knocked out. But when women try to play that type of hockey, it doesn't fit traditional gender norms dictating how women and girls should behave. In 2022, more than thirty years after that rule change, the Swedish Women's Hockey League (in Swedish, Svenska damhockeyligan, or SDHL) decided to allow body checking for the 2022–23 season as part of a temporary pilot project. "It feels inspiring that we now make a decision for our own league and not only pave the way for Swedish women's hockey, but for the entire women's hockey world," Gizela Ahlgren Bloom, the sports manager for the SDHL, said in a statement.[54] In 2023, the league heralded the pilot program as a success and announced it would be extended, including down to the lower levels. A study of the body checking experiment found positive feedback from 86 percent of the players, who also reported better overall competition and entertainment during the games, as well as lower rates of injury.[55] Myriad other aspects of organized women's sports as they are currently structured continue to prevent women athletes from reaching their true potential. Not only are women's sports hindered by rules and regulations that may have unintended negative consequences; the rules also serve as a distraction from addressing larger systemic issues at play in women's sports.

The sports world exposes and replicates chronic problems in our societies, including wealth disparity, racism, sexism, and other forms of discrimination and abuse. These issues are often exacerbated by fiercely protective gatekeepers and the self-governing nature of sports leagues that can promote a culture of secrecy and toxicity. Much is made about the need—whether well-founded or not—to protect women's sports by protecting the athletes when they're participating in a particular sport. But the abuse experienced by these athletes when they're *not* competing is far more prevalent, much more insidious, and has been ignored for far too long. The global scale and scope of the abuse, especially sexual abuse, faced by women athletes is overwhelming and hard to keep track of. At the end of 2023, the Canadian federal government announced it would launch a commission to investigate sexual abuse, human rights violations, and other types of misconduct and harassment within various sports. "I absolutely think this is a systemic problem," Sport Minister Carla Qualtrough told CBC News. "I think it is a crisis."[56] Other countries across the globe are plagued by sports abuse scandals, from France and Germany to South Korea and Australia. Recent scandals in the US alone include abuse in women's gymnastics, soccer, running, fencing, and rowing. A 2021 survey of eight hundred adults who attended private or public universities found that one in four college athletes—regardless of gender—endured sexual abuse during their collegiate athletic careers.[57]

American swimming, which we have described as one of the key battlegrounds for trans inclusion, has also been a hotbed of abuse perpetrated by white cisgender men coaches and administrators. An in-depth investigation by the Southern California News Group in 2018 revealed how USA Swimming ignored hundreds of allegations of sexual abuse against swimmers in the girls' division under the age of eighteen. The swimming administration botched investigations into (cisgender) men coaches, clearing them to continue coaching, therefore allowing them to continue their predation and abuse.[58] The swimming scandal mirrors the rampant and well-documented abuses in USA Gymnastics involving athletes such as Aly Raisman. Acknowledging and tackling these issues is necessary to improving all sports.

These abuses and failures to protect women's leagues from physical, sexual, and emotional abuse are compounded by the ongoing and shocking pay disparities between women's and men's divisions. Earlier chapters scratched the surface of the disparities in pay and media coverage between men's and women's sports, but let's dig deeper. Women can make good money in some professional sports such as tennis, golf, and basketball. At this point, the same cannot be said about women's hockey. Until a few years ago, women's professional hockey players in North America were all unpaid volunteers, with many of them being forced to pay out of pocket to buy their own equipment. For decades, the only professional women's hockey league on the continent was the Canadian Women's Hockey League (CWHL). It wasn't until 2015 that women hockey players in Canada were actually paid to play, and it wasn't until the last couple years that their salaries were considered a living wage. The highest amount Harrison made playing in the Premier Hockey Federation (formerly known as the NWHL) was $19,500 for seven months of work. The average annual salary for professional women's hockey players in 2023 was around $55,000; one player made headlines that year for striking a $150,000 deal with the Toronto Six, shortly before it was bought by the now-defunct PHF.[59] Compare that to the average NHL player's salary, which is more than $3 million; the highest paid player in 2024 made $16.5 million.[60]

Let's take elite basketball as another example. The opportunities to play in the top professional league in the US are far greater for men than they are for women. There are 450 roster spots in the NBA, more than three times the number of spots in the WNBA, 144.[61] The highest-paid NBA player, Stephen Curry, made the equivalent annual salary of 350 WNBA players during the 2023–24 season—a number that far surpasses the number of total WNBA roster spots.[62] A viral TikTok video helps illustrate this inequality in college-level basketball. In 2021, NCAA Oregon Ducks basketball player Sedona Prince posted a video from the March Madness tournament showing how the women's leagues had access to a single rack of dumbbells as part of their weight training area, while the men's leagues had access to a spacious, state-of-the-art weight facility with numerous types of equipment.[63] Ultimately, the NCAA was shamed into apologizing for the situation, and the women's weight area was quickly upgraded for the rest of the tournament.[64] This was a small glimpse into the widespread discrimination faced by women and girls in all levels of sport. And it still did not lead to systemic change within the NCAA.

BANS IN THE NAME OF PROTECTION

Anti-trans and sexist policies aren't the only examples of efforts that are framed as a way to maintain the integrity and safety of women's sports but actually do the opposite. The case of Asmahan Mansour, the eleven-year-old Canadian girl who fought the international ban against hijabs on the soccer field, provides a good example of policies designed to control athletes on the women's side that have no scientific basis. The policy, which focused on proper "headgear," was implemented without consultation with Muslim women, just as policies pertaining to trans athletes are also often implemented without consultation from those with lived experience and who are actually trans. It was clear that the hijab ban was rooted in misogyny and Islamophobia. In 2007, Mansour tried to wear her hijab at a tournament in Quebec and a referee refused to allow her to play because of her headscarf, citing potential danger to herself and other players.[65] The prohibition was completely unfounded, as there's no evidence that wearing a hijab can inflict any harm to the player who wears one or anyone else on the field. Thousands of Muslim girls were prevented from playing soccer due to the ban. Although a concern with "religious symbolism" was the reason that FIFA, the international body governing soccer, gave for banning head coverings on the field, it's clear that this justification was a ruse and a case of hypocrisy, as cisgender men soccer players' bodies are often covered in tattooed crosses and other religious symbols. FIFA quickly walked back the "religious symbolism" reason and stuck to "health and safety" concerns.[66]

By 2014, in response to strong advocacy and educational campaigns, the hijab ban was overturned; it remains unclear how many prospective young soccer players on the girls' side were lost over the course of the seven-year ban.[67] And even though FIFA overturned its hijab ban, one still exists in France.[68] At the same time, there's a highly organized and courageous contingent of players fighting against it. This provides hope and precedent for those fighting against anti-trans bans, which may come and go depending on several factors, including the extent to which the successes of trans women athletes get proper media attention.

Imagine the possibilities for equality that could come from pushing for adequate investments in women's sports, instead of transphobic and racist efforts to exclude a small percentage of athletes. Why are we more focused on targeting a small group of trans woman athletes for their successes than rectifying our larger societal failures and the widening funding disparities between men's and women's sports? Instead of succumbing to hysteria and panic over the inclusion of trans women, we ought to focus on creating a world in which all women athletes are adequately valued for their power, strength, and potential. Paving the way for young women athletes with a focus on empowerment rather than exclusion—this starts at the school level, where clashes over gender diverse youth are perhaps the most urgent.

CHAPTER 7

SCHOOL BATTLEGROUND

"**I** Was the Fastest Girl in Connecticut. But Transgender Athletes Made It an Unfair Fight." The 2021 op-ed by Connecticut high school runner Chelsea Mitchell opens with a description of being at the starting line in a state championship race.[1] "This should be one of the best days of my life. I'm running in the state championship, and I'm ranked the fastest high school female in the 55-meter dash in the state. I should be feeling confident. I should know that I have a strong shot at winning," Mitchell writes. "Instead all I can think about is how all my training, everything I've done to maximize my performance, might not be enough, simply because there's a runner on the line with an enormous physical advantage: a male body." Even though Mitchell opines about being at a disadvantage against her trans competitor, and even though the reader is led to believe that she lost the race to a trans woman (whom Mitchell refers to using derogatory and incorrect language), Mitchell went on to actually *win* that race.[2]

Two of Mitchell's competitors in Connecticut were trans teens Andraya Yearwood and Terry Miller, whose participation sparked the ensuing lawsuit, filed by Mitchell, three other cisgender runners, and their families. The lawsuit marked the apex of the battle against trans youth in the US. By age sixteen, Yearwood, who realized she was trans before high school, had won myriad state titles in the 100- and 200-meter races.[3] Miller, who has rarely spoken to the media, followed in her father's footsteps as a high school track runner in Jamaica.[4] Both she and Yearwood had been undergoing hormone suppression treatments over the course of competing as runners that aligned their testosterone levels with those of their cisgender competitors. Yearwood and Miller, two Black students in a town made up of more than 90 percent white people, garnered national media attention in 2018 after coming in first and second place, respectively, in the 100- and 200-meter races at a regional track championship. That's where the pair also met for the first time and continued staying in touch, forging a strong bond as they dealt with the onslaught of criticism and vitriol.[5]

As Yearwood and Miller's winning streaks continued—with fifteen championship race wins between 2017 and 2019—they became the targets of lawsuits and campaigns by parents, fellow athletes, and anti-trans organizations that sought to oust them from their chosen teams and strike down the policies that allowed them to compete. In 2020, the families of three cisgender women and girls' high school students, including Chelsea Mitchell's, filed a lawsuit against the Connecticut Association of Schools and other public school organizations, seeking to block Yearwood and Miller from participating in girls' sports leagues in high school, including the upcoming spring track meets, which ended up being canceled because of the COVID-19 pandemic. The cisgender girl students argued they were unfairly forced to compete against Yearwood and Miller. On top of that, they also sought to have all the records set by trans athletes between 2017 and 2020 erased. Their legal proceedings were represented and funded by attorneys for the Alliance Defending Freedom (ADF), the well-funded evangelical Christian legal group founded in 1994 that's on a mission to roll back rights for LGBTQ+ people and women in the US and around the world. The group has supported legal efforts in places such as India and Belize to criminalize same-sex intercourse.[6] In recent years, the group has been on a winning streak, with at least fourteen victories before the US Supreme Court, including the 2018 *Masterpiece Cakeshop* case, in which the court sided with a Colorado baker who refused to make a wedding cake for a gay couple because doing so would violate his Christian faith. A more recent victory was the overturning of *Roe v. Wade* in 2022. The successful arguments that helped overturn *Roe* are expected to be adapted in future challenges to *Obergefell v. Hodges*, the Supreme Court case that legalized gay marriage. Now, ADF is at the root of the panic and backlash against the less than 2 percent of youth in the US who identify as trans. Since 2019, the group has ramped up much of its efforts and energy on challenging policies in schools and in the realm of healthcare that are meant to support transgender children and youth, including the participation of trans girls in sports. At least twenty-three states have passed legislation to that effect with the backing and lobbying of ADF. The group's chief executive and general counsel, Kristen Waggoner, told the *New Yorker* in 2023 it is fighting "the radical gender identity ideology infiltrating the law." For Waggoner, the reason why more and more youth are identifying as trans owes to a "social contagion" being foisted on them by popular culture, schools, and the law.[7]

One of the ADF's latest targets is the state of Connecticut, a state that allows trans kids to play on sports teams according to their gender identity. The Connecticut Interscholastic Athletic Conference, part of the Connecticut Association of Schools, says its policy follows a state anti-discrimination law that students must be treated in school by the gender with which they identify, and the group believes the policy is "appropriate under both state and federal law." The athletic conference has said that prohibiting students from playing on the sports team that aligns with their gender identity would not only be discriminatory but would deprive them of the meaningful opportunity to participate in educational and extracurricular activities.[8] Although the Justice Department and the Department of Education's Office for Civil Rights under the Trump administration had backed the cisgender runners in the Yearwood and Miller case, the Biden administration withdrew the federal government's support in 2021 and the case was dismissed, a decision that was then appealed by the cisgender students and parents.[9] It could be years before there's a full resolution in this case—long after the students have graduated high school and even college—as the parents and ADF are determined to pursue every avenue and loophole possible to get some sort of win. It's beyond the scope of the book to dig into the legalese of this particular process, but it's important to note that a three-judge panel on an appeals court in 2022 found that, given that the cisgender runners had actually placed first in some track and field events against Yearwood and Miller, the plaintiffs (the cisgender girls) lacked standing on the matter because their concerns over being deprived of wins, state titles, and scholarships were speculative in nature, meaning that they were hypothetical and not based on something that happened.[10] "The plaintiffs simply have not been deprived of a 'chance to be champions,'" one judge wrote.[11] Mitchell and the two other cisgender women runners went on to receive running scholarships at prestigious US colleges. Yearwood and Miller, on the other hand, did not get any such offers and stopped running by the time they got to college. In fact, exactly zero trans women have ever been granted an NCAA scholarship to date.

While this lawsuit involves concerns about competition, placing, and other tangible results in sports, what's at stake here is the less tangible aspects of sports, especially for youth—things like community, sense of self, physical well-being, and emotional fulfillment. Trans youth, especially trans girls, are the subject of ridiculous notions that they will automatically be elite athletes and always take potential college team spots away from their cisgender peers whenever they compete. The truth is that most youth athletes, regardless of gender identity, do not go on to compete at elite levels after high school, nor do they aspire to. Most youth who continue playing sports into adulthood do so solely for recreational purposes. Recent studies show that only 2 percent of high school athletes—one in fifty-seven—go on to play their sport as Division I athletes in the NCAA.[12] There is a whole other group, consisting of 98 percent of athletes and students (cisgender and gender diverse), that is being left out of these discussions, intentionally or not. We've spoken to numerous young trans kids and their families who worry about the ways in which this next generation is being deprived of their full rights and vital childhood experiences as the climate for LGBTQ+ youth becomes increasingly hostile.

THE STORY OF SUNNY

Sunny Bryant is a ten-year-old trans girl who lives with her family in the Houston area. She's got bright blond, shoulder-length hair and a wide, infectious smile. She enjoys teasing her mom Rebekah and running around with her puppy. When you speak with Sunny, she's immediately engaged in the conversation, and you can tell she's deeply curious and inquisitive. She's excited to share things about her life with you, and she's open and full of energy and spunk. But, most importantly, she likes to brag about how fast she can run and that her middle name, Jet, fits her well. When Rebekah was pregnant with Sunny, one of her baby shower gifts was a stopwatch in order to time how fast her future child would be. Rebekah and her husband, Chet, love sports and play recreational softball, so it was the perfect gift for parents like them who want to pass down their love of sports to their children. You could say the stopwatch worked, as these days, Sunny is excelling at softball, but is eager to try rock climbing. But amid all the positivity and happiness that surrounds Sunny, there's an undeniable hum of anti-trans sentiment in their home state of Texas, and what Sunny's future, athletic and otherwise, looks like remains uncertain.[13]

Even at such a young age, Sunny has become embroiled in the battle for trans inclusion in sports and a symbol for the ways in which harmful rhetoric and regulations impact kids like her. Just two years ago, when she was eight, Sunny and Rebekah testified before state legislators to halt proposed laws that would ban trans girls from participating on sports teams that aligned with their gender identity. Sunny and her family joined a growing number of trans youth and their allies who were standing up to the government in the name of equality and fairness.[14] Throughout 2021, Rebekah went to the Capitol at least six times—at a personal financial cost of more than $3,000 for taking time off work—to advocate against the bills. Sunny herself testified against the sports bans twice. While testifying, she told congresspeople about her love of baseball, tennis, gymnastics, and soccer. None of her classmates cared that she was trans, she said. "Kids care about what's in your heart," Sunny continued. "Only old people can't see that." Even the Republicans chuckled at Sunny's jab.[15]

The second time that Sunny testified was after midnight, long past her bedtime. Up until this point, Sunny's experience testifying had been relatively positive. She and her family had come away from these sessions feeling energized and supported in their advocacy efforts. But this time, things took a darker turn. Sunny left the session feeling dejected and discouraged. She broke down in tears to Rebekah when they returned to their hotel room. "Why do so many people not like me?" Sunny asked her mother. It was the first time she had expressed any pain or anguish toward this issue and this process. These are feelings that no child should have to endure, especially at such a young age. For the next little while, Sunny began to show signs of anxiety, though those eventually dissipated. It was a rude awakening for Sunny and her entire family. Rebekah hasn't brought Sunny back to the Capitol since, seeing it as a potential trigger for her child, who only wants to be loved and accepted for who she is and be free to do the things she loves just like her cisgender classmates. They're trying to live their lives in peace as best they can for now.[16]

A parent will do anything to protect their children, and some outsiders viewing these sports bans from afar may question why parents of trans children stay in these hostile environments. Why not move away to a state or place that's more welcoming and inclusive? Families like Sunny's, who are being attacked at all angles, should not be driven out from their homes and forced to move away from a community they've built to protect their child from harm. "We built a life here and I love my job. I have a great career and position that I've worked really hard for," Sunny's mother, Rebekah, told us in the summer of 2023. "We have a great community. We live in a little bubble. They love their school. My husband likes his job. We have everything set up pretty comfortably." Rebekah had never decorated a home before, and she recently did so for the first time with theirs, from top to bottom, with furniture accessories that she loves. "We're sort of digging our heels in, and yeah, we know if we move to L.A., we're going to be in a tiny apartment. The cost of living is different even with good jobs. We'd like to keep it [our house] as much as possible," Rebekah continued.[17]

Part of what makes Sunny so special is how resilient she is, despite her struggles, which she knows might continue. Her ability to move forward with such a brightness of spirit is attributed to her family and their unconditional support. Luckily, the Bryants are far from the only example.

THE STORY OF LIBBY

Before Sunny and her family took up the mantle of advocating for trans inclusion in sports in Texas, there was Libby Gonzales, who took on the state's infamous bathroom bill years earlier. It's jarring to think of the burden these young children must endure to achieve basic equality and dignity, but they are the ones who are being impacted and harmed the most. Libby was three years old when she began identifying as a girl. During a trip from their home in Texas to California, this became clear to Libby's mom and dad, Rachel and Frank, when Libby expressed a strong desire to purchase a fairy costume with a pink skirt and matching wings from a toy store they stopped at along the way. Libby grew out her hair and felt her best when wearing clothing that was "girly." By the time she turned six, Libby asked her mom whether Santa could make her a girl for Christmas. Rachel told Libby that she didn't have to wait to get girl's clothes. Over the following six months, she started wearing feminine clothes and eventually changed her name and pronouns. The transition for Libby, and the entire family, wouldn't be without its challenges and learning curves, but seeing Libby live as her authentic self became a gift for the family.[18] And it would help lay a positive foundation for Libby's mental health going forward. A 2017 study in the *Journal of the American Academy of Child and Adolescent Psychiatry* found that parents who allow their transgender children to socially transition nearly eliminate the high risks of depression and feelings of low self-esteem they might otherwise experience.[19]

By the time she was seven, Libby had become a warrior for trans rights in her home state. It was July 2017, years before the most recent attacks on trans rights and trans athletes, and Republican state legislators were trying to push a bill that would restrict trans people from accessing public restrooms that aligned with their gender identity. Libby, along with her mother and younger sister Cecilia, who was four, and her two-year-old brother Henry, joined hundreds of others at the Texas Capitol building to protest that bill and speak to legislators directly about the detrimental impacts of the proposed law.[20] It was the third time in as many months that Libby and her family made the nearly four-hour trek to the Capitol to advocate against the bill and try to bring as many legislators as they could to their side. The last time the Gonzales family was there in April, they weren't called to testify until 2 a.m., by which time Libby had fallen fast asleep and couldn't give the speech she had spent hours preparing. So while she slept in her father Frank's arms, he pleaded to legislators on her behalf to not force his daughter to use men's bathrooms in public. "It would force her into a hostile environment to publicly out her every time she needed to use the restroom," Frank urged.[21]

The Gonzales family formed part of a burgeoning network of families of trans kids who decided, out of necessity, to become activists in the wake of the anti-trans bathroom legislation being pushed by Texas governor Greg Abbott, who remains in office as of this writing. This type of activism meant taking time from work, opening themselves up to harassment online and in real life, and speaking to Republican lawmakers, many of whom had already firmly made up their minds on the matter, and weren't open to listening to their perspectives. That hot summer day in 2017, Libby finally had her turn to address the lawmakers who were trying to keep her from using the bathroom of her choice—a basic human right. "I love my school and my friends, and they love me, too," Libby said. "I don't want to be scared to go to the restroom in [public]. And I never ever want to use the boys' bathroom. It would be so weird. Please keep me safe. Thank you." Libby's mother then took the mic, saying she was tired of having to defend her daughter and her rights. "Please, please keep in mind that we need to keep every single child in this state safe," Rachel said. The Gonzales family left the room and Libby broke down crying. Her father embraced her and said he loved her.[22]

A month later, the bathroom bill died after losing ground and support that summer. LGBTQ+ activists were obviously relieved and pleased with that outcome, but it would just be a few short years before they would be confronted with an even bigger fight.[23] Today, trans rights and those of all LGBTQ+ people are under threat in Texas, perhaps more than any other state. The ironic part of the bathroom bill was that it lost ground largely as a result of sports governing bodies and large corporations putting their foot down against transphobia. Companies including IBM, Apple, American Airlines, Capital One, and Ben & Jerry's, along with more than 650 business interest groups and chambers of commerce, staunchly opposed the law and threatened to boycott the state if it passed.[24] They pointed to a similar, successful corporate initiative in North Carolina that in 2017 led to legislators rolling back a bathroom bill passed the year before. The state had suffered millions of dollars in losses as a result of the bill—with a projected $3.76 billion in total losses had the ban remained in place—through major event cancellations and boycotts, including the NCAA's ban on holding championships there.[25] In the end, sports leagues and organizations actually have the potential to protect trans kids like Libby from discriminatory measures. Now, five years later, sports are being weaponized against them, and have become one of the biggest threats to trans kids and their ability to live freely in the United States.

Now, in 2023, Libby is thirteen and attends middle school in Dallas. Once again, Libby and her family have found themselves on the front lines of the war against trans people and youth. Having to constantly fight for your rights to access public spaces and other things like health care can make anyone exhausted, especially when you've been doing it for half of your life like Libby has. In June 2023, Abbott signed into law new piece of state legislation, SB 15, dubbed the "Save Women's Sports Act," that bans transgender athletes from participating on collegiate sports teams that align with their gender identity. This expanded legislation that came into effect in 2021 that prevents trans women and girls in public schools from kindergarten to twelfth grade from participating on sports teams that align with their gender identity, forcing them to instead play on teams that match their original birth certificate. The latest wave of trans sports bans has hit the Gonzales family particularly hard. "It feels exhausting on top of everything else, and much more personal," Libby's mom Rachel told us over dinner one spring evening in 2023, a couple months before the latest Texas sports ban officially came into effect. "Sports are obviously mostly not just about the competition. It's about the team camaraderie, learning how to work with a bunch of people, having body movement, that kind of relief in your day."[26] But lately, sports have become a politicized environment that Libby and many kids like her—trans or not—are being forced to think about and reconsider in a new and troubling way.

Even before the sports ban came into effect in Texas, Libby played soccer at her school for a short while; however, shifting attitudes and curiosity about her gender identity began to heighten, particularly among other parents and players from competing teams. Becoming a preteen meant contending with puberty both for herself and those around her. Children who would not have known otherwise were suddenly becoming aware of their bodies and hers as well. "She was so uncomfortable knowing the hate rhetoric from people we didn't know," Rachel said.[27] Because Libby has for years been so public about her trans identity, she worried about facing hatred and being targeted if people recognized her and had an issue with trans people—for instance, parents or players on opposing teams. So, she stopped playing soccer.

Even before any anti-trans legislation was pursued, trans youth like Libby already felt unable to be fully themselves at school and on sports teams. According to a 2022 survey by the Trevor Project, 83 percent of transgender and nonbinary youth said that they have worried about trans people being denied the ability to play sports due to state or local laws.[28] Additionally, in a 2022 poll also conducted by the Trevor Project, 86 percent of transgender and nonbinary youth said the recent debates over state laws restricting the rights of trans people have negatively affected their mental health, which can already be precarious as they grapple with their gender identity.[29] Further, recent research shows that trans-inclusive sports programs for youth improves the participation rates of cisgender youth, especially girls. Researchers warned in a 2023 opinion piece for the journal *JAMA Pediatrics* that bans on trans athletes at schools and colleges could discourage them from playing sports entirely, contributing to "lasting deterioration of the physical and mental health of this at-risk population."[30]

These fears have become a reality for too many trans youth in just the past couple of years. A prominent example is the troubling case of a young teen trans girl at a high school in Broward, Florida. The reaction to her simply playing sports at her school led to her being outed against her will, teachers and administrators being punished for letting the girl play, students protesting in support of her, and an entire school district in upheaval and shot into international headlines. It all started in 2021, the year the trans girl, whose identity is not public, played on the girls' soccer team and girls' volleyball team at her middle school. This was also the year that Governor Ron DeSantis signed the "Fairness in Women's Sports Act" that barred trans girls from playing on girls' sports teams in Florida. At the age of eleven, the girl began hormone blockers, at the recommendation of her endocrinologist, that would halt the testosterone-driven puberty she would otherwise undergo. She eventually started taking estrogen hormone therapy as well, something that she plans to do for the rest of her life. The girl and her parents filed a lawsuit against the state, using only their initials so as not to be publicly identified, challenging the constitutionality of the 2021 sports ban. The girl, her parents argued, "cannot play safely on the boys' team or be in the boys' locker rooms." By early 2023, when the girl was in high school, a US District Court rejected their legal challenge, citing the biological differences between girls and boys, but gave the girl's family more time to file a new amended legal challenge.[31]

That fall, the school district launched an investigation into "allegations of improper student participation in sports" at the school and the teen girl's participation on the high school varsity girls' volleyball team. In late November, news broke that the principal and several other staffers were reassigned by the district to non-school sites. The reassignments are believed to be retribution for allowing the girl to play on the girls' team, something that violates the state law.[32] Hundreds of students at the high school staged a walkout to protest the investigation and staff reassignments. The national outcry and spotlight on the high school prompted the girl's mother to issue a public statement in which she thanked the community for their outpouring of support, but decried the fact that her daughter was publicly outed and the danger she was now facing amid the resulting firestorm. "A lot of things were taken from my family," the mother wrote, "our privacy, sense of safety, and right to self-determination. There is a long history of this country outing people against their will—forced outing, particularly of a child, is a direct attempt to endanger the person being outed." The mother concluded the statement by asking for privacy and space to process what happened. By the end of the year, the district punished the high school by putting it on a one-year administrative probation and fining it $16,500—all because a young girl played volleyball. The girl was also declared "ineligible to represent any member school" for sports for at least a year.[33] This is only the beginning of the enforcement of these laws if they remain in place.

The support that this trans athlete and her family received from the school's employees in the face of extreme legislation exemplifies how important allies are in this battle, and the real risks they are taking on. Educators are on the front lines, and they see firsthand how this discrimination is affecting their young students, unlike the government officials who very likely don't personally know any transgender people or understand how their proposed laws intimately affect them. Teachers, parents, coaches, and students are at a crossroads and must decide whether to toe the line or fight in defense of vulnerable youth.

SPORTS ARE NONNEGOTIABLE

Candy Gwyn is one of Libby Gonzales's teachers at her private Montessori middle school in the Dallas area. Gwyn describes the school as being situated in a protective bubble in a state that has become exponentially more hostile toward progressive ideas and basic human rights. Through classes and activities, the school promotes advocacy and awareness regarding social justice and environmental issues. There are no curriculum constraints, which allows the school and its teachers to discuss issues and go deeper on topics that might otherwise be excluded or even forbidden in public school settings. This includes conversations about racism and gender identity. In the summer of 2023, Texas governor Greg Abbott signed a ban restricting books deemed "sexually explicit" in school libraries, along with other measures to further empower parents' involvement in the classroom.[34] Opponents of Abbott's law have decried the efforts as targeting reading materials about members of the LGBTQ+ community and therefore infringing on children's right to read. They have further sounded the alarm over the fact that what counts as "sexually explicit" under the law is vague and therefore could be applied arbitrarily. Texas currently has more than 438 bans on books, the most out of any other US state.[35]

"There is not a single person I know in Texas who is not afraid right now," Gwyn told us. "Educators are scared they're going to lose their job, they're afraid of overstepping the line. Doctors are terrified."[36] She added that while adults have perspective and years of experience that might allow them to see the light at the end of the tunnel, children and adolescents don't have that foresight and wisdom. Even though Libby is wise beyond her years, Gwyn says, she's still a thirteen-year-old girl who is scared, and that fear seeps into other aspects of her life. "And there's no real shielding kids from the fear. I can't see any way to protect her from that fully. It's out there. She feels it. We all feel it."[37]

But for Gwyn, sports for children are nonnegotiable. And she will defend her students' right to be able to participate. An avid runner herself, Gwyn started an amateur running club at the school with the simple aim of getting children outdoors and active. It's not competitive, and so the goals and approach are calmer and looser.

"I think physical activity and being able to do something with your body is so empowering," Gwyn said.[38] In running and other similar activities, there are more opportunities to connect with your teammates in a way that wouldn't necessarily happen outside that environment. In fast-paced team sports where you are chasing either a ball or a puck, you range all over whatever playing surface you are on throughout the course of a game. In running, it's less erratic, and runners have the ability to carry on conversations. In the running club, Gwyn and her students chat about interactions with their parents as they run, and even talk about how they came out as gay or trans to their families. "It's totally unselfconscious. We are just openly talking. We are laughing about the awkwardness of things [that they're dealing with]," said Gwyn.[39]

When Harrison reflects on what drew him to sports, and why he found so much solace in the hours during the day when he was on the ice or at the gym, it's because that was the only time his mind would become quiet and calm. When he wasn't playing sports, he was constantly ruminating on his gender dysphoria, the future, or anything—the inner monologue was relentless and chaotic. He also felt out of control of his own body, especially during puberty when all these changes were happening, such as developing breasts and getting a period. He also felt helpless when changes that he wanted to happen to his body didn't occur, such as experiencing a growth spurt, voice drop, and an overall masculinization. When he played sports, he could control what his body did, how it looked in terms of building muscle, and he gained a new relationship with what it was capable of doing. He didn't think so much about what he didn't have in terms of speed, dexterity, and strength; the mentality shifted to where he felt like he had a say and could play an active role in becoming what he wanted in terms of athletic performance through training. Outside of sports, he felt like a bystander who just had things happen to him, just watching life. While playing sports, he felt like an active participant whose actions made a tangible impact. He's truly not sure who he would be, or even if he would be here at all, without sports.

Chris Mosier, the trans triathlete and duathlete who helped overhaul the Olympics' trans policy, sums this perspective up well in his advocacy, calling on us to consider the implications of excluding trans people from sports and also lift up the voices of trans people to confront the moral panic. "Taking away sports isn't going to make me not trans, and it's not going to make a kid not trans. . . . It's just going to make our life incredibly more challenging," Mosier told sports reporter Shireen Ahmed in a podcast interview in 2022. "And so, by telling trans people to lean into their joy, to celebrate their victories and accomplishments and celebrate the love that they have for themselves and other people in their community, that is a form of resistance."[40]

Libby is only one example of the countless trans youth who have decided not to continue playing sports, or even try to play for the first time, out of fear of rejection or condemnation. When Libby told us about team sports, her demeanor became more closed off and guarded, and understandably so. When there are constant headlines about disgruntled parents demanding proof of a child's biological sex, it portrays sports as a terrifying battleground. Why would any transgender kid want to join sports and subject themselves to this on top of anxieties they may already feel about being scrutinized in society, having their autonomy policed, and their very identity questioned at every turn? Sports have been weaponized against the transgender community, and the damage that this does to transgender youth who are trying to find their place in society runs deep.

WHAT ABOUT TRANS BOYS?

Trans women and girls are usually at the center of the controversies around trans inclusion in sports. But the policies that impact them also impact trans men and boys. Though other trans kids who don't live in Texas face a less restrictive environment than Libby and Sunny's, they nonetheless feel the impacts even if they are two thousand miles away. One such example is an eleven-year-old trans boy named Tommy, who lives in a town just outside Boston, where the state government is fortunately supportive of the full inclusion of trans children in sports.[41] His father, Brian, describes Tommy as the "1950s, prototypical kind of all-American boy's boy."[42] (Owing to privacy concerns, Tommy's family requested we use a pseudonym for him and the other members of his family.) Every morning, Tommy phones up his friends so they can all coordinate which hockey jersey they're going to wear to school that day. Tommy has a wide array of jerseys from teams he's played on and those of the players he idolizes. There's an Auston Matthews Toronto Maple Leafs jersey, a Brad Marchand Boston Bruins jersey. And recently, he has hung one of Harrison's jerseys among his hockey heroes. "Everything about him is just a jock; he's just about sports," Tommy's dad, Brian, told us in the summer of 2023.[43]

For the last five years, Tommy has been playing ice hockey. His interest began when he was watching a game one day with his friends. He was struck by how fun it looked and knew right away it was the sport for him. So, he started learning how to skate and eventually played on a mixed team with both boys and girls. Before getting bit by the hockey bug, Tommy had played soccer, starting out on mixed teams as well, and eventually going on to play on the girls' team, where the jerseys were purple. For him, purple was too girly, and he wanted nothing to do with it—and therefore soccer altogether. Every week, Tommy wanted to quit. Brian and Tommy's mother, Kate, tried to coax him into staying on the team. One day, they finally said to Tommy, "Fine, do you want to go play with the boys?" He did, and now that he no longer had to wear the purple jersey, he never asked to quit again. Tommy's needs to feel accepted were not that complicated. There were no special requests or any framework changes required by the entire league or team. He just wanted to play where he felt the most comfortable, as anyone would.[44]

Tommy and Brian have always shared a deep love of sports—it's a crucial part of their father-son relationship that just clicks. Brian is not only a big fan of Tommy as an athlete, but he also serves as his son's coach on their local co-ed club hockey team. For Brian, this role allows him to shape the team and the environment into what he wants it to be: a more inclusive space in sports. For Tommy, having his dad as the coach makes him feel unconditionally supported and safe. Even though he's only eleven years old, he has an acute awareness that being trans comes with a lot of unknowns and potential safety risks. He's a young child who understands that not every space is welcoming and safe for him. Although his parents surround him with protection and vigilance, he is constantly watching his own back, though no child should have to do this.[45]

When people talk about the relationships that are built through sports, the focus is frequently on the friendships that athletes build, sometimes for life, through being part of a team. What is often left out of the conversation is the connection that parents and caregivers can have with their kid through sport. Whether that's physically transporting them to the sporting arena and spending quality time together, receiving praise and affirmation for excelling, or simply participating, practicing together. A parent may be an athlete themselves and can be excited to impart the wisdom that they have learned through their own experiences to their child. Being able to raise an athlete can be a source of pride for a parent, and the exclusion of trans athletes is taking that pride away from them too. There are far more people who stand to lose—among them parents, siblings, and friends—when trans kids are excluded from sports.

Tommy's parents have empowered him to know that he has the choice whether and to whom he discloses his identity as a trans boy. Some of his teammates are aware that he is trans, while others are not. Since he is currently playing on a co-ed team, he's just seen as a cisgender boy and blends in with the majority of the team, which is made up mostly of cisgender boys. Still, he has already witnessed gender discrimination play out on his team and it's upset him. Some of the boys targeted one of the only girl players on the team by excluding her from the locker room and not talking to her on the bench during games. Tommy, as one of the team's leaders, tried to stand up for his teammate, and his dad Brian had to talk to the entire team about respect for all teammates no matter their differences. Seeing how someone is treated based on their gender identity can make any young trans kid feel fearful of receiving that same or even worse kind of treatment.

Although Massachusetts does not have a trans sport ban for youth, the ripple effects and the anti-trans rhetoric that are moving through from states like Texas can make trans youth and their caregivers fearful of their place in sports and how they will be accepted in team environments. "If there was a ban in Massachusetts or if he lived in a place where there already was a ban, and if his choice was play on a girls' team or don't play, he wouldn't," Brian explained. "He just wouldn't do it." That would be something that would take a terrible toll on Tommy. "Thinking about how much of him would be lost from doing that, it's really hard to think about."[46] Although Tommy is currently on a co-ed team, he is on the cusp of puberty and at the age where kids start to branch off into teams segregated by gender. His future within sports is unknown, but he told us he aspires to play on the men's hockey team at Boston University. We hope he does.

CHAPTER 8

VOICES FROM INSIDE
THE LOCKER ROOM

I n 2014, Jesse Thompson, a seventeen-year-old trans boy and minor league hockey player in a boys' league in Ontario, filed a human rights complaint against Hockey Canada after being denied access to the locker room used by the rest of his team. Thompson said this resulted in him being "outed" as transgender and ostracized from team bonding and other important team interactions. He said he was also subjected to harassment and bullying as a result. Thompson's mother, Ailsa, told reporters it was "very upsetting" when the coach booted Thompson from the boys' locker room on the basis that "she's a girl."[1]

At the time, Hockey Canada's co-ed locker room policy required players of all genders older than eleven years old to change in separate locker rooms. The policy was based on one's sex assigned at birth, not the gender identity of the players. "Once you get to a certain age, you are forced into a different room, or basically a closet," Thompson said. "Sometimes they didn't even have change rooms for girls." Thompson went on to settle his complaint with Hockey Canada. As part of his settlement agreement, the national organization's policy was amended to allow amateur hockey players to access the locker room that corresponds with their gender identity and ensure privacy and confidentiality with respect to their status as a transgender person. Hockey Canada also agreed to provide training to all Ontario coaches on gender identity and discrimination and harassment. "I just hope that kids can see this and know that they don't have to hide anymore," Thompson later told the *Canadian Press*. "They can come out and play their sport that they love, and they don't have to stop playing it just because of how they are or who they are."[2] By going public in this courageous way, especially at a time when broad public awareness, understanding, and empathy toward transgender issues was far more lacking than it is today, Thompson was able to bring about some positive changes. But for every Thompson, there are many other gender diverse athletes who likely suffer in silence. And the problems raised by Thompson in 2014 about locker room culture are far from resolved.

Inclusion in the locker room can be a tricky and emotional issue for all LGBTQ+ athletes, from recreational to competitive levels. The division and setup of locker rooms has become an even more charged topic for some parents and caregivers of young athletes, and the broader sports community, as debates about where transgender athletes fit in continue to ramp up. Parents of young athletes, for example, are often worried about the optics of having different bodies and different gender identities in the same change rooms, the result of fearmongering about the supposed risk of sexual assault against their cisgender children. "By building coed locker rooms, you'll be intentionally placing our children, my daughter in particular . . . at much greater risk of sexual assault," a father of a high school swimmer in Los Angeles declared at a school board meeting in 2020 in opposition to a plan to construct gender-neutral locker rooms.[3] The rhetoric espoused by this father not only is misguided and detrimental to transgender and nonbinary people who are being villainized, but also harms cisgender men. There are many progressive voices who fall into this trap.

Progressives who may advocate for the inclusion of trans people broadly speaking may not be able to wrap their heads around spaces such as co-ed locker rooms. But when trans women are perceived as posing an inherent threat, this perception points to the harms perpetuated by systems of patriarchy, highlighting the very worst traits of cisgender men. Trans people, mostly women, then become a distraction from the work of dismantling the effects of toxic masculinity. One survey conducted in 2021 by GLSEN, an education advocacy group, found that 45 percent of LGBTQ+ students in the US avoided using school bathrooms segregated by gender, and 44 percent avoided locker rooms altogether because they felt unsafe or uncomfortable in them.[4] In reality, it's trans (and queer) people who are particularly at an increased risk of victimization and abuse in these settings, not the cisgender athletes.

Around the world, countless efforts have been made to ban trans people from public spaces such as bathrooms, homeless shelters, and prisons that align with their gender identity—a trend we have seen happen against many marginalized communities over time. Before locker rooms, controversies around restroom access were at the center of fights for basic civil and human rights. A 1739 masquerade ball held in Paris is believed to be the site of the first gender-segregated public restroom on record in the Western world, though there's some debate around whether the practice predated this instance.[5] In 1887, Massachusetts enacted the first state law to require restrooms for women and men to be separate. Black people were banned from "whites only" restrooms in the Jim Crow era beginning in the late nineteenth century and extending into the 1960s. Samuel Younge Jr., a student in Alabama, was the first college student to die in the struggle for civil rights after he was shot and killed for trying to use a "whites only" bathroom in 1966. In subsequent decades, several states promoted fear-based public messaging around gay people's use of public toilets. A Florida state legislative committee released a report in 1964 that warned that gay men loitered around bathroom stalls and "posed a threat to the health and moral well-being of a sizable portion of our population, particularly our youth."[6] And it wasn't until 1990 that the Americans with Disabilities Act came into effect to guarantee public restroom access to people with disabilities.[7]

Fast-forward to 2017, when trans people became the subject of bathroom restriction bills. Lawmakers in sixteen states debated bills that proposed restrictions or bans on trans people accessing restroom facilities aligning with their gender identity. This included restrooms, locker rooms, and the like. Bills were pursued in both Republican and Democratic states including Kentucky, New York, Washington, and Tennessee. Young trans and gender nonconforming children such as Libby Gonzales in Texas took time off from school to urge their state legislators to vote against these bills to uphold their privacy and ability to use the restroom in peace. Unlike the similar anti-trans legislation that's being pursued across the US today, every single one of these bills ultimately failed. Still, the impact was palpable: calls by LGBTQ+ youth to suicide prevention services jumped in many states after such bills were proposed, according to 2021 research conducted by the Trevor Project.[8] These bathroom bill efforts and discussions laid the groundwork and infrastructure for the efforts now being pursued to perpetuate fears around trans participation in sports and in society. Trans sports bans are largely focused on the actual competition and how to keep sports "fair." But what's left out of the conversation is the ways in which trans athletes will miss out on locker rooms and the friendships forged in that space that are equally as important as, if not more so, the emotional and physical enrichment provided by the act of playing sports. Figuring out how to make the locker room safe is key to ensuring that sports themselves are more inclusive for all athletes.

Given the high incidence of cases like Jesse Thompson's, it makes sense that the dropout rate for transgender athletes and LGBTQ+ individuals is staggeringly higher than that of their cisgender and heterosexual peers. A 2019 study by Out on the Fields, a research group that studies homophobia and transphobia in sports, found that almost 90 percent of LGBTQ+ people believe that homophobia and transphobia remain problems in sport, while 73 percent of all participants, regardless of gender identity and sexual orientation, believe that it's not safe for queer youth to come out publicly in sports environments.[9] One of the contributing factors to these feelings of exclusion and fear are the locker room environments, where homophobia and transphobia impact athletes who clash with the predominantly heterosexual culture ingrained in sports. Fear of discrimination and harassment also prevents many LGBTQ+ youth from joining sports at all, according to a 2021 survey by The Trevor Project. "I'm scared I will be harassed because of my sexuality," one youth told researchers. Locker rooms were a particular source of stress, another youth shared: "I hated how I was treated by kids and adults who played sports. The locker room was always a nightmare, the athletic kids at my school hated me, the coaches at my school hated me . . . I avoided athletic activities out of terror, not disinterest."[10]

Every sport has its issues, and no space is completely devoid of problematic views and actions, but when it comes to toxicity—whether that's misogyny, racism, homophobia, or transphobia—hockey (particularly men's hockey) is amid a culture reckoning. In recent years we've seen countless headlines about brutal hazing, targeting of LGBTQ+ individuals, racism, sexual and physical assault, and emotional abuse. Hockey serves as a useful case study to examine the dynamics of locker room culture and the possibilities for it to either be a hotbed of hatred or a sanctuary.

Understanding the culture and unique dynamics that take place in both men's and women's hockey locker rooms, which are radically different from each other, is important because they reveal what happens when athletes are exposed to and work with people who have varying gender identities and sexualities. Women's hockey, on the one hand, has long been an environment in which LGBTQ+ athletes have felt safe and embraced. Men's hockey, on the other hand, is homogenous and rigid in every regard, from wealth to race to gender and sexuality. It is also notorious for abuse on and off the ice, including racism and sexual assault by its players. Its environment and culture are intrinsically linked.

On top of this, hockey locker room design is somewhat unique in that players all shower communally. For the most part, players shower together. At least from Harrison's experience, being naked in the women's shared locker rooms and the showers was a kind of rite of passage. As someone who advanced to elite levels (Hockey Canada, NCAA, etc.), he found that the higher level of hockey you played, the more it was expected of you to shower naked. Some teammates would not feel comfortable with this at the beginning and would shower in a bathing suit, but that would make them stand out as awkward and maybe prudish. There was status in being naked. And the culture around nudity also exists on the men's side. Harrison had previously established a confidence in his body in the women's locker room, whereas the thought of being naked in a locker room full of cisgender men scared him enough to make him walk away from the sport he had played, excelled at, and loved for sixteen years. It scared him because he knew about the anti-LGBTQ+ environment that is rampant in men's hockey locker rooms.

After physically transitioning, Harrison played on a couple men's teams in charity tournaments, where he didn't know where he fit in or how the men there would react to him and his body. At one of the charity events, a cisgender man player used the f-word and other homophobic slurs. No one called him out on it. It struck Harrison deeply. He would turn to the wall to change. He didn't shower there because he didn't want to expose his body. History speaks for itself: most men's hockey locker rooms are not safe for people in the LGBTQ+ community. Harrison felt the risk of having those fears confirmed was too great.

Harrison's experience is not unique, and we wanted to understand how other players from the LGBTQ+ community have grappled with the harsh realities of men's hockey, in particular, and the locker room culture that makes it one of sport's most exclusionary and hostile spaces for marginalized athletes. The best way to learn and create avenues for true culture change is to hear directly from athletes who have lived it. While these athletes come from different parts of the LGBTQ+ community, they shed light on how those who do not align with the stereotypical player are often "othered" and forced to choose whether to fight for change or suffer in silence.

VOICES FROM INSIDE THE LOCKER ROOM

Jessica Platt, the first openly trans woman to play pro hockey, is soft-spoken, almost bashful, yet gets visibly passionate when you mention hockey. She has a dry sense of humor and conveys a sense of warmth and authenticity. Growing up in a small lakeside town in southwestern Ontario, Platt attended a Catholic high school, where she played men's hockey. "I loved playing hockey so much that I put aside all of the horrible feelings in the [men's] change room," Platt told us in 2023 during a Pride Night for the PHF's Toronto Six. She loved playing so much that she delayed both her social and medical transitions. "I tried to hide who I was and how I felt and suppressed it all for so long. Just because I didn't feel like I could play hockey and express who I really was." During her time in men's hockey, Platt was steeped in the rampant homophobia typically found in men's leagues, on the ice and in the locker room. "There were constantly gay jokes, people calling each other the f-word," she said. "If you did anything remotely effeminate, they called you 'gay.' People talked derogatorily about women, about girls' bodies, things they wanted to do to them."[11]

Though Platt might have tried to play for the juniors, the top-tier youth league, she ended up playing in a beer league, something that was not at all her cup of tea. Some beer leagues have more aggressive players, "but you really get that bro attitude. And you feel like you can't be different from anyone else," Platt told us. "It's almost a little worse . . . than playing in my rep league [also known as a representative, or club, league]." As Platt and her teammates on the men's side got older, they would naturally discuss their personal lives; their jobs, girlfriends, and the like. There were so many things she just couldn't really relate to, and that divide continued to deepen. "They were going on one journey and I was starting to go on a journey in the complete opposite way," Platt said. So she decided to quit hockey altogether in 2007, not because she didn't love the sport, but because the environment and locker room culture she was in didn't fully love her in return.[12] Either the sport itself would somehow need to change, or she would need to somehow find another way back to it.[13]

Platt, as a trans woman, did not fit into the mold of a stereotypical cisgender man hockey player. This is a similar story shared by many cisgender man hockey players who are gay or bisexual. In 2009, a couple years after Platt initially left hockey behind, the hockey world was rocked when Brendan Burke, son of Brian Burke, the general manager for the Toronto Maple Leafs at the time, came out as gay. Brendan's hockey playing career stopped at high school, but, even though he wasn't an NHL professional, his coming out was a huge moment for hockey, and the sports world as a whole, because there were no openly gay players in the NHL then, or on any prominent men's professional league. It's not a mystery as to why, as of this writing, there's never been an openly gay NHL player. However, Luke Prokop, an NHL prospect for the Nashville Predators, did come out in 2021. Statistically, the actual number of LGBTQ+ players in the NHL is likely much higher.[14] For example, some estimates show that at least 5 percent of the US adult population of men is gay, trans, or bisexual.[15]

Though Brendan himself wasn't playing at an elite level at the time he came out, he represented a hockey dynasty and was putting himself on the line. Even as a highly privileged player with a known last name, he was not immune from the pervasive homophobia and toxicity in the locker room. He quickly became an advocate for change. "The important thing is that it's started a discussion," Brendan told the newspaper the *Globe and Mail* in 2009, after his coming out was mysteriously leaked to ESPN.[16] "And people realize there could be a gay person next to them in the locker room." He cited his high school in Massachusetts as the place where he experienced homophobia on his hockey team, particularly in the locker room, something that forced him to quit over his worries about what would happen if his teammates discovered that he was gay. Brendan's older brother Patrick, who is now the NHL's vice president of player safety and played hockey at the same high school, talked about his time there in a 2021 NHL short film about his brother. "I left behind a locker room that was homophobic. . . . That locker room was unsafe for [Brendan]," he said.[17] "My biggest regret comes from that I left him in an unsafe position. That I left a culture that wasn't what it should have been, and what I have tried to do since then is rectify that."

In 2010, a few months after coming out, Brendan died in a tragic car accident in Indiana, but his legacy sparked the inception of efforts to overhaul hockey to promote inclusion and diversity. His brother Patrick, along with his father, Brian, co-founded You Can Play in Brendan's honor. The organization campaigns for the eradication of homophobia in all sports by creating communities of allies. Patrick and Brian have been outspoken advocates of improving the culture in locker rooms by discouraging homophobic slurs and attitudes in an attempt to have LGBTQ+ players feel accepted and welcome. One of the main contributions that You Can Play has had in the NHL in its efforts to shift hockey culture, including inside the locker room, is its themed Pride Nights. The teams within the NHL participate in a few themed nights every year, from Military Appreciation Night to Hockey Fights Cancer Night, to raise funds and show support for different communities and causes. At one point, every team in the league hosted a Pride Night, where the rinks would be decked out in rainbows, and members of the LGBTQ+ community would be activated for special ambassador treatment such as being honored during the ceremonial puck drop. Players of each team had opportunities to show their support and allyship through special team logos and player numbers on their jerseys that were usually made up of elements from the Pride flag.[18]

As Pride Nights expanded, so did another effort for inclusion in the form of rainbow hockey tape known as Pride Tape. Pride Tape was founded by Canadians Jeff McLean and Kristopher Wells as an awareness tool and a way to start positive conversations about how to make hockey locker rooms safer for the LGBTQ+ community. The idea emerged after the two of them learned of hockey's staggering dropout rate for gay and bisexual cisgender boys, which they attributed to homophobic language and attitudes in the sport. The rainbow-colored tape replaces the standard white-and-black tape that players typically use on their hockey sticks, immediately bringing a symbol for inclusion and acceptance within the very walls that have been known to have the opposite effect. Pride Tape quickly became synonymous with the NHL, You Can Play, and the Pride Nights, as it was such an amazing visual for fans and players to connect with and was used by many prominent players in the league. A player McLean and Wells first turned to was Andrew Ference, captain of the Edmonton Oilers at the time, who showed unwavering support for the community through wearing Pride Tape on his stick and attending Pride parades over the years. As the initiative gained momentum and You Can Play became more established in the nonprofit space, it seemed as if hockey culture was moving in the right direction. And it was. The NHL for a time was seen as a shining example that other professional sport leagues could look to on how to properly celebrate and include a community that is often vilified by the sporting world. That was until the 2022–23 NHL season.[19]

On January 17, 2023, the Philadelphia Flyers hosted their annual Pride Night, where the players were all expected to wear their specialty Pride jerseys for the on-ice warmups. After the game the jerseys were to be sold through an auction to raise money for You Can Play and other LGBTQ+ initiatives. A Philadelphia Flyers defender, twenty-six-year-old Ivan Provorov from Russia, refused to wear the jersey, citing religious reasons, and a media firestorm ensued.[20] Provorov's stance caused a ripple effect on other teams in which a handful of players also declined to wear the jerseys, citing religious objections and other reasons. His stance also exposed the role that anti-LGBTQ+ ideologies and policies from countries outside the US play in the league. Russia, Provorov's homeland, is notoriously hostile toward LGBTQ+ people, which was perhaps most manifest in the country's Supreme Court ruling in 2023 that the worldwide movement for LGBTQ+ rights is an "extremist organization," and that anyone accused of supporting LGBTQ+ rights could be punished with time in prison.[21] The ruling also declared the rainbow flag an illegal symbol. This is significant because many prominent NHL players come from Russia. (Alexander Ovechkin, whose Instagram profile photo features him posing with Russian president Vladimir Putin, is second only to Wayne Gretzky in total number of goals scored.) The oppressive ideologies that the large majority of Russian players espouse are then compounded by the already homophobic culture of the NHL and its fandom. When these players are seen as idols by young players, of all genders, it can hinder LGBTQ+ initiatives or set them back greatly.

Because of the Provorov controversy, every team that hosted a Pride Night after that was under intense public and media scrutiny to see how it would handle a player refusing to participate in the evening's festivities. Some teams preemptively canceled their Pride Nights or scrapped wearing the jerseys out of fear of triggering media attention and scrutiny from the LGBTQ+ community. The PR for the league was such a disaster that for the 2023–24 season, the NHL had taken matters into its own hands with a league-wide ban of themed nights, including Pride Night.[22] The league had gone so far as to ban players from choosing to wear Pride Tape on their stick at any point in the season.[23] This ban stands in stark contrast to women's hockey, where rainbow flags, tape, and other accessories are so common on and off the ice that virtually no player, administrator, or fan would bat an eye. The prevalence and support for LGBTQ+ players had become inherently engrained in the culture of the sport. However, when men's hockey was in a dire need of a culture shift, the NHL's choice to remove a player's ability to show visible support for the LGBTQ+ community really called into question whether "Hockey Is for Everyone," as the NHL claims in its so-called inclusion slogan.

In the first few weeks of the start of the 2023–24 season, twenty-six-year-old Canadian defenseman Travis Dermott of the Arizona Coyotes fought back against the Pride Tape ban and displayed it on his stick. Dermott, who is straight and cisgender, told reporters that he simply felt it had to be done. "[It's] important to be that role model that isn't just doing the right thing when you're allowed to do the right thing," he continued.[24] "It's about making waves when something isn't going the right way, something isn't being handled correctly." By forcing the NHL's hand and calling out the league, Dermott is credited with being responsible for the NHL rescinding the ban a few days later. Players, including allies, are allowed to use the tape if they so choose—for now.

That periodic uncertainty in the men's league about symbols like Pride Tape and the flip-flopping of support for LGBTQ+ players and fans does not exist on the women's side. It's one of the only sports that is very often a place of solace and support for players and fans of all genders and sexualities. The experiences of transgender and nonbinary athletes highlight the inclusion discrepancies between the men's and women's leagues. Jessica Platt, as discussed earlier, quit men's hockey in the wake of experiencing toxic masculinity and homophobia. She would never go back to men's hockey, and it would be years before she eventually found her way back to the sport as well, this time on the women's side. Following a years-long hiatus, she put on her skates for the first time in 2014, after she started teaching kids to skate and fell in love all over again with the sport she'd left behind. She eventually felt inspired to join a league and set her sights on the CWHL, the now-defunct Canadian league for top talent in the women's league. "I actually cared about my body and wanted to take care of myself and wanted to see how good I could be. That was when I trained nonstop," Platt told us.[25]

After securing a spot on the Toronto Furies for the 2017–18 season, Platt disclosed to CWHL coaches and administrators that she was transgender. The idea of coming out terrified her at first. Would they accept or reject her? Would she feel alienated, as she had on the men's side? But, to her relief, she was met with acceptance by the league—including her teammates. "Everyone just treated me like normal," Platt recalled. It was a vastly different experience from what she went through playing in the men's leagues. She no longer worried about people judging her. She became the first openly transgender woman to compete in professional ice hockey, coming out publicly through an Instagram post on January 10, 2018.[26] She cited Harrison as one of the reasons she felt empowered to do so. "I saw how the women's hockey community accepted him, and I was like, 'I can do this too,'" Platt later told reporters.[27]

While Platt had found her way back to hockey through the more accepting women's side, Harrison, as a trans man, has not been able to feel the same comfort from the men's league, which aligns with his gender identity. After retiring from playing professionally, he attempted to play recreationally and still stayed on the women's side after he began hormone replacement therapy. But when he entered spaces filled with people who were no longer his long-term teammates, he felt strange speaking with a lower voice and showing off a flat chest and thought he would confuse the women, making them wonder why a man was in their space. He also would get long stares from parents and spectators as he entered the women's locker rooms. So, he stopped playing with his previous teammates and friends on the women's side. He felt he didn't have a space there and was stuck in a sort of limbo between not playing at all and attempting to switch to the men's side. Given what we know and have explored here about the culture in men's hockey, Harrison is understandably reticent to make the switch, even though he still desires to play hockey.

EXPLORING SOLUTIONS THROUGH HOCKEY CANADA

The stories of these athletes have provided a window into the negative culture that can pervade hockey locker rooms, especially on the men's side. These experiences alone are enough to raise concern, but they don't even scratch the surface or account for the many individuals who have received the same or even worse treatment yet have not come forward for a multitude of reasons. After recognizing the harm done to the sport behind closed doors, Hockey Canada, the nation's governing body for hockey, felt compelled to create a revised policy specifically tailored to the locker room in a way that addresses the intimacy of that space. Here we break down two important components within this policy that most affect LGBTQ+ athletes and trans athletes.

The first is the implementation of the Rule of Two. This rule states that two adults who have been screened and have completed training and a background check must be present at all times in the locker room when athletes are present, or in any space where coaches or other team officials are not consistently there to supervise team interactions.[28] This in theory helps LGBTQ+ individuals, as the presence of screened adults serves to ensure that homophobic slurs, language, and harassment are addressed right away. The second rule is the "base layer rule." This policy states that an athlete is not allowed to disrobe in the locker room beyond the base layer, which can include compression shorts, spandex, thermal underwear, and so on. One must either arrive to the locker room with the base layer on or change into it in a private space such as a bathroom. Hockey is a sport where girls and boys often play together in the younger age brackets, thus making the changing space more gender neutral for all and allowing teammates to change together regardless of gender identity. By eliminating the aspect of being exposed in the locker room, the rule is also designed to bring a lot of peace of mind to trans individuals worried about how their intimate body parts will be viewed by their teammates. Unfortunately, as nice as these rules are, they're hard to enforce and monitor, and there are many teams that don't follow them.

Thinking back on his experiences in the locker room, Harrison feels that having adult supervision there would have felt out of place. If adults had been present, they would have been a barrier to the joy, the healthy sense of discomfort, the discoveries, and the camaraderie that teammates would have otherwise experienced, as it's common for players' demeanors and behaviors to naturally adapt and change, if only temporarily, in the presence of adults. Hockey friends of Harrison who have gone into coaching and who are technically required to uphold the Rule of Two policy admit they don't enforce it for that very reason. For them, it potentially takes away a special element of hockey culture, as it likely would if the policy were implemented in other similar sports settings. Instead of relying on surveillance tactics, the preference is to have appropriate and respectful behavior originate within each athlete. Athletes instead should be encouraged to abide by the motto of "doing the right thing when nobody's watching," to be informed and engaged bystanders and leaders, as many coaches say.

Some of the initial discussions about transgender inclusion in sports, particularly around the locker room, have focused on overly simplistic solutions that could potentially perpetuate harms against the trans person and threaten the cohesion and bonding within the team. Such solutions include giving trans and nonbinary people their own locker room, where they'd be alone. This so-called solution is in the same vein as pursuing trans-only sports leagues, which have fallen flat. Requiring athletes to use locker rooms of their sex assigned at birth, rather than a gender-neutral facility or that of their gender identity, can potentially put them at risk for ridicule or even violence. As Jesse Thompson's case highlights, it also forces them to out themselves as gender nonconforming when they might not otherwise be ready to do so.

The rationale behind proposals for separate gender-neutral locker rooms is they will make trans people feel safe and meet their needs. It's assumed that they would prefer to be alone. These goals might seem laudable at first; however, it's just another form of "othering" and ostracization. Having trans and nonbinary athletes change alone, away from their teammates, means they're excluded from a crucial component of team building. Having isolated and trans-specific locker rooms further fuels transphobia, as well as the notion that trans women and girls are not "real" women and girls and that trans men and boys are not "real" men and boys. Instead of rectifying any deep-rooted fears or prejudice toward trans and nonbinary people, solo locker rooms are just a band-aid solution meant to placate and provide comfort to cisgender teammates, coaches, and parents who are not properly informed. The American Kinesiology Association, for one, has endorsed inclusive sports locker rooms that are open to transgender athletes on the basis of their gender identity.[29] But there are questions around the practicalities of this proposal. While it's great in theory, how can this be realized in practice?

In 2021, Athlete Ally teamed up with global architecture firm Gensler to produce a design concept of what a more inclusive locker room could look like, called "Inclusion Utopia: A Locker Room Experience Where Difference Is the Norm."[30] "With bathrooms and locker rooms [being] such heated topics in the country's culture wars, making a one-size-fits-all design solution [is] unlikely," states a document with a rendering of the design. In this ideal locker room built from scratch, "all athletes would be offered a diverse assortment of spaces with varying degrees of privacy, and their preferences would be protected from the judgment of others."[31] Some of the proposed design features include partitions for bathroom stalls that go from floor to ceiling, extendable locker room doors that can create "a cubicle-like space," combined shower and locker areas, and adjustable curtains. Other recommended solutions and principles include signage that welcomes everyone regardless of their gender identity, privacy, gender-neutral design, robes, and seating that can be rearranged to reduce "opportunities for spectacle and situations of overexposure." The designers recognize that only parts of this plan might be achievable, but having goals and standards to strive for is important. "What inclusiveness can do for integrated design is make the experience less jarring," Santiago Rivera, a regional leader at Gensler, told the *Architect's Newspaper*. "The utopia itself may not be within full reach today, but we can work towards implementing design that promotes equity and safety."[32]

Although locker room restructuring and policies such as Hockey Canada's Rule of Two show that sports organizations are making efforts to address and improve the culture of the locker room, these policies alone are not enough to bring about the seismic shift that's needed. The best way to drive change is through grassroots action and young people's own engagement. The more the next generation of hockey players can embody and embrace different attitudes and worldviews, the more likely a true overhaul can occur. One way to do this is to expose youth to different types of people and different life experiences from their own. Men's hockey, as we've shown, is predominantly white and straight, leaving very little room for exposure to diverse people and life experiences. LGBTQ+ organizations like You Can Play combat this by dispatching a roster of speakers and ambassadors, many of whom are athletes themselves, to educate young players at team events and functions through storytelling. This is something that has emerged only in the last decade or so, meaning that most athletes from previous generations have not been immersed or introduced to these types of people, especially on the boys' and men's sides. This is the only way for hockey, and all sports, to move past performative allyship and foster true empathy for LGBTQ+ athletes, coaches, and fans alike. There's still so much work to be done, but it's efforts like these, led by allies, that can help move the needle in a positive direction for the next generation as it pursues its college athletic dreams, though it's not without its own controversies.

CHAPTER 9

THE TRIALS AND TRIBULATIONS OF THE NCAA AND COLLEGE SPORTS

One Saturday morning in February 2019, twenty-four-year-old CeCé Telfer anxiously woke up an hour earlier than her alarm in anticipation of the big day ahead. It was the Northeast-10 Indoor Track & Field Championship at Franklin Pierce University, an NCAA Division II school in Rindge, New Hampshire. Telfer's whole life had been building up to this moment. Growing up in Jamaica, she struggled with her gender identity and experienced hate in her community that embodied strict gender roles and the intense homophobia and transphobia rooted in colonialism and conservative Christianity. Telfer was assigned male at birth, but always gravitated toward feminine clothing and toys that the girls played with. Her experiences with shame and suppression in her childhood are painful to relive. Telfer was bullied and taunted for not fitting in with the boys. Some of Telfer's best memories are of playing Double Dutch and doing gymnastics; she always wanted to be around other girls and play on their team. Still, Telfer officially remained on the boys' sports teams throughout her youth. Though she struggled with her gender identity, physical activity always served as a refuge from the depression and anxiety that permeated her mind. "On the track, my mind could focus on my performance, my speed. All of the pain, the hate, the judgment, could fade away like the scenery I sprinted past," she said.[1] "Sports saved me. I could stay at school longer because I had track practice, and running kept my mind distracted from the reality of my situation outside of school. I don't know if I would be here if I didn't have sports."

Telfer eventually immigrated to Canada and then moved to the US, where she was accepted onto the men's track team at Franklin Pierce. For three years, Telfer ran on the men's team before deciding to medically transition with hormones, as she wanted to live out her identity as a trans woman. College had provided her the space to experiment with her identity, and she finally felt safe to express her true self, a woman. She could finally breathe. The hormone transition process included more than a year of testosterone suppression coupled with estrogen pills. Telfer quit the men's team and graduated with a bachelor's degree in psychology. She thought this was the end of her track career, but the possibility of resuming it emerged after she returned to the college for a fifth year to complete her second major in biology. While back at school and out as a woman, she began going to the gym every day with her roommate, who was on the women's track team. Telfer realized that while she had finally embraced the most important aspect of herself, she was denying another part of it: running. And so, she decided to try returning to her athletic sanctuary, but this time on the women's team.[2]

Telfer worked alongside the sports administrators and medical team at the university to ensure that she was in full compliance with the rules set forth for trans women athletes by the NCAA, the organization that regulates collegiate sports in the US, specifically the policy that was put in place a few years earlier in 2011 that required trans women to have at least one year of testosterone suppressant therapy in order to compete. And because Franklin Pierce didn't yet have its own specific trans policy, Telfer and her administrators helped craft one, thereby laying the groundwork for future inclusivity and acceptance for other athletes on campus and beyond. Telfer, in full compliance with the NCAA transgender policy, eventually joined the school's women's track team for the 2018–19 season. She went on to be a champion, and a prime example for how regulations at this elite level can serve both the aims of inclusion and fairness.[3]

On that exciting day at the Northeast-10 Indoor Track & Field Championship in February of 2019, Telfer came in first place in a few events, becoming the first openly trans woman to win a NCAA Division II championship. At the track, it was a joyful celebration for the team. Telfer was named Most Outstanding Female Athlete, and her accomplishments were met with applause and support. But outside this supportive bubble, hatred was festering in the form of misinformation and misgendering. An article was published shortly after Telfer's win by the far-right site the *Daily Caller*, founded by former Fox News host Tucker Carlson, with the headline: "Biological Male Is Top-Ranked NCAA Women's Track Star."[4] The first sentence of the article states that a "top-ranked runner in NCAA women's track is dominating the competition and setting records one year after competing as a man at the same level." The article was tweeted by Donald Trump Jr., someone who's recently become preoccupied with trans athletes, who wrote: "Yet another grave injustice to so many young women who trained their entire lives to achieve excellence. Identify however you want, to each his own, but this is too far and unfair to so many."[5] What the article, which is chock-full of transphobia and misinformation, failed to mention was that in the 60-meter hurdle race, Telfer tied for first place with cisgender competitor Olivia Dexter, at 7.63 seconds.[6] Telfer also came second in the preliminaries—the races before the finals to determine the participants' starting positions on the track—at 7.69 seconds, behind Dexter, who had a time of 7.62 seconds. Neither Telfer nor Dexter really dominated in the final race, as all eight finalists crossed the finish line within 0.4 seconds of each other.[7] Despite the close proximity of the race times in this event, it nonetheless became one of the most scrutinized instances of trans participation in elite sports at the time and shone a spotlight on the participation of trans athletes at the collegiate level. The controversy swirling around Telfer laid the foundation for what swimmer Lia Thomas would soon come to face.

With outsized media attention and the subsequent backlash against trans women reaching a fever pitch, Lia Thomas infamously won the 500-yard women's freestyle at the NCAA Division I Swimming and Diving Championships in March 2022, becoming the first trans woman to win an NCAA Division I championship. Thomas's win was quickly followed by another win by Telfer in the 400-meter hurdle at the NCAA Division II Outdoor Track and Field Championships. It was a perfect storm for those looking to latch onto something to bolster their anti-trans rhetoric and agendas. In Telfer's case, it's important to keep in mind that she was competing in Division II, not in the top division. Yet, the public outcry and paranoia around the issue only grew. Again, the race time results are important here, as Telfer won that race with a time of 57.53, while the NCAA Division I record as of 2024 in the same event is 53.21, which was achieved more than a decade ago by a cisgender woman named Kori Carter from Stanford University.[8] Still, Thomas's and Telfer's wins added fuel to the flame, and right-wing media outlets became even more vicious in their coverage, giving false accounts (describing both athletes as "dominating" in their events) and employing shocking and incorrect terminology (such as "biological male") as sure-fire clickbait.

The NCAA itself made a drastic move regarding its existing policy for transgender athletes in response to the backlash over Thomas's win, seemingly to calm the hysteria. However, it only served to placate and validate misinformation and transphobia. Under the previous policy, trans inclusion was overseen only by the NCAA. Now, each sport association oversees trans policies themselves, leaving the door open for inconsistencies and discrepancies. In other words, some trans and nonbinary athletes will receive support and be welcomed onto the teams of their choice. Others could be forced to play their sport in a hostile or discriminatory environment, depending on the culture and awareness of the sports association—or not even allowed to play at all. This has a ripple effect well beyond the confines of college sports, as many leagues around the world look to the NCAA for inspiration on inclusion policies. They set the tone. Danne Diamond, who was the director of policy and programs at Athlete Ally, summed up the NCAA situation well. "I would kill to get the previous [2011] NCAA policy back," Diamond told us. "And I never thought that I would say that."[9]

What the public outcry, exemplified by the *Daily Caller's* coverage of Telfer and Thomas, fails to comprehend is that trans-inclusive policies are not put in place to stop trans athletes from winning altogether. They exist to ensure as much competitive parity as possible. The reality of what happened at the beginning of 2019 was not that the NCAA's transgender policy had failed cisgender women and jeopardized the sanctity of women's sports. It was just two athletes, out of hundreds of thousands, performing well—and those two happened to be trans. These cases nonetheless sparked unprecedented scrutiny into existing elite sports policies regarding this tiny fraction of athletes. In neither case did Thomas or Telfer win her respective competition by a large margin; their races were extremely competitive, with their cisgender opponents finishing within milliseconds of the trans athletes in some cases. If the second-place and the first-place athletes in the races were both cisgender women, the race time differences would likely not have made headlines, nor have captured the outrage of the Trump family. A closer examination of Thomas's and Telfer's stories shows that the 2011 NCAA trans athlete policy that was in place when they won was, actually, effective in achieving fairness. Part of the reason why the policy changed in January 2022 was not due to some mass influx of trans women beating their cisgender counterparts, but because of rabid media and political attention coupled with misunderstanding and ignorance.

To hammer home that trans athletes need not have been suddenly reevaluated after a small percentage from that community performed well, we are going to take a closer look at the NCAA's 2011 transgender policy and compare it with the 2022 policy that replaced it. While it was not perfect, the 2011 version served as a strong example for what athlete inclusion within one of the largest elite, multi-sport regulatory bodies could look like. Let's go back to 2006. It was a year after Keelin Godsey, who was assigned female at birth, came out as a trans man on the Division III women's hammer throw team at Bates College in Maine. At the time, no policy existed for trans athletes, but Godsey was allowed to remain on the women's team because he hadn't yet started a physical transition with testosterone. (But he was nonetheless forced to use a separate locker room from the rest of his teammates, something that wouldn't happen today.) In determining an athlete's eligibility, the NCAA mainly deferred to the athlete's gender as provided on their state-issued identification, such as their driver's license. This was a problem because each state has its own requirements for changing one's gender marker. Some require simply filling out a form, while others require that various types of surgeries have been completed. Therefore, athletes could be excluded from teams that reflect their gender identity simply because of their home state's harsh eligibility rules.[10]

In 2006, the NCAA's Office for Inclusion convened a roundtable to come up with a consistent transgender policy for the organization, a process that would take about five years to complete.[11] The goal was to create rules and procedures distinct from the 2003 transgender policy of the International Olympic Committee in place at the time. That IOC policy stated that any trans person who transitioned *after* puberty was allowed to compete in the sport that aligned with their gender identity, but only if they underwent gender-affirming surgery, provided legal recognition/documentation of their gender, had been on hormone therapy for at least two years, *and* had lived publicly in their gender identity for the same amount of time.[12]

While the 2003 IOC trans policy was praised for its aim of promoting inclusion, it also included measures that didn't need to be replicated at the collegiate level, namely the redundant requirement for both surgery *and* two-year hormone replacement therapy. Critics also questioned the lack of science behind the two-year hormone requirement and pointed out that many trans individuals may not wish to undergo surgeries for a variety of reasons. The NCAA ought to be even more inclusive and permissive than the Olympics, which does not exist to build character or develop emerging adults, nor exists to support students' academic pursuits—not to mention the fact that a two-year hormone requirement is far too restrictive for a college athlete whose career usually lasts only four years. A college athlete is under a much more condensed and finite timeline; therefore, the rules should reflect that.

Fast-forward to 2011, when the NCAA released its first official transgender policy after a five-year deliberation. This groundbreaking policy had stipulations for both trans women and trans men regarding their participation. There was the one-year hormone suppression requirement for trans women who wanted to compete on the women's side, and trans men were allowed hormone replacement therapy if they switched to the men's side.[13] While some experts pointed out that the one-year hormone requirement was rooted in scientific evidence that was only preliminary, the NCAA's trans policy was not deeply criticized by participants or coaching staff, nor did it garner much controversy or media attention over the course of the decade that it was in effect. Following suit, in 2015, the IOC also adjusted its trans policy and loosened its hormone rules for trans women, reducing the two-year hormone requirement to one year, bringing it in line with the NCAA.[14] By this time, the IOC had also done away with its surgery requirements, something the NCAA never had in the first place.

In November 2021, the IOC made a stunning announcement when it issued new guidelines for trans athletes that scrapped all hormone requirements, including for trans women, deeming them "medically unnecessary."[15] The IOC also announced it would no longer require athletes to undergo any hormone modifications to be able to compete, something that came in response to calls to uphold the human rights and dignity of intersex athletes and those with hyperandrogenism, as we explored earlier through the stories of Caster Semenya and Dutee Chand. The IOC was praised for taking a progressive step forward for trans inclusion and recognizing that focusing on testosterone levels was limiting, harmful, and, not to mention, potentially abusive. "This new IOC framework is groundbreaking in the way that it reflects what we know to be true—that athletes like me and my peers participate in sports without any inherent advantage, and that our humanity deserves to be respected," Quinn, the trans nonbinary Canadian soccer player and first trans athlete to win an Olympic gold medal, told reporters.[16] However, the new IOC framework is *not* a policy. It is a framework without teeth or enforcement provisions. It is simply a document that international and national sport governing bodies can take or leave. Simultaneously, it has both represented a huge opportunity for inclusion and left a vacuum for potential discrimination and uneven policies across sports.

A few months later, in January 2022, the NCAA Board of Governors voted for a policy change in which the new trans policy that replaced the 2011 one would adopt a sport-by-sport approach to transgender participation and increase hormone testing for athletes throughout the season, stating that the new policy "preserves opportunity for transgender student-athletes while balancing fairness, inclusion and safety for all who compete."[17] The 2022 policy defers to whatever stance the national governing body or international federation has adopted for the specific sport in question. This mirrors the approach taken by the IOC, which some, including runner and academic Joanna Harper, have decried as "passing the buck" on implementing and promoting leadership on trans inclusion.[18]

With this new policy, the NCAA, like the IOC, has backed away from the conversation of trans inclusion for its own athletes and left it in the hands of the national governing body, or NGB, of that sport. If there is no NGB policy for a sport, that sport's international federation policy would be followed, and if there is no international federation policy, the IOC framework would be followed. "It is disappointing to me that after years of discussions and calls for more research, a new policy could be quickly assembled under pressure from people who don't want to see a great athlete who is transgender succeed," Chris Mosier said in a statement.[19] The new NCAA policy also prompted the public resignation of one of the administration's facilitators, Dorian Rhea Debussy, who was one of only a few trans and/or nonbinary facilitators. Debussy stated in their resignation letter: "I'm deeply troubled by what appears to be a devolving level of active, effective, committed, and equitable support for gender diverse student-athletes within the NCAA's leadership."[20]

The consequences of the NCAA's and IOC's guidelines are that some trans athletes are now beholden to anti-trans policies that have been implemented by the international governing body for their sport. For example, if a trans woman wants to compete on an NCAA swim team or any other aquatic sport, she is forced to follow the same discriminatory regulations that World Aquatics (as FINA is now known) has put forth, stating that no trans woman who has gone through a testosterone-driven puberty is allowed to participate. (Again, this policy is virtually impossible to abide by for the majority of trans people in the United States as there are laws in place in many states that bar any medical intervention for trans youth.) This is a way for the NCAA to absolve itself from any accountability for the athletes they are now leaving behind and to blame it on the NGB. Mark Emmert, the NCAA president, stated that "approximately 80 percent of U.S. Olympians are either current or former college athletes. This policy alignment provides consistency and further strengthens the relationship between college sports and the U.S. Olympics."[21] To bring the discussion back to the NCAA's 2011 policy, the precedent was that the NCAA did *not* align with the IOC. One of the reasons it sought to adopt this policy separate from the IOC in the first place was that it recognized the short duration of a college athlete's four-year career. The NCAA was implicitly and explicitly differentiating college athletes from Olympians, even if they went on to compete in the Olympics. Different stages of an athlete's competitive career call for different regulations and protocols.

No sports policy is perfect, and it's worthwhile to critically examine them. But changes to policies regarding trans people should be made only after a full cross section of stakeholders, including trans people, has been properly consulted. Although the NCAA has largely absolved itself from dealing with transgender participation policies on a case-by-case basis, some postsecondary institutions and sports governing bodies in Canada are revisiting their own policies in favor of inclusion.

VOLLEYBALL GIRL: A STORY OF ACCEPTANCE AND PUSHING BOUNDARIES

CL Viloria, who was assigned male at birth, began playing volleyball as a young child on the boys' teams in elementary and high school. After she moved with her family to Canada in 2017 and entered the eleventh grade, she continued playing on the boys' team at her new school. "At that time, I didn't think about it that much, [being] on the men's team," Viloria told us in an interview over Zoom in the summer of 2023. "I wasn't really thinking about transitioning." Viloria loved the sport and was especially great in the position of right-side hitter, in which the player has pass, attack, serve, block, and defense duties.[22]

It was on the men's high school varsity team that Viloria began to feel uneasy both physically and mentally. Her cisgender men teammates knew she was different from the rest of them, and that before coming out as trans, she was seen as an openly gay man. Viloria says her teammates weren't necessarily hostile toward her, but she still didn't feel like she belonged in the way she would have hoped as a valued player. She started feeling like her teammates were gawking at her, so she started changing alone in the washroom, a self-imposed exile, while the rest of her teammates changed together in the shared locker room. "They made me feel that I'm not wanted on that team." After playing a few games, Viloria couldn't bear her discomfort anymore, so she approached her coach to let him know that she wanted to quit. The coach wasn't receptive to her concerns and made her feel like she was overreacting. But he tried to convince her to stay because she was a solid player. "I told him that I really can't stay because of how uncomfortable I was. He didn't really say anything [to that]," Viloria said. "It was hard." She left. It was a time of great change in her life, as she had also just started physically transitioning, something she felt more confident in pursuing after speaking about it with her other transgender friends. After researching hormone suppression therapy and consulting her doctor, who referred her to a specialist, she started the process. At age nineteen, she officially began undergoing hormone replacement therapy.[23]

After high school, Viloria enrolled part-time in the practical nursing program at Seneca College of Applied Arts and Technology (which has since been rebranded as Seneca Polytechnic), a public college in the Greater Toronto Area. She had been on a volleyball hiatus ever since she quit her men's high school team, and embarking on a new athletic journey wasn't top of mind. Viloria hadn't done much research on the athletics programs at Seneca but was scrolling through the school's Instagram account one day when she saw an announcement for a volleyball tryout. Intrigued by the possibility of getting back on the court, she tried to register for it, but wondered if the school would let her participate as a trans woman who had been on hormone suppression therapy for only four months. She was openly trans on campus but felt trepidation about pushing this boundary. Viloria messaged the sports coordinator asking if she could try out. To her surprise, the answer was yes, she would be welcome to join the tryouts. Viloria did well and the coach asked to speak with her privately afterward. It was unclear which way this was going to go; Viloria wondered whether he would accept her or shut her down for being trans. She was pleasantly surprised by his response. "I would love to give you a spot on the team," the coach told her.[24]

However, under the rules of the Ontario Colleges Athletics Association (OCAA), the province's governing body for collegiate sports, trans athletes weren't allowed to participate unless they had been on hormones for one year, similar to the 2011 NCAA rules.[25] Viloria desperately wanted to join the team and get back to the sport she loved. If she couldn't play on the women's team, she wouldn't play at all. She couldn't bear the thought of joining a team that did not align with her gender identity. She went back to the sports coordinator, who suggested they could try to change the rules altogether to accommodate Viloria. While four months of hormone suppression therapy is too short under the NCAA policy for trans women, the new IOC framework does away with hormone-based restrictions, meaning that Viloria, just by her attestation alone, is eligible for the women's team. Even before the IOC framework was released, the Canadian Centre for Ethics in Sport, a national nonprofit, multi-sport organization, put forward a policy guidance report in 2016 stating that "hormone therapy should not be required for an individual to participate in high-performance sport. . . . Trans athletes should be able to participate in the gender with which they identify, regardless of whether or not they have undergone hormone therapy." The report adds that exceptions to this guidance could be made if a sport organization "is able to provide evidence that demonstrates hormone therapy is a reasonable and bona fide requirement."[26]

Viloria's request to join the women's volleyball team was approved with unanimous support from the OCAA, and she became the first openly trans varsity athlete at any Canadian college. Gillian McCullough, Seneca's director of sport and recreation, applauded the decision and told the student newspaper that trans athletes shouldn't have to disclose where they are in their transition process or whether they have begun one at all. "Not everybody can do what Viloria did—she did have to come forward for us to challenge the rule," McCullough said. "That took leadership and courage."[27]

Though Viloria had been on hormones for only four months by the time she joined the team, she says she could already feel the impacts that it had on her body. It affected her strength. "I hit harder before, but now, it's not like I don't hit harder now, but it reduces my strength to hit," she said. "I felt different physically after four months because I'm starting something that I know I'm going to like for myself." She was feeling mentally better than before. Her friends warned her that she was going to be weaker, but that can be improved upon by practicing and training harder. Interestingly, Viloria says she had a less muscular body before starting hormones. "Training made me physically stronger, and I have a very strong physique right now. That's because of me training so hard," she said. For Viloria, even though the rules were changed in her favor (and meet the IOC framework), having zero restrictions on hormones for trans women athletes gives her pause and makes her wonder about fairness.[28]

Although Viloria's case would have caused major outcry and upheaval in the US, it didn't in Canada; there is something to be said about the measured media coverage of her story. This is a Canadian women's college volleyball program that isn't a very prominent or widely followed sport compared to, say, hockey or basketball in North America. There's a striking contrast between the response to Viloria's story and the controversy unfolding in the NCAA's women's swimming category over Lia Thomas and in women's track and field over Cecé Telfer. The main outcry comes from people who neither watch the sport nor are truly invested in women's sports and ensuring its "fairness." The obsession is rooted in transphobia and control. If the critics of trans participation in sports truly cared about athletes in women's leagues in the way that they claim to, they would be fighting much harder for things such as an equal level of sports media coverage and equal pay.

REFLECTIONS FROM HARRISON

My mind goes back and forth on the issues with respect to hormones, inclusion, and athletic ability. There's clearly a gap in the research, and I hope there's more rigorous study of this on the horizon. I deeply sympathize with Viloria and all other trans athletes who are anxious to compete on the team that aligns with their gender identity. It's great to see a news story focused on how we can include, rather than exclude, a trans athlete's participation in a sport. But I'll admit that when I initially heard about Viloria's story, I felt that changing policies to make room for one athlete could set a dangerous precedent. On the basis of the research and science done to this point, a requirement that trans women be on hormone therapy for twelve months before joining the women's division seemed sound to me—until recently. Even Viloria herself said she thought the policy change was perhaps too lenient, even if it did work in her favor. Viloria's participation did *not* compromise the legitimacy of the varsity sports program at Seneca, but her story could add fuel to the argument of those opposed to trans inclusion in sports.

What I appreciate about the policy change is the way it occurred within the varsity and college realms without input from external forces who might have ulterior motives or a lack of pertinent lived experience. Viloria's school supported her own direct request and desires to play on the women's side, working alongside her instead of against her. Colleges should do what they deem is best for their own students and not, as the NCAA did when it rolled back its 2011 policy, acquiesce to noisy and inflammatory media coverage. Colleges are allowed to make mistakes, but they also must be accountable for their actions. It seems that Seneca and the OCAA are pleased with how they moved forward with Viloria's case, and it is refreshing to see a sports entity like this embodying inclusivity. Ultimately, any advantages held by Viloria, or other trans women athletes who haven't been on hormones for over a year, are not going to make or break the sanctity of women's sports. This is especially so when it comes to team sports like volleyball, hockey, and soccer. Unlike individual sports, where the athlete's physicality stands alone, trans athletes on teams could be given more leeway with respect to their physical transition, as Viloria exemplifies. To be clear: I'm talking about trans athletes who have been on hormones for less than a year, or not at all, and are seeking exemptions from more restrictive policies. I don't see why exemption-seeking athletes can't be approached on a case-by-case basis and considered from a place of empathy and humanity.

Hormones are but one small factor in the success of a particular athlete, so I am questioning my own logic and biases behind why this ruling on Viloria's inclusion initially gave me pause. I've had to reframe my own thinking around testosterone and my internalized trans misogyny when it comes to the way it affects my physicality. We have been so deeply conditioned to this notion that testosterone equals better athletic performance when it isn't even half of the story of what makes a specific athlete successful.

In my experience with testosterone, the most polarizing substance to date in the trans inclusion and rights debate, the biggest tangible impacts that comes to mind are the way it has shaped my chest and shoulders and the increased weight that I can bench-press. Before I was on testosterone, and at the height of my elite hockey career, I maxed out at around 130 pounds. In the five years that I've been on testosterone, I haven't been training nearly as much as I was during my time in the NCAA, and I've been able to press 160 pounds and climbing. I'm also nearly a decade older than I was in college, which means I'm far removed from my prime years as an elite athlete. To sum up: testosterone has markedly improved my weight training metrics. Has being on testosterone improved my hockey skills in terms of my stickhandling, shooting, and skating? Maybe marginally, but it's hard to tell. Right now, trans exclusionists are preoccupied with stats in the gym that can't necessarily be linked to the actual skills required in one's specific sport.

In 2017, NHL top prospect Casey Mittelstadt failed to complete a single pull-up at the league's top scouting event. But this didn't prevent Mittelstadt from getting drafted eighth overall. This proves that skill on the ice outweighs strength in the gym in terms of what makes an elite hockey player.[29] Perhaps an individual sport, such as weightlifting, might be able to put forward a science-based argument for such a restriction, or maybe not. But other sports, such as hockey and volleyball, might not even be affected by varying hormone levels in men's and women's leagues. So, as I'm writing this, I have come to realize that I had written off this policy prematurely, and the OCAA might have done exactly the right thing.

CHAPTER 10

THE FUTURE IS TRANS

Aidan Cleary, who uses he and ze pronouns, felt he was always different, but he didn't have the language to define exactly what made him feel this way. As an adult, he now identifies as trans nonbinary. He was always into musical theater and, as a hockey player, hated when things got violent on the ice. That didn't go over well with his cisgender hockey teammates in Santa Rosa, California, who he says verbally and physically abused him when he was between twelve and fourteen years old because he didn't fit in with the stereotypical mold of toxic masculinity embodied by most of his team. He says the coaches and the teammates' parents participated as well by letting it happen without intervening. One day, when Cleary was fourteen, the violence spilled over onto the ice during a scrimmage toward the end of the season. One of the most incessant bullies saw Cleary in a corner and skated across the ice and cross-checked him from behind. "I think he was absolutely trying to paralyze me," Cleary recalled. "I was writhing on the ground in pain." Cleary left and moved to a different town for the next season, and, after that, he drifted away from hockey and devoted more of his time to the theater and his academic studies.[1]

It wouldn't be until years later that he would step back fully into hockey culture, particularly the locker room, later co-creating Team Trans, partly in response to the way he was alienated and mistreated as a younger hockey player by his cisgender men teammates. Team Trans is an international hockey team made up of transgender men, transgender women, and nonbinary players from amateur to pro.

In November 2019, transgender hockey players from around North America gathered for what was coined a Friendship Series between Team Trans and members of the Boston Pride Hockey organization, a co-ed team for LGBTQ+ hockey players. The aim of this gathering was to create spaces for transgender people to feel the camaraderie that most cisgender athletes take for granted—being in a room full of people with similar life experiences and points of reference. This game was the first such event where athletes who are usually marginalized or even demonized could play together in an inclusive and celebratory environment, with no reason to hide anything. A moment to be authentically and openly themselves as hockey players—and people. This vibe extended to the locker room, where all members of Team Trans used a single unsegregated communal space with no gender-based restrictions.

For Harrison, who played in the 2023 Friendship Series, the Team Trans locker room experience was the first time he felt an alignment with his body in this type of environment. It wasn't the first time that he had been in a hockey locker room since his top surgery, but that was a locker room filled with cisgender people. Being in a room filled with individuals who understood his journey, knew what a trans body looked like (pre- and post-op), and understood what dysphoria feels like was something he had never experienced. Now he was getting a glimpse of what it must feel like to be surrounded by those who identify the same way as you. For the first time, Harrison didn't worry about how he would be viewed walking to the shower with just a towel around his waist and top-surgery scars exposed. He was just a body among other bodies. A teammate among other teammates. Gone were the little nagging voices or thoughts that would always be a constant commentary in his head when he was in cisgender-dominant spaces.

In November 2023, around seventy-five transgender hockey players from across the US and Canada descended on Madison, Wisconsin, to represent Team Trans for another Friendship Series, this time against the Madison Gay Hockey Association (MGHA). What made this different from the first time Team Trans took the ice was that both organizations had five co-ed teams representing them in game play at various skill levels over the course of three days. The event was sponsored by the NHL's Minnesota Wild, and the league sent over one of its employees to play with the MGHA. A nonprofit, all-gender hockey league for the LGBTQ+ community, the MGHA currently has 180 skaters.[2] Organizations like this come from a long line of others, such as the National Gay Flag Football Leagues and the Gay Rodeo, that strive to create a safe space for LGBTQ+ athletes to participate in sports where they otherwise wouldn't.

Harrison was invited to attend the event in Wisconsin as a guest professional player. With the exception of a charity hockey tournament, it had been years since Harrison had played in a game. In that time, he had been struggling with a desire to get back on the ice but was always hesitant to do so because he wasn't sure which division he wanted to play in—men's or women's—and whether it would be safe to play alongside cisgender men. When Mason LeFebvre, one of the Team Trans co-founders along with Aidan Cleary, reached out to Harrison and invited him, it seemed like a safe way for him to get back into hockey and the locker room environment that he deeply missed.

Harrison arrived at the Capitol Ice Arena for a three-hour practice. Because of how many players were there, there were four different locker rooms that were mixed gender, as all the locker rooms would be for the whole weekend. Harrison entered his locker room with some hesitancy at the prospect of not only meeting new people but also being in an intimate space like this, where people of all genders and body types would be getting changed together in the open. But that sense of anxiety quickly dissipated after some joking around and teasing, also known as "chirping"—the love language of hockey teammates—lightened the mood, or broke the ice (pun intended). Since the 2019 Team Trans Friendship Series had established a tradition of the team traveling all over the country, many of the same players here also played in that original series. Harrison felt a little out of place, as many of these players had developed bonds and camaraderie, but the team was quickly finding its rhythm. Still feeling a bit hesitant in front of strangers, Harrison faced the wall when changing his undergarments; then he tied up his skates and was ready to hit the ice.

The practice kicked off with more than fifty trans and gender diverse people swirling around the ice at any given time. At this point, everyone was skating together regardless of skill level or which team they were assigned to for the weekend. They were all laughing and smiling during the drills and scrimmages, while lovingly pushing each other around in a way that only makes sense when you are part of a sports team. In these moments, Harrison watched the community that has been targeted and successfully excluded from sports experience immense joy, while playing in that same environment in which they had been barred. Just one month earlier, in October 2023, the Republican-controlled Wisconsin State Assembly approved legislation limiting the participation of trans high school youth and collegiate athletes in sports. The law also banned gender-affirming surgeries for minors. Skating together with jubilant and carefree gender diverse athletes against this backdrop was not only bittersweet, but a bit mind-blowing. That these athletes have the sheer resilience and courage to do what they love and be who they are, unapologetically, in spite of the horrors being perpetrated against them is truly inspiring. This event on the ice encapsulated the tension of the present moment, as rules and regulations are being pushed without the input of the gender diverse community, but it still moves forward without backing down.

The Friendship Series coincided with the annual observance of the Transgender Day of Remembrance. Before each game the announcer gave an explanation of the day's origins and why it's observed, and a moment of silence was held to honor those we have lost due to anti-trans violence. There were more than 320 murders of transgender and gender diverse people in 2023 globally, a 15 percent increase from the year before.[3] For the rest of the weekend, each Team Trans division played against a team in the MGHA that matched its overall skill level. To state the obvious, Team Trans divisions were composed of trans and gender diverse players, whereas the MGHA divisions were mostly cisgender gay men and women. The rosters included some players with junior level experience and some at the college level. Some had only a couple years under their belt while others had decades of playing experience. If we were to follow the logic and assumptions of those who believe that anyone who had gone through a testosterone-driven puberty—including cisgender men and trans women—would automatically dominate, only trans women would represent the top division of Team Trans. But this was not the case at this tournament, nor has it been the case on any team anywhere where Team Trans has been involved. The divisions were not based on what type of puberty the player had gone through; they were purely based on merit and proficiency. A mixture of trans women and trans men, as well as nonbinary people, was represented on each team.

The inclusion of these players revealed a possible future where not only mixed-gender teams, but gender-diverse teams, were possible, and competitively matched with one another. Up until this point, Harrison had yet to experience a truly successful mixed-gender tournament where players were properly matched. It was often the case that teams would be lopsided, meaning players would have to either hold back or be in over their heads, trying to compensate for not being as experienced. In Madison, however, it helped to have a high volume of players from various hockey backgrounds that allowed for more evenly matched teams. It was good hockey—and it was fair. It showed a promising future where hormone levels didn't matter and athletes were just athletes, treated with humanity and dignity. Athletic prowess wasn't assumed—it was proven. For team sports, especially, it's possible to not only tolerate but to celebrate gender diverse inclusion. While the Friendship Series only lasted for a weekend, the format could be used not just as a template for hockey, but as inspiration for the creation of successful inclusive policies.

WELCOMING TRANS AND NONBINARY PLAYERS INTO THE HOCKEY FOLD

One such example for how inclusion ought to look is the transgender policy for the now-defunct Premier Hockey Federation (PHF, previously called the NWHL), the professional women's hockey league in which Harrison played before he retired to medically transition. In 2021, just before the IOC revealed its revised framework for trans athletes that moved away from testosterone-based restrictions, the PHF announced its new and groundbreaking policy for nonbinary and trans athletes that took effect immediately that season.[4]

As the first professional league in North America for individuals who play women's hockey, the PHF had already broken barriers and was exemplary in terms of sports inclusion and gender equality. As well as fighting for its cisgender players to have a better future and a place to play while being paid after college, the PHF had long been a leader on progressive policies for trans players, creating the first trans policy in US and Canadian professional team sports after Harrison came out. However, the new PHF policy signaled a whole different level of inclusion that distinguished the league from most others at the collegiate, Olympic, or professional level of sport. Unlike most of those entities, this PHF policy did not tie itself to hormones. Trans men, according to the PHF, would not only be eligible and welcome to play in the league, but would also *not* be rendered ineligible if they were taking testosterone as part of their medical and physical transition, though they would be required to consult with the league if they were taking testosterone to formalize their exception. This was a dramatic departure from the previous policy, which had made trans men players, like Harrison, ineligible to compete if they were undergoing testosterone treatment. The revised PHF guidelines also stated that trans women were eligible to participate if they had been living in their transgender identity for at least two years.[5] Had this policy regarding trans men players been in place while Harrison was grappling with choosing to go on testosterone or play another year of hockey, he may have played longer. Other leagues ought to make the same decision; lifting the hormone requirement on trans and nonbinary people will open opportunities for individuals who would otherwise feel that their athletic careers need to end because of their identity or because they have to choose between themselves and their sport.

What is also unique about the PHF's policy was that it explicitly included and mentioned nonbinary players, a group of players who are often overlooked in these discussions. The nonbinary guidelines were in keeping with those for trans athletes, stating that nonbinary athletes assigned female at birth who did not undergo hormone therapy were welcome to compete in the league without restrictions. Those who were assigned female at birth and taking testosterone as part of their transition were, like trans men, allowed to compete, but were also required to consult with the league's medical team. Nonbinary athletes assigned male at birth were also eligible to compete as long as they had been living out their identity for at least two years and were in consultation with the league.

Though the PHF policy might have appeared to fully satisfy advocates for trans inclusion, that wasn't necessarily the case, as the critics raised some important points. First, there were parts of the PHF policy that were vague. What exactly does it mean for someone to "live" in their identity for two years? And when does that clock start? When they come out to themselves, or to other people? And why set a minimum time threshold in the first place? As Mike Murphy, managing editor at women's hockey online news site The Ice Garden, notes in a piece from October 2021, "If the league believes that trans and nonbinary athletes do not transition to gain a competitive advantage in sports (true), then why would the league set a minimum amount of time that an athlete has been 'living in their trans identity' before they can join the PHF?"[6] Murphy's criticism is that the policy required the athlete to "prove" their trans identity to league administrators, something they shouldn't have had to do if the organization rightly believed that trans athletes were not trying to be deceptive about their trans identity.[7] Building off Murphy's arguments, it's worth imaging a world where inclusion is possible without forms of surveillance and infantilization, and privacy is upheld wherever possible.

Even before the PHF announced its new policy, sports leagues in Australia came together in 2020 to announce an admirable approach for supporting trans athletes.[8] In a "world-first" initiative spearheaded by an Australian non-governmental organization called ACON, which promotes health and wellness among LGBTQ+ people, eight sport federations including the top governance bodies for tennis, rugby, football, hockey, water polo, and university sports announced new participation guidelines for trans athletes. Much like the IOC guidelines for trans athletes, these are not enforceable regulations that must be adhered to; they're merely suggestions. The move came after years of criticism by advocates who accused the national sports bodies of neglecting trans athletes. One of Australia's first trans athletes to come out in the early 1990s, former middle distance runner Ricki Coughlan, complimented the new guidelines for allowing athletes the space to deal with "concerns about size, or weight, or performance." Coughlan added: "I'd just say that every transgender person is different and that let's begin with inclusion."[9] Though there's an overarching aim of promoting inclusion, the guidelines greatly vary across the different sports and different levels. The result is a disjointed patchwork of policies, where one sports federation can be much stricter than another.

Rugby Australia, for one, requires trans athletes to obtain consent from a medical specialist that attests to the fact that their "physical development, skill level and experience are appropriate" given the full-contact nature of the sport.[10] Tennis Australia is more lenient and progressive, actively discouraging sport officials from questioning athletes about their physical or medical transition; it does not require medical consent for trans participants. The Australian Football League released a policy for its community clubs that allows players to play for the team that aligns with their gender identity; nonbinary players also are encouraged to play on the team of their choosing.[11] Trans football players are under no obligation to "confirm" their gender identity or disclose that they are trans at all. Not all football clubs in Australia, however, put their own trans-inclusion policies in writing; some say their strategy is simply "to be nice."[12] The policies of the professional level of Australian football are drastically different from the lower levels. For example, all trans women athletes are still required to meet the testosterone threshold of less than 5 nanomoles per liter. Australia is a place, like many other countries, where the debate over trans athletes is fierce, yet there are some positive movements toward inclusion and efforts to promote it, at least.

MIXED-GENDER UTOPIA

With so much contradiction and confusion around the world when it comes to this issue, it's a useful exercise to imagine starting from scratch. What would it look like if mixed-gender sports were the default as opposed to gender segregation? What if gender segregation never happened in the first place? This is where Harrison's friend River Butcher comes back in. Butcher is a trans man and stand-up comedian residing in Los Angeles. His work includes a Comedy Central half-hour special called *A Different Kind of Dude* that provides a hilarious social commentary on gender roles, from the perspective of someone who has been on both sides of it. Butcher is passionate about co-ed sports and Title IX, which he talked about at length in his sport-based podcast, *Three Swings*. While he is a staunch advocate for gender equality, he takes issue with legislation like Title IX that purports to uphold equality but, for him, legitimizes the myth that women are inherently worse than men at sports. "It bolsters the illusion that women need protection, that they will be embarrassed and obviously will lose if they compete against/with cisgender men. But the reality is we don't want men to be embarrassed because there's a possibility they might lose to cisgender women," Butcher told us.[13]

Butcher shares with Harrison a similar schooling and sports background, including attending a Christian all-girls school as well as participating on girls' sports teams in his youth. Through the many conversations he's had with people who play on the women's side of sport, Harrison has come to realize that women athletes' view of themselves differs from that of society in general, which holds that women need to be protected and are less physically able than men. For cisgender men, who haven't had the opportunity to be teammates with or play against cisgender women, they have been conditioned by a society that teaches them it's not okay to play rough with girls, that girls need to be protected and taken care of, that they aren't capable of handling competition and physicality in a way that men are. In other words, they are not allowed to be treated equally. As Butcher has continued to play recreational baseball while he physically transitions, he has been privy to being treated as "one of the guys" on his co-ed team. He recalls talking to his pitcher, a cisgender man, who found it hard to pitch when a woman was at bat, sharing with Butcher that "it's hard because you're conditioned your whole life, 'Don't hit girls, don't hurt them.' Now, I'm throwing a ball at one and it's really hard. The pitcher wanted to play with women, and wants to be fair, but was expressing his difficulty with how he was raised culturally." Butcher chalks up this notion that men don't feel that they can play sports as hard with cisgender women as they would their cisgender men counterparts to that social conditioning. "When you are constantly separated out to be with people who look like you, it warps your perception of who you can be neighborly with; competitive with," he said. "It's putting obstacles between two people to show up in a game and have fun."[14]

Is gender segregation in sports necessary? What if far more sports were co-ed? What if boys and girls played together from the start and continued to do so? Take a look at soccer and T-ball. T-ball is a completely co-ed sport, while soccer is a sport that most kids have played as a member of a co-ed team. Why is it okay for six-year-olds to play together no matter their gender, but it's not okay for ten-year-olds? To not enable girls to compete with boys who are not remotely close to puberty is arbitrary and rooted in misogyny. It's especially arbitrary given that, as they get older and develop their athletic skills, some boys cannot compete with others, which is why there are different divisions within gendered categories. But what if those different divisions were not separated by gender, but rather by skill and commitment? It would mean more cisgender men athletes would be exposed to women athletes and see them as equals, thus expanding their understanding of what girls and women are truly capable of. Respect and camaraderie would not just be limited to people like them, as co-ed competition would promote a practice in which spectators more often saw athletes as athletes, plain and simple, without the gender distinction. In this kind of sports world, there would be no conversation about where trans athletes fall in sports; their skill level and dedication would be the only thing up for debate, as it already is for their cisgender counterparts. This is the definition of true equality and a way forward for sports.

Before Harrison went to play in the latest Friendship Series with Team Trans in Wisconsin at the end of 2023, he was skeptical of this ideal world described by Butcher. When he had spoken with Butcher a few months earlier, the idea of a sports world with no gender binary sounded great in theory, but in practice, Harrison's own inner misogyny and sexism cast doubt on the abilities of cisgender women athletes to truly succeed in these spaces. Yet, playing on a co-ed team, and seeing it involve adults of all sorts on a larger scale, proved Butcher's argument that people of all genders can respect each other as teammates and competitors and not hold back at all in terms of their strength, speed, and agility. In Wisconsin, everybody wanted to do their best, without altering their playing style according to the skill level of the player opposite them. And they did just that.

TRANS-SPECIFIC SPORTS TEAMS?

People and sports bodies around the world frequently point to trans-specific categories as a solution to the so-called problem of transgender athletes. These types of proposals are often vague and do not answer crucial questions: Would trans men and trans women be allowed to compete against each other? What's more, if trans-specific leagues or teams were to be pursued, it's easy to imagine how much more marginalized and stigmatized these athletes would become. Think about all the ways that women's competitive sports, by and large, are seen as lesser to men's. Imagine how much inferior trans teams and leagues would be perceived. The concept of trans-specific categories and leagues is merely a way to make cisgender athletes and administrators feel better about themselves and place their comfort above the basic rights and dignity of trans people. These proposals are also often made by cisgender (and white) men without the input and consultation of trans and gender diverse people. This type of initiative should not be regarded as in the same vein as Team Trans, because Team Trans was created by and for gender diverse people as a safe haven, and was a necessary response to the increasingly hostile and dangerous environments of heteronormative and binary sports teams. For the majority of competitors who also play in more established and formalized leagues, Team Trans is a symbolic act of protest and subversion. If Team Trans were the only option for trans and nonbinary hockey players, they would only be playing a couple times a year in various infrequent series. So, in short, no, trans-specific teams and leagues are not the answer.

Even just on a numerical basis, trans-specific categories and leagues don't make sense. You would have one sports category with 49.5 percent of people, another with 49.5 percent of people, and a third category with 1 percent of people. A trans category is thus nearly unfeasible just based on the numerical limitations. This is the case for all levels and ages, beginning with recreational youth leagues.

As mentioned briefly in the "Myth of Saving Women's Sports" chapter, World Aquatics, previously known as FINA, the international governing body for swimming, introduced a trans-specific open category on a trial basis in 2022 as a response to the outcry over Lia Thomas. World Aquatics claimed the move was to promote trans inclusion, with the president, Husain Al-Musallam, declaring that "everybody has the opportunity to compete at an elite level," but so far, the World Aquatics experiment has been a failure.[15] In October 2023, Berlin hosted the World Aquatics Swimming World Cup, an annual event that attracts athletes from around the world in part because of its considerable prize money. In 2022, a total of $1.2 million was awarded to the top 20 athletes in both the men's and women's categories. In the first event for the open transgender category, *zero* participants signed up for the slated 50-meter and 100-meter races, and the open category was scrapped altogether.[16] In a statement, the organization said it was continuing its work and engagement with the aquatics community on open category events. "Even if there is no current demand at the elite level, the working group is planning to look at the possibility of including Open Category races at Masters events in the future," World Aquatics added.[17] This fiasco helped further debunk the myth that trans women only want to compete in a particular division in order to obtain medals and high-ranking glory, whether it's on the women's or another side. In this open aquatics category, which would have had much less competition and therefore offer a higher probability of winning, doesn't it seem likely, if this myth were true, that at least some trans women would want to enter it? Or maybe, just maybe, their stated explanation is the correct one—that they simply wish to compete on the side that aligns with their gender identity.

World Aquatics isn't the only sporting body exploring contentious trans-specific categories, though what happened in Berlin should serve as a warning sign that this isn't a good solution. In the UK, various national sporting bodies have either introduced, or are looking at, open categories, including Swim England, British Cycling, British Triathlon, UK Athletics, and British Rowing. The World Boxing Council (WBC) announced in 2022 that it planned to introduce a separate transgender category in 2023 that would consist solely of transgender fighters.[18] "It is the time to do this, and we are doing this because of safety and inclusion," WBC president Mauricio Sulaimán told reporters, which coincided with the organization issuing a global call for trans athletes to enter the category. "We have been the leaders in rules for women's boxing, so the dangers of a man fighting a woman will never happen because of what we are going to put in place," he added.

As of this writing, this trans-specific division has yet to come to fruition. But transgender professional boxer Patricio Manuel, whom we first mentioned in the "Brief History of Gender Diverse Athletes" chapter, has described this effort as "dehumanizing." In a 2023 *Rolling Stone* article, Manuel is quoted saying he had no interest in being in a transgender division. "I understand there may [be] some people that feel more comfortable with that label, and I can't speak for them, but every time I walk into a gym, every time I go sparring, I'm perceived as a man," he said. WBC president Sulaimán is quoted saying that he is "concerned for Manuel's safety" when he fights cisgender men, who, according to Sulaimán, had "different bone and neck structure" from Manuel. This sentiment is far from warranted given the fact that Manuel has won most of his fights against cisgender men throughout his professional boxing career. "For me, there is no other way to compete other than in the male division," Manuel explained. "To have a leader of my sport saying that I don't get to be a man, that I can't compete even though I've been out here doing just that, you know, it really hurts."[19]

HUMANITY IS NOT UP FOR DEBATE

Where so-called progressives and other supposed allies are truly failing the trans community is in their thinking that they are not the problem and that they're not perpetuating the talking points and propaganda of the extreme conservative groups. They think they can pat themselves on the back for merely saying that they support trans people. We've seen performative allyship too many times to count. But this veneer of acceptance and support can quickly be exposed as transphobia the more we drill down into these conversations. The hard truth is that this isn't a debate; this is an all-or-nothing proposition. There is no room for sentiments like, "I support trans women, BUT . . ." or "I support trans men, BUT . . ." For those who are struggling to see trans women as women, ask yourself why that is. Consider reflecting on the story of Lia Thomas. One self-identified "progressive" parent of an athlete at the University of Pennsylvania told *Sports Illustrated* reporter Robert Sanchez in 2022 that while the hate and vitriol Thomas was receiving was unacceptable, they nonetheless opposed Thomas's inclusion on the women's side: "It's not transphobic to say I disagree with where she's swimming."[20] Sanchez described this parents' take as "disingenuous." There is no such thing as "half-support," he wrote. "Either you back her fully as a woman or you don't."

River Butcher said, "I try not to debate things that are not up for a debate. Once I engage in debate about whether my trans identity is real or valid or important, I've given in to the debate."[21] For him, so much of the debate over the fears around trans people, particularly trans women, participating in women's sports is based on fictionalized fears or conceptions. As American sportswriter Dave Zirin wrote in a March 2023 column in *The Nation*, "Republicans are not stopping with sports in their project of trans eradication. Either we stand with our trans friends, or we lose them. . . . Either we stand with our trans friends, or we're next."[22] It can't be overstated that this is a matter of life and death, as rates of violence and murder against trans and gender diverse people continue to rise year over year.

This journey into fairness and inclusion in sports for all has been a roller coaster both in terms of emotions and facts. Cutting through the noise and the opinions on these issues, which have far-reaching impacts, is a nearly impossible task. For Harrison, it's unearthed raw and sometimes uncomfortable feelings regarding his place in sports. The conversations about trans and gender nonconforming people have made him feel alienated; many people do not want his community within the sports fold at all, or if they do, it's only if it abides by their often-baseless rules rooted in fear. He, like the naysayers, used to think of trans people in terms of their physical bodies and hormone levels, especially trans women. But after immersing himself in this research, having hours-long conversations with fellow athletes, and participating alongside trans women on the ice, he's realized they are all just devoted athletes who want the same things: to be part of a team, make friends, and do their best. An inclusion-first mentality, rather than succumbing to a scarcity mentality and creating barriers, is the only way forward.

The common refrain among the numerous gender diverse athletes with whom we spoke was that they would not be alive were it not for their sport. Sports save lives; they provide an escape, a refuge, for those participating or those on the sidelines. Throughout history, we've seen it serve as a way to bring people from disparate factions together to celebrate achievements, be entertained, and pursue common goals. Sports are meant to bring people together, not tear them apart. We're at a crossroads: we can either continue to allow barriers against those who need sports the most, or open pathways for empathy and an expansion of sports as we know them. Choosing humanity over winning, humanity over everything else, is the way we all succeed.

APPENDIX

Thank you for taking the time to read and engage with our book. Researching and writing it was an eye-opening and even uncomfortable process for us, as we learned. Being pushed in our thinking exposed us to new ideas and inspiration for action. Reading books like this that confront our preexisting biases is just a first step in bringing about real change in our own circles and communities and beyond. It can be scary to take action and daunting to know where to start, whether you're trying to be an informed individual navigating this fraught topic, practicing greater empathy for the gender diverse people in your life, or seeking to bring about broader systemic change. There's always something—big or small—we can do. We need people like you to feel equipped and empowered to act, for the sake of a better environment and world for not just athletes, but everyone. We've put together the following list of action items and discussion topics for anyone who wants to ensure that no trans or nonbinary person is denied their right to play sports and be included in all areas of life.

INSPIRATION FOR ACTION FOR COACHES AND SPORTS ADMINISTRATORS

- Support children of all genders and sexualities in exploring mixed-gender teams.
- Encourage boys, girls, and nonbinary youth to see each other as peers and worthy opponents and competitors in sports.
- Attend, watch, or participate in local amateur and professional women's sports. Women's hockey, for example, is one of the main sports at the forefront of promoting and championing transgender inclusion, including Jessica Platt. Supporting these types of organizations will help support their initiatives around transgender inclusion.

INSPIRATION FOR ACTION FOR TEACHERS AND PARENTS

- Reach out to a local organization in your area that's dedicated to supporting children in sports, especially marginalized children. Donate your time or resources, if you can.
- Speak to your local city councilperson or representative about whether they support women's and youth sports teams in disenfranchised neighborhoods. See if they have any existing mandates or campaigns devoted to this issue and, if not, urge them to take it on.
- Confront your bias when it comes to transgender people and athletes.
- Imagine sports as an end in itself, not just a means to something else.
- Make an effort to speak directly with trans and nonbinary youth about how they are feeling when they participate in organized sports. How might their experiences be improved? What do they need to feel safe?
- Encourage cisgender students and administrators to support their trans and nonbinary peers in sports and outside of sports.
- Start a club or afterschool program that involves non-competitive physical activity.

INSPIRATION FOR ACTION FOR EVERYONE

- Speak with young athletes about their experiences in the locker room and ask them if there are any adjustments or changes that would help them feel safer.
- Facilitate group team discussions about how to foster a more inclusive and safer environment for all.
- Call out transphobia and hatred in all areas of sport, including the locker room. Research bystander intervention techniques against transphobia and anti-trans violence. We recommend "Draw the Line Against Transphobic Violence in Schools," a guide by Egale Canada, as a starting point.
- Educate yourself! Seek out at least three to five transgender or nonbinary folks to follow on social media. We recommend Schuyler Bailar (Instagram: @pinkmantaray), Chase Strangio (Instagram: @chasestrangio), Raquel Willis (Instagram: @raquel_willis), Katie Barnes (Instagram: @katie_barnes3), and Katelyn Burns (X/Twitter: @transscribe).

- Attend a Team Trans event (or other LGBTQ+ sports league event) in your area.
- Avoid consuming (and call out) content or organizations that are rooted in or perpetuate transphobia and hatred.
- Take a listen to the September 2023 episode of the podcast *Armchair Expert*, featuring an interview with Jonathan Van Ness (aka JVN) in which the subject of trans athletes comes up. (Trigger warning: this episode contains discussions of suicide and transphobia.) Compare and contrast this conversation to JVN's subsequent podcast interview with Keke Palmer on *Baby, This Is Keke Palmer*.
- We want to leave you with this: A cliché expression used in the debates about the participation of trans athletes is, "I support trans women, but it's not fair for them to compete against women in sports." We challenge anyone who feels this way to name three—or even two—trans women athletes who have participated at the elite level of any sport. Now we ask you to name one trans woman who holds an Olympic medal. Are you stumped? If so, that might reveal to you that trans participation in sports is not much of a threat at all.

ACKNOWLEDGMENTS

For me, Harrison, sports saved my life. It's that simple. Sports was the one place that I felt I belonged and the one place I could celebrate my body instead of feeling trapped by it. Even though I'm not engaging in sports these days as much as I used to, I still feel its influence and impact in almost everything I do. I would truly be lost if I didn't have the relationships, the lessons, and the memories of my time as an athlete guiding me today. Everyone has a right to find themselves as I did through sports—no matter how they identify.

For Rachel and me, our hope through this book is to bring humanity to the front of people's minds when it comes to the fraught debate of trans and gender diverse athletes and their right to play sports, and to champion stories from amazing athletes and advocates within the community and empower the voices that are being impacted the most.

We have been so lucky to be surrounded by an amazing community as we've worked on this book. It has truly been a team effort. We'd like to thank our incredible agent, Carly Watters, for believing in us from the beginning and supporting our book with tenacity and care every step of the way. Thank you to our editor, Joanna Green, for your enthusiasm, thoughtfulness, and passion for this topic and for supporting LGBTQ+ voices and perspectives at a time when it is so desperately needed. You helped push our thought processes and conception of the book in exciting and meaningful ways. We are so grateful to have the opportunity to work and learn from you throughout this process. And thank you to Brian Baughan, Susan Lumenello, Alison Rodriguez, and the rest of the team at Beacon Press.

Thank you to everyone who spoke with us for this book during our research and reporting journey. (Thank you to the Gonzales family for our special dinner in Dallas!) Learning from your stories and life experiences helped create pathways of empathy, and we can't thank you enough for your openness and trust in us.

To all of those who read earlier drafts and chapters, we so appreciate your feedback and guidance in helping us shape our book and considering things we hadn't before.

To every coach, teammate, trainer, and fan I encountered during my time playing women's hockey: Thank you for embracing me as Harrison. You empowered me to be myself and for that I will be forever grateful. Thank you to our parents, Russ and Joan, for supporting us both: Harrison through his hockey journey, and Rachel through her journalism career, and providing us with every opportunity to be the best athlete and journalist we can be. We wouldn't have gotten very far without you both.

We also owe a debt of gratitude to the authors and advocates who have published and continue to publish books seeking to educate and elevate the perspectives of gender diverse athletes and help push the narrative for more inclusivity and empathy overall. This includes Katie Barnes's book *Fair Play*, Schuyler Bailer's book *He/She/They*, and CeCé Telfer's memoir *Make It Count*. We're privileged and honored to share space with great works like these and have our book be just one voice in the ongoing conversation.

Thank you to our partners, Louis and Nicolette, for your love and support, and for putting up with our hours-long writing sessions! And thank you for being there when we felt insecure or had writer's block. You got us through the hard parts and helped us complete this book.

And, of course, thank you to our readers for engaging with this material and being curious and open to new possibilities both for yourself and your community.

ABOUT THE SERIES

The Queer Ideas/Queer Action series from Beacon Press addresses pivotal issues in the LGBTQ+ movement today. Written by a wide range of scholars, journalists, activists, and academics, the Queer Ideas/Queer Action series presents provocative, deeply researched, and accessible titles that push the boundaries of discourse surrounding a contemporary queer issue. Every book in the series identifies a contemporary critical social and political issue and offers insights that transcend the political moment, informing conversations for years to come.

> What makes *Queer Ideas/Queer Action* unique is the fact that it understands that there must be a direct connection between how we think about LGBTQ+ issues and what we do with those thoughts in the actual world. To pretend that creative thinking and action—the mind and the body—are not, and should not be, connected is a fallacy that has hurt both queer academic writing and activism.
>
> —Series editor Michael Bronski

ABOUT THE SERIES EDITOR

Michael Bronski has been involved in gay liberation as a political organizer, a writer, and an editor for more than four decades. The author of several award-winning books, including *A Queer History of the United States*, Bronski is Professor of the Practice in Activism and Media in the Studies of Women, Gender, and Sexuality at Harvard University and lives in Cambridge, Massachusetts.

NOTES

INTRODUCTION

1. Marta Lawrence, "Transgender Policy Approved," NCAA, Sept. 13, 2011, https://ncaanewsarchive.s3.amazonaws.com/2011/september/transgender-policy-approved.html.

2. Katie Thomas, "Transgender Man Is on Women's Team, *New York Times*, Nov. 1, 2010, https://www.nytimes.com/2010/11/02/sports/ncaabasketball/02gender.html.

3. Matt Higgins, "Leaving Women's Hockey to 'Fly Under the Radar,' as Himself," *New York Times*, Mar. 14, 2017, https://www.nytimes.com/2017/03/14/sports/hockey/nwhl-transgender-player-harrison-browne.html.

4. Sneha Day, "Texas Health Providers Are Suspending Gender-Affirming Care for Teens in Response to GOP Efforts," *Texas Tribune*, Mar. 22, 2022, https://www.texastribune.org/2022/03/22/texas-transgender-teenagers-medical-care.

5. "British Cycling Bows to the Inevitable," Fair Play For Women, May 26, 2023, https://fairplayforwomen.com/british-cycling-bows-to-the-inevitable/.

6. Fiona McAnena, Zoom interview with authors, 2023.

CHAPTER 1: THE MORAL PANIC MACHINE

1. Madison Reeve, "Girl, 9, Accused of Being Trans at Kelowna Track Meet," *Castanet*, June 12, 2023, https://www.castanet.net/news/Kelowna/431500/Girl-9-accused-of-being-trans-at-Kelowna-track-meet.

2. Gordan McIntyre, "Girl Verbally Abused at Kelowna Track Meet Hopes Devastating Incident Can Bring About Change," *Vancouver Sun*, June 14, 2023, https://vancouversun.com/news/local-news/girl-verbally-abused-at-kelowna-track-meet-hopes-devastating-incident-can-bring-about-change.

3. Matt Lavietes, "'Groomer,' 'Pro-Pedophile': Old Tropes Find New Life in Anti-LGBTQ Movement," NBC News, Apr. 12, 2022, https://www.nbcnews.com/nbc-out/out-politics-and-policy/groomer-pedophile-old-tropes-find-new-life-anti-lgbtq-movement-rcna23931.

4. Staff Reporter, "'Strong and Perfect the Way You Are': Kelowna Girl Harassed at Track Meet Speaks Out," *Vancouver Sun*, June 14, 2023, https://vancouversun.com/news/local-news/in-her-own-words.

5. Staff Reporter, "'Strong and Perfect the Way You Are.'"

6. Staff Reporter, "'Strong and Perfect the Way You Are.'"

7. RCMP, "Statement in Response to Public Concerns over Sports Day Incident," RCMP Newsroom, June 6, 2014, https://kelowna.rcmp-grc.gc.ca/.

8. Gordon McIntyre, "Girl Verbally Abused at Kelowna Track Meet Hopes Devastating Incident Can Bring About Change," *Vancouver Sun*, June 14, 2023, https://vancouversun.com/news/local-news/girl-verbally-abused-at-kelowna-track-meet-hopes-devastating-incident-can-bring-about-change.

9. McIntyre, "Girl Verbally Abused at Kelowna Track Meet Hopes Devastating Incident Can Bring About Change."

10. Erich Goode and Nachman Ben-Yehuda, "Moral Panics: Culture, Politics, and Social Construction," *Annual Review of Sociology* 20, no. 1 (1994): 149–71, https://www.jstor.org/stable/2083363.

11. Goode and Nachman Ben-Yehuda, "Moral Panics."

12. Katie Barnes, "Young Transgender Athletes Caught in Middle of States' Debates," ESPN, Sept. 1, 2021, https://www.espn.com/espn/story/_/id/32115820/young-transgender-athletes-caught-middle-states-debates.

13. M. M. Johns et al., "Transgender Identity and Experiences of Violence Victimization, Substance Use, Suicide Risk, and Sexual Risk Behaviors Among High School Students—19 States and Large Urban School Districts," *Morbidity and Mortality Weekly Report* (Jan. 25, 2019): 67–71, http://dx.doi.org/10.15585/mmwr.mm6803a3.

14. Human Rights Campaign, "Get the Facts About Transgender & Non-Binary Athletes," https://www.hrc.org/resources/get-the-facts-about-transgender-non-binary-athletes, accessed Aug. 15, 2024.

15. Erin Reed, "It Was Never About Sports: The Strategy of the Anti-Trans Right," *Erin in the Morning* (Substack), Jan. 11, 2023, https://www.erininthemorning.com/p/it-was-never-about-sports-the-strategy.

16. Alex Paterson, "Spotify's Joe Rogan Suggests Trans Are Sign of 'Civilizations Collapsing," *Los Angeles Blade*, Jan. 28, 2022, https://www.losangelesblade.com/2022/01/28/spotifys-joe-rogan-suggests-trans-are-sign-of-civilizations-collapsing.

17. Matt Walsh, X, Oct. 3, 2022, https://x.com/MattWalshBlog/status/1577043574222622720/.

18. Bil Browning, "Marjorie Taylor Greene Says Straight People Will Soon Be Extinct," *LGBTQ Nation*, May 31, 2022, https://www.lgbtqnation.com/2022/05/marjorie-taylor-greene-says-straight-people-will-soon-extinct/.

19. Peter Wade, "CPAC Speaker Calls for Eradication of 'Transgenderism'—and Somehow Claims He's Not Calling for Elimination of Transgender People," *Rolling Stone*, Mar. 6, 2023, https://www.rollingstone.com/politics/politics-news/cpac-speaker-transgender-people-eradicated-1234690924/.

20. Judith Adkins, "'These People Are Frightened to Death': Congressional Investigations and the Lavender Scare," *Prologue Magazine* 48, no. 2 (Summer 2016), https://www.archives.gov/publications/prologue/2016/summer/lavender.html.

21. Suyin Haynes, "You've Probably Heard of the Red Scare, but the Lesser-Known, Anti-Gay 'Lavender Scare' Is Rarely Taught in Schools," *Time*, Dec. 22, 2020, https://time.com/5922679/lavender-scare-history/.

22. Ethan Watters, "The Forgotten Lessons of the Recovered Memory Movement," *New York Times*, Sept. 27, 2022, https://www.nytimes.com/2022/09/27/opinion/recovered-memory-therapy-mental-health.html.

23. H. L. Comeriato, "'There Will Be Blood': How Neo-Nazis and White Supremacists Are Fueling Ohio's Anti-LGBTQ+ Movement," *Buckeye Flame*, Dec. 22, 2023, https://thebuckeyeflame.com/2023/12/22/there-will-be-blood/.

24. Movement Advancement Project, "Equality Maps: Restrictions on Drag Performances," www.mapresearch.org/equality-maps/criminaljustice/drag_restrictions, accessed Aug. 15, 2024.

25. Campaign for American Principles, "Wrestler 7," YouTube, posted Sept. 27, 2019, https://www.youtube.com/watch?v=Qm1gEdtl06M.

26. Ben Jacobs, "This 'NRA for Families' Is Attacking Trans Kids—and the GOP Is Listening," *VICE*, June 28, 2021, https://www.vice.com/en/article/wx5zxn/meet-the-nra-for-families-making-the-war-on-trans-kids-a-core-gop-issue.

27. Sara Murray, "Republicans Build Momentum as They Drive Anti-LGBTQ Legislation Nationwide," CNN, Apr. 22, 2022, https://www.cnn.com/2022/04/22/politics/republicans-anti-lgbtq-legislation/index.html.

28. Zachary Oren Smith, "Terry Schilling, Son of a Republican Candidate for Iowa's 2nd District, Defends Deleted Tweets, Saying They Won't Hurt His Father's Chances," *Iowa City Press-Citizen*, May 28, 2020, https://www.press-citizen.com/story/news/politics/2020/05/28/terry-schilling-defends-deleted-tweets-bobby-schilling-2nd-district-candidate/5276039002.

29. Jeffrey M. Jones, "More Say Birth Gender Should Dictate Sports Participation," Gallup, June 12, 2023, https://news.gallup.com/poll/507023/say-birth-gender-dictate-sports-participation.aspx.

30. Alex Kirshner, "The Trans Athletes Debate Is Not Really About 'Fairness,'" *Slate*, June 28, 2023, https://slate.com/culture/2023/06/transgender-athletes-sports-debate-lance-armstrong.html.

31. Erich Goode and Nachman Ben-Yehuda, "Moral Panics: Culture, Politics, and Social Construction," *Annual Review of Sociology* 20 (1994): 149–71, https://www.jstor.org/stable/2083363.

32. Judith Butler, "Why Is the Idea of 'Gender' Provoking Backlash the World Over?" *The Guardian*, Oct. 23, 2021, https://www.theguardian.com/us-news/commentisfree/2021/oct/23/judith-butler-gender-ideology-backlash.

33. Andrew DeMillo, "Arkansas Malpractice Bill Restricts Trans Youth Medical Care," Associated Press, Feb. 13, 2023, https://apnews.com/article/arkansas-state-government-gender-health-586e773f62600b34e4ed55422a5a3de8.

34. Justia US Law, AR Code § 5-1-109 (2020), https://law.justia.com/codes/arkansas/2020/title-5/subtitle-1/chapter-1/section-5-1-109/, accessed Aug. 2, 2023.

35. Gillian Brockwell, "How the Homophobic Media Covered the 1969 Stonewall Uprising," *Washington Post*, June 8, 2019.

36. Alex Paterson, "'Doom & Gloom': Fox News Has Aired 170 Segments Discussing Trans People in the Past Three Weeks," Media Matters for America, Apr. 8, 2022, https://www.mediamatters.org/fox-news/doom-groom-fox-news-has-aired-170-segments-discussing-trans-people-past-three-weeks.

37. James P. Walsh, "Social Media and Moral Panics: Assessing the Effects of Technological Change on Societal Reaction," *International Journal of Cultural Studies* 23, no. 6 (2020), 840–59, https://www.ncbi.nlm.nih.gov/pmc/articles/PMC7201200.

38. Anna Baeth and Anna Goorevich, "Mediated Moral Panics: Trans Athlete Spectres, the Haunting of Cisgender Girls and Politicians as Moral Entrepreneurs in 2021," in *Justice for Trans Athletes: Challenges and Struggles*, ed. Ali Durham Greey and Helen Jefferson Lenskyj (Bingley, UK: Emerald Publishing Limited, 2022), 137–49.

39. TransLash, https://translash.org, accessed Aug. 15, 2024.

40. Serena Sonoma, "The New York Times' Inaccurate Coverage of Transgender People Is Being Weaponized Against the Transgender Community," GLAAD, Apr. 19, 2023, https://glaad.org/new-york-times-inaccurate-coverage-transgender-people-being -weaponized-against-transgender.

41. Sonoma, "The New York Times' Inaccurate Coverage."

42. Emily Bazelon, "The Battle over Gender Therapy," *New York Times*, June 15, 2022, https://www.nytimes.com/2022/06/15/magazine/gender-therapy.html.

43. Schuyler Bailar's Instagram and TikTok accounts: https://www.instagram.com /pinkmantaray/; https://www.tiktok.com/@pinkmantaray.

44. Ayden Runnels, "After Controversy, Texas School Board Says Transgender Student Can Sing in School Musical," *Texas Tribune*, Nov. 10, 2023, https://www.texas tribune.org/2023/11/10/texas-trans-student-musical-sherman-oklahoma/.

45. International Chess Federation, "FIDE Laws of Chess," in *FIDE Handbook*, https://handbook.fide.com/chapter/E012023, accessed Aug. 15, 2024.

46. TarjeiJS, "FIDE Publishes Controversial New Transgender Policy," Chess.com, Aug. 18, 2023, https://www.chess.com/news/view/fide-publishes-controversial-new -transgender-policy.

47. Yosha Iglesias, X, https://x.com/IglesiasYosha/status/1692092172001071122, Aug. 17, 2023.

48. Matthew Impelli, "Why Do Women Have Own Chess Tournaments? Transgender Ban Raises Questions," *Newsweek*, Aug. 17, 2023, https://www.newsweek.com /women-chess-tournament-transgender-ban-fide-1820632.

49. Erin Reed, "International Chess Org: Trans Women Have 'No Right to Participate' in Women's Chess," *Erin in the Morning* (Substack), Aug. 16, 2023, https://www .erininthemorning.com/p/international-chess-org-trans-women.

50. Jeremy Wilson, "Angling Bans Transgender Women from England Ladies Team Following Protest," *The Telegraph*, Nov. 28, 2023, https://www.telegraph.co.uk/sport /2023/11/28/angling-transgender-women-ban-england-ladies-fishing/.

51. Shannon Bond, "Children's Hospitals Are the Latest Target of Anti-LGBTQ Harassment," NPR, Aug. 26, 2022, https://www.npr.org/2022/08/26/1119634878 /childrens-hospitals-are-the-latest-target-of-anti-lgbtq-harassment.

52. Matt Walsh, X, Oct. 3, 2022.

53. Delphine Luneau, "ICYMI: Leading Medical Organizations Call for Action to Counter Threats, Abusive Behavior Targeting Health Care Facilities, Workers and Families," Human Rights Campaign, Oct. 3, 2022, https://www.hrc.org/press-releases/icymi -leading-medical-organizations-call-for-action-to-counter-threats-abusive-behavior -targeting-health-care-facilities-workers-and-families.

54. Kail Cheng Thom, "The Moral Panic over Trans Rights Is a Distraction from Society's Real Issues," *Globe and Mail*, Mar. 4, 2023, https://www.theglobeandmail .com/opinion/article-the-moral-panic-over-trans-rights-is-a-distraction-from -societys-real.

CHAPTER 2: A BRIEF HISTORY OF GENDER DIVERSE ATHLETES

1. Helen Lenskyj, "We Want to Play . . . We'll Play," *Women and Sport in the Twenties and Thirties* 4, no. 3 (Spring 1983): 15–18, https://cws.journals.yorku.ca/index.php/cws/article/download/13853/12906/13892.

2. Sarah Pruitt, "How Title IX Transformed Women's Sports," *History*, Aug. 16, 2023, https://www.history.com/news/title-nine-womens-sports.

3. "Joan Benoit," International Olympic Committee (IOC) website, https://olympics.com/en/athletes/joan-benoit, accessed Dec. 2023.

4. "Triple Jump," World Athletics, https://worldathletics.org/disciplines/jumps/triple-jump, accessed Dec. 2023.

5. "Stacy Dragila," IOC, https://olympics.com/en/athletes/stacy-dragila, accessed Dec. 2023.

6. "20 Kilometres Race Walk," World Athletics, https://worldathletics.org/disciplines/race-walks/20-kilometres-race-walk, accessed Dec. 2023.

7. Nick Zaccardi, "Race Walkers Lose Bid to Add Women's 50K to Olympics," NBC Sports, Feb. 4, 2020, https://www.nbcsports.com/olympics/news/race-walk-womens-50k-olympics; Luca Lovelli, "What's New at Paris 2024?" IOC, Oct. 16, 2023, https://olympics.com/en/news/whats-new-paris-2024-marathon-race-walk-mixed-relay.

8. Eric Anderson, Rory Magrath, and Rachael Bullingham, *Out in Sport: The Experiences of Openly Gay and Lesbian Athletes in Competitive Sport* (Oxon, UK: Routledge, 2016), 84.

9. Anderson, Magrath, and Bullingham, *Out in Sport*, 84.

10. Joe Hernandez, "Why There Are Few Openly Gay Athletes in Men's Professional Sports," NPR, July 21, 2021, https://www.npr.org/2021/07/21/1018404859/openly-gay-athletes-in-mens-pro-sports-few.

11. Sara Lentati, "Tennis's Reluctant Transgender Pioneer," BBC News, June 26, 2015, https://www.bbc.com/news/magazine-33062241.

12. Renée Richards, *No Way Renée: The Second Half of My Notorious Life* (New York: Simon & Schuster, 2007).

13. Richards, *No Way Renée*.

14. "'The Second Half of My Life,'" *Talk of the Nation*, NPR, Feb. 8, 2007, https://www.npr.org/2007/02/08/7277665/the-second-half-of-my-life.

15. Jon Wertheim, "She's a Transgender Pioneer, but Renée Richards Prefers to Stay Out of the Spotlight," *Sports Illustrated*, June 28, 2019, https://www.si.com/tennis/2019/06/28/renee-richards-gender-identity-politics-transgender-where-are-they-now.

16. Emily Bazelon, "Cross-Court Winner," *Slate*, Oct. 25, 2012, https://slate.com/culture/2012/10/jewish-jocks-and-renee-richards-the-life-of-the-transsexual-tennis-legend.html.

17. Rob Picheta, "Martina Navratilova Dropped by LGBT Group over Trans Athletes Row," CNN, Feb. 20, 2019, https://www.cnn.com/2019/02/20/tennis/martina-navratilova-dropped-lgbt-group-scli-spt-intl/index.html.

18. RNZ, "Laurel Hubbard: I Have to Block Out the Criticism," YouTube, Dec. 7, 2017, https://www.youtube.com/watch?v=7JYerP_Ysts.

19. Samantha Lock, "Who Is Laurel Hubbard? Weightlifter and First Transgender Athlete to Compete at Olympics," *Newsweek*, Aug. 1, 2021, https://www.newsweek.com/laurel-hubbard-transgender-athlete-weightlifting-olympics-japan-lgbt-controversy-new-zealand-1613341.

20. Tariq Panja, "Laurel Hubbard Had Her Moment. Now She'd Like Her Privacy," *New York Times*, Aug. 3, 2021, https://www.nytimes.com/2021/08/03/sports/olympics /laurel-hubbard-transgender-weight-lifter.html.

21. Panja, "Laurel Hubbard Had Her Moment."

22. Joe Kinsey, "Transgender Weightlifter Closes In on a Spot in the Olympics," *OutKick*, May 6, 2021, https://www.outkick.com/olympics/transgender-weightlifter -closes-in-on-a-spot-in-the-olympics.

23. Panja, "Laurel Hubbard Had Her Moment."

24. RNZ, "Laurel Hubbard."

25. RNZ, "Laurel Hubbard."

26. RNZ, "Laurel Hubbard."

27. Nate Stuhlbarg, "Transgender Pioneer Laurel Hubbard Makes History Competing in Olympic Weightlifting," NBC Olympics, Aug. 2, 2021, https://www.nbcolympics.com/news/ transgender-pioneer-laurel-hubbard-makes-history-competing-olympic-weightlifting.

28. Stuhlbarg, "Transgender Pioneer Laurel Hubbard Makes History."

29. Newshub, "NZ Weightlifter Laurel Hubbard's Post-Tokyo Games Interview," YouTube, Aug. 2, 2021, https://www.youtube.com/watch?v=j97PZjE1aZE.

30. McCann, "Laurel Hubbard Speaks."

31. thequinny5, Instagram, https://www.instagram.com/p/CRoPrQvs4Ev/?igsh =NjZiM2M3MzIxNA==.

32. thequinny5, Instagram.

33. Quinn, Zoom call with the authors, 2023.

34. thequinny5, Instagram, https://www.instagram.com/thequinny5/p/CE42Vt6Jje4/.

35. thequinny5, Instagram.

36. Martha Gumprich and Nicola Hare, *The Canadian Non-Binary Youth in Sport Report*, 2023, https://ankorstransconnect.com/wp-content/uploads/2023/10/non-binary -youth-in-sport-report.pdf; Solutions Research Group Consultants, Inc., "Canadian Youth Sports Rebound After Pandemic Disruptions, but Rising Costs Raise Concerns About Affordability," June 26, 2023, https://www.srgnet.com/2023/06/26/canadian -youth-sports-rebound-after-pandemic-disruptions-but-rising-costs-raise-concerns -about-affordability.

37. Patricio Manuel, Zoom call with the authors, 2023.

38. Manuel, Zoom call.

39. Manuel, Zoom call.

40. Manuel, Zoom call.

41. Manuel, Zoom call.

42. Manuel, Zoom call.

43. "IOC Consensus Meeting on Sex Reassignment and Hyperandrogenism November 2015," International Olympic Committee, https://stillmed.olympic.org /Documents/Commissions_PDFfiles/Medical_commission/2015-11_ioc_consensus _meeting_on_sex_reassignment_and_hyperandrogenism-en.pdf.

44. Kevin Baxter, "Transgender Male Boxer Patricio Manuel Makes History with a Win in His Pro Debut," *Los Angeles Times*, Dec. 8, 2018, https://www.latimes.com /sports/boxing/la-sp-pat-manuel-fight-20181208-story.html.

45. Samantha Riedel, "Trans Boxer Patricio Manuel Says Proposed Trans-Only League Is 'Dehumanizing,'" *Them*, Jan. 11, 2023, https://www.them.us/story/patricio -manuel-trans-boxing-league.

46. Karleigh Webb, "Trailblazing Trans Boxer Patricio Manuel Pushes Back Against the WBC's Proposed Trans Division," *Outsports*, Jan. 10, 2023, https://www.outsports .com/2023/1/10/23548163/patricio-manuel-wbc-boxing-transgender-division.

47. Athlete Ally, "Athlete Ally, interACT, NWLC and NCTE Respond to AMA Inclusive Policy," press release, Nov. 17, 2022, https://www.athleteally.org/athlete-ally -interact-nwlc-and-ncte-respond-to-ama-inclusive-policy/.

48. Morty Ain, "Chris Mosier: 'I Finally Feel Very Comfortable with My Body,'" *ESPN The Magazine*, June 28, 2016, https://www.espn.com/olympics/story/_/page /bodychrismosier/duathlete-chris-mosier-breaking-barriers-repping-team-usa-body -issue-2016.

49. Frederick Dreier, "For Transgender Triathlete, a Top Finish in New York Is Secondary," *New York Times*, Aug. 5, 2011, https://www.nytimes.com/2011/08/06/sports /for-transgender-triathlete-a-top-finish-is-secondary.html.

50. Jim Buzinski, "Transgender Triathlete Chris Mosier Tells About Competing in the N.Y. Triathlon," *Outsports*, Aug. 16, 2011, https://www.outsports.com/2011/8 /16/4051688/transgender-triathlete-chris-mosier-tells-about-competing-in-the-n-y.

51. Ain, "Chris Mosier."

52. Talya Minsberg, "Trans Athlete Chris Mosier on Qualifying for the Olympic Trials," *New York Times*, Jan. 28, 2020, https://www.nytimes.com/2020/01/28/sports /chris-mosier-trans-athlete-olympic-trials.html.

CHAPTER 3: FAIRNESS FALLACY

1. "Marie-Philip Poulin," Canadian Olympic Committee, https://olympic.ca/team -canada/marie-philip-poulin/, accessed Dec. 2023.

2. Hannah Cechini, "Del. 'Fairness in Women's Sports Act' Opened to Public Comment," WMDT, Mar. 23, 2022, https://www.wmdt.com/2022/03/del-fairness-in-womens -sports-act-opened-to-public-comment.

3. Dwayne McBean, "Australia's Prime Minister Backs Controversial Bill Targeting Trans Athletes," *Xtra Magazine*, Feb. 28, 2022, https://xtramagazine.com/power /politics/australias-prime-minister-backs-controversial-bill-targeting-trans-athletes -218863.

4. Sean Gregory, "How Kids' Sports Became a $15 Billion Industry," *Time*, Aug. 24, 2017, https://time.com/4913687/how-kids-sports-became-15-billion-industry/.

5. Rick Westhead, "Canadian Youth Sports Industry Worth $8.7 Billion, Company Says," CTV News, Mar. 1, 2019, https://www.ctvnews.ca/w5/canadian-youth-sports -industry-worth-8-7-billion-company-says-1.4316678?cache=piqndqvkh.

6. National Recreation and Park Association, *Youth Sports at Park and Recreation Agencies*, 2022, https://www.nrpa.org/globalassets/research/nrpa-youth-sports-at-park -and-recreation-agencies-research-report.pdf.

7. Carolyn B. Maloney, Senior House Democrat, US Congress Joint Economic Committee, "The Economic State of the Black Community in America," Jan. 21, 2019, https://www.jec.senate.gov/public/index.cfm/democrats/2019/1/the-economic-state -of-the-black-community-in-america.

8. E. J. Staurowsky et al., *Chasing Equity: The Triumphs, Challenges, and Opportunities in Sports for Girls and Women*, Women's Sports Foundation, 2020, https://www .womenssportsfoundation.org/wp-content/uploads/2020/01/Chasing-Equity-Full -Report-Web.pdf.

9. Editors, "Kids Need More Places to Play, Not Fat Shaming," *Scientific American*, July 1, 2023, https://www.scientificamerican.com/article/kids-need-more-places-to -play-not-fat-shaming.

10. Matt Richtel, "The Income Gap Is Becoming a Physical-Activity Divide," *New York Times*, Mar. 24, 2023, https://www.nytimes.com/2023/03/24/health/sports -physical-education-children.html.

11. "Snoop Dogg Says Sens Bid Could Boost Hockey Among Black Youth," CBC News, May 2, 2023, https://www.cbc.ca/news/canada/ottawa/snoop-dogg-ottawa -senators-espn-first-take-1.6829452.

12. Étienne Lajoie and Salim Valji, "In Canada, the Cost of Youth Hockey Benches the Next Generation," *New York Times*, Feb. 22, 2020, https://www.nytimes.com/2020 /02/22/sports/hockey/canada-youth-hockey-cost.html.

13. Lajoie and Valji, "In Canada, the Cost of Youth Hockey Benches the Next Generation."

14. Lajoie and Valji, "In Canada, the Cost of Youth Hockey Benches the Next Generation."

15. Greg Wyshynski, "NHL's First Diversity and Inclusion Report Finds Workforce 84% White," ESPN, Oct. 18, 2022, https://www.espn.com/nhl/story/_/id/34824468 /nhl-releases-first-diversity-inclusion-report.

16. Terrence Doyle, "The NHL Says 'Hockey Is for Everyone.' Black Players Aren't So Sure," *FiveThirtyEight*, Oct. 19, 2020, https://fivethirtyeight.com/features/the-nhl -says-hockey-is-for-everyone-black-players-arent-so-sure.

17. Wyshynski, "NHL's First Diversity and Inclusion Report Finds Workforce 84% White."

18. Malcolm Gladwell, *Outliers: The Story of Success* (New York: Back Bay Books, 2009), 15.

19. Gladwell, *Outliers,* 23.

20. Jeff Merron, "Q&A with Malcolm Gladwell," ESPN, Dec. 8, 2008, https://www .espn.com/espn/page2/story?page=merron/081208.

21. Stephen Cobley et al., "Annual Age-Grouping and Athlete Development: A Meta-analytical Review of Relative Age Effects in Sport," *Sports Medicine* 39, no. 3 (2009), https://pubmed.ncbi.nlm.nih.gov/19290678/.

22. Cobley et al., "Annual Age-Grouping and Athlete Development."

23. "Disaggregated Trends in Poverty from the 2021 Census of Population," *Statistics Canada*, Nov. 9, 2022, https://www12.statcan.gc.ca/census-recensement/2021/as -sa/98–200-x/2021009/98–200-x2021009-eng.pdf.

24. Bianca D. M. Wilson et al., *LGBT Poverty in the United States: Trends at the On- set of COVID-19,* UCLA School of Law, Williams Institute, Feb. 2023, https:// williamsinstitute.law.ucla.edu/publications/lgbt-poverty-us/.

25. Ali Durham Greey and Helen Jefferson Lenskyj, *Justice for Trans Athletes: Chal- lenges and Struggles* (Bingley, UK: Emerald Publishing Limited, 2022).

26. "Transphobia Rife Among UK Employers as 1 in 3 Won't Hire a Transgender Person," *Crossland* (blog), June 18, 2018, https://www.crosslandsolicitors.com/site /hr-hub/transgender-discrimination-in-UK-workplaces.

27. Stuart G. Wilson et al., "Parental Sport Achievement and the Development of Athlete Expertise," *European Journal of Sport Science* 19, no. 2 (Dec. 2018), https://www .researchgate.net/publication/329361287_Parental_sport_achievement_and_the _development_of_athlete_expertise.

28. Wilson et al., "Parental Sport Achievement and the Development of Athlete Expertise."

29. Katie Barnes, "They Are the Champions," ESPN, May 29, 2018, https://www.espn.com/espnw/feature/23592317/how-two-transgender-athletes-fighting-compete-sports-love.

30. Mark Zeigler, "Column: Norway's Hands-off Approach to Youth Sports Might Explain Why They're So Good When They Get Older," *San Diego Union-Tribune*, July 20, 2022, https://www.sandiegouniontribune.com/sports/sports-columnists/story/2022-07-20/zeigler-norway-youth-sports-track-field-world-athletics-championships-eugene-karsten-warholm.

31. USAFacts Team, "Are Fewer Kids Playing Sports?" USAFacts, Mar. 21, 2024, https://usafacts.org/articles/are-fewer-kids-playing-sports/.

32. Zeigler, "Column: Norway's Hands-off Approach to Youth Sports."

33. "Pyeongchang 2018," International Olympic Committee website, https://olympics.com/en/olympic-games/pyeongchang-2018/medals, accessed Dec. 2023.

34. "U.S. and World Population Clock," US Census, https://www.census.gov/popclock/world, accessed Sept. 2024.

CHAPTER 4: THE HORMONES QUESTION

1. Katherine Kornei, "This Scientist Is Racing to Discover How Gender Transitions Alter Athletic Performance—Including Her Own," *Science*, July 25, 2018, https://www.science.org/content/article/scientist-racing-discover-how-gender-transitions-alter-athletic-performance-including.

2. Kornei, "This Scientist Is Racing to Discover How Gender Transitions Alter Athletic Performance."

3. Ross Tucker, "Letter to BJSM Reinforcing Call for Retraction of IAAF Research on Testosterone in Women," *Science of Sport*, Aug. 2, 2018, https://sportsscientists.com/2018/08/letter-to-bjsm-reinforcing-call-for-retraction-of-iaaf-research-on-testosterone-in-women/.

4. Melissa Block, "Olympic Runner Caster Semenya Wants to Compete, Not Defend Her Womanhood," NPR, July 28, 2021, https://www.npr.org/sections/tokyo-olympics-live-updates/2021/07/28/1021503989/women-runners-testosterone-olympics; World Athletics, "IAAF Publishes Briefing Notes and Q&A on Female Eligibility Regulations," press release, May 7, 2019, https://www.worldathletics.org/news/press-release/questions-answers-iaaf-female-eligibility-reg.

5. "Hormones," Cleveland Clinic, https://my.clevelandclinic.org/health/articles/22464-hormones, last reviewed Feb. 23, 2022.

6. Matthew C. Leinung and Jalaja Joseph, "Changing Demographics in Transgender Individuals Seeking Hormonal Therapy: Are Trans Women More Common Than Trans Men?" *Transgender Health* 5, no. 4 (Dec. 2020): 241–45, https://www.ncbi.nlm.nih.gov/pmc/articles/PMC7906237.

7. Erin Digitale, "Better Mental Health Found Among Transgender People Who Started Hormones as Teens," Stanford School of Medicine, Jan. 12, 2022, https://med.stanford.edu/news/all-news/2022/01/mental-health-hormone-treatment-transgender-people.html.

8. Diane Chen et al., "Psychosocial Functioning in Transgender Youth After 2 Years of Hormones," *New England Journal of Medicine* 388, no. 3 (Jan. 2023): 240–50, https://www.nejm.org/doi/10.1056/NEJMoa2206297.

9. Chen et al., "Psychosocial Functioning in Transgender Youth After 2 Years of Hormones."

10. David J Handelsman et al., "Circulating Testosterone as the Hormonal Basis of Sex Differences in Athletic Performance," *Endocrinology Review* 39, no. 5 (Oct. 2018): 803–29, https://www.ncbi.nlm.nih.gov/pmc/articles/PMC6391653.

11. Jonathon W. Senefeld, "Sex Differences in Youth Elite Swimming," *PLOS ONE* 14, no. 11 (Nov. 2019), https://journals.plos.org/plosone/article?id=10.1371/journal .pone.0225724.

12. "Speedo / Tom Dolan Invitational," Potomac Valley Swimming, Dec. 2013, https://www.pvswim.org/1314meet/14-26-ma.pdf.

13. "2024 PVS LC 12 & Under Championships Qualifying Times," Potomac Valley Swimming, https://www.pvswim.org/2324meet/2024-LC-12U-Champs-Qualifying -Times.pdf.

14. Schuyler Bailar, Zoom interview with authors, 2023.

15. Blair Crewther et al., "The Effect of Steroid Hormones on the Physical Performance of Boys and Girls During an Olympic Weightlifting Competition," *Journal of Human Kinetics* 28, no. 4 (2016), https://journals.humankinetics.com/view/journals /pes/28/4/article-p580.xml.

16. Rebecca M. Jordan-Young and Katrina Karkazis, *Testosterone: An Unauthorized Biography* (Cambridge, MA: Harvard University Press, 2019).

17. Timothy A. Roberts et al., "Effect of Gender Affirming Hormones on Athletic Performance in Transwomen and Transmen: Implications for Sporting Organisations and Legislators," *British Journal of Sports Medicine* 55, no. 11 (Apr. 2021): 577–83, https://bjsm.bmj.com/content/55/11/577.

18. Jordan-Young and Karkazis, *Testosterone*.

19. 5 News, "Usain Bolt: A Woman Would Beat Me over 800m," YouTube, Sept. 19, 2013, https://www.youtube.com/watch?v=veSqmr-HIWs.

20. Jordan-Young and Karkazis, *Testosterone*.

21. Alyssa Rosenberg, "A New Low in Anti-trans Bills," *Washington Post*, June 6, 2022, https://www.washingtonpost.com/opinions/2022/06/06/ohio-bill-transgender -athletes-gender-confirmation-exams/.

22. Susan Tebben, "Ohio Trans Athletes Ban Moving Forward with Genital Inspections Replaced by Birth Certificates," *Ohio Capital Journal*, Dec. 7, 2022, https://ohio capitaljournal.com/2022/12/07/ohio-trans-athletes-ban-moving-forward-with-genital -inspections-replaced-by-birth-certificates.

23. Molly Walsh, "'We Would Have to Leave the State': What It's Like Being a Transgender Student in Ohio as Lawmakers Push Anti-trans Bills," Cleveland.com, July 20, 2023, https://www.cleveland.com/news/2023/07/we-would-have-to-leave-the-state -what-its-like-being-a-transgender-student-in-ohio-as-lawmakers-push-anti-trans -bills.html.

24. Megan Henry, "Ohio House Passes Bill Blocking Gender-Affirming Care and Trans Athletes," *Ohio Capital Journal*, June 22, 2023, https://ohiocapitaljournal.com /2023/06/22/ohio-house-passes-bill-blocking-gender-affirming-care-and-trans-athletes -from-playing-sports.

25. Roberts et al., "Effect of Gender Affirming Hormones on Athletic Performance in Transwomen and Transmen," 577–83.

26. Roberts et al., "Effect of Gender Affirming Hormones on Athletic Performance in Transwomen and Transmen," 577–83.

27. Roger Marshall, "Sen. Roger Marshall: Biden's Gender Discrimination Executive Order Will Destroy Women's Sports," Fox News, Mar. 1, 2021, https://www.fox news.com/opinion/womens-sport-destroyed-biden-executive-order-roger-marshall.

28. Miriam Valverde, "Kansas Senator Leaves Out Context in Claim About Transgender Athletes," Poynter Institute/PolitiFact, Mar. 9, 2021, https://www.politifact .com/factchecks/2021/mar/09/roger-marshall/kansas-senator-leaves-out-context -claim-about-tran/.

29. Valverde, "Kansas Senator Leaves Out Context."

30. Parker Dunn, Zoom call with authors, 2023.

31. Scott Gleeson, "'It's a Life or Death Issue': Trans Athletes Fight for Their Humanity While Battling Anti-trans Laws," *USA Today*, June 9, 2021, https://www.usa today.com/story/sports/2021/06/09/its-life-death-issue-trans-athletes-fight-draconian -laws/5290074001.

32. Harrison Browne, "Trans Tips: Trans Athletes in Sport," Harrison Browne YouTube channel, Jan. 11, 2018, https://www.youtube.com/watch?v=SFkCGhOCmkA.

33. Tyler Santora, "Why Trans Kids Need to Be Allowed in Sports, According to a Trans Athlete," *Fatherly*, May 30, 2023, https://www.fatherly.com/health/why-trans -kids-need-to-be-allowed-in-sports-according-to-transgender-athlete-schuyler-bailar.

34. Jordan-Young and Karkazis, *Testosterone*.

35. Dan Roan and Katie Falkingham, "Transgender Athletes: What Do the Scientists Say?" BBC Sports, May 11, 2022, https://www.bbc.com/sport/61346517.

CHAPTER 5: PANIC AT THE OLYMPICS

1. "Dora Ratjen," International Olympic Committee, https://olympics.com/en /athletes/dora-ratjen, accessed Dec. 2023.

2. Rob Tannenbaum, "The Life and Murder of Stella Walsh, Intersex Olympic Champion," *Longreads*, Aug. 18, 2016, https://longreads.com/2016/08/18/the-life-and -murder-of-stella-walsh-intersex-olympic-champion/.

3. Rachel Giese, "Women Are Finally Getting Their Fair Share of the Olympics— Almost," *Chatelaine*, June 15, 2017, https://chatelaine.com/news/women-athletes -olympics.

4. Giese, "Women Are Finally Getting Their Fair Share of the Olympics."

5. Alyssa Rosenberg, "A New Low in Anti-trans Bills: Genital Exams for Female Athletes," *Washington Post*, June 6, 2022, https://www.washingtonpost.com/opinions /2022/06/06/ohio-bill-transgender-athletes-gender-confirmation-exams.

6. Robert Ritchie, "Intersex and the Olympic Games," *Journal of the Royal Society of Medicine* 101, no. 8 (Sept. 2008), https://www.researchgate.net/publication/23156663 _Intersex_and_the_Olympic_Games.

7. Ritchie, "Intersex and the Olympic Games."

8. Robyn Ryle, *Throw Like a Girl, Cheer Like a Boy: The Evolution of Gender, Identity, and Race in Sports* (Lanham, MD: Rowman & Littlefield, 2020), 19.

9. Kathryn E. Henne, *Testing for Athlete Citizenship: Regulating Doping and Sex in Sport* (New Brunswick, NJ: Rutgers University Press), 100.

10. Ryle, *Throw Like a Girl, Cheer Like a Boy*, 73–74.

11. Louis J. Elsas et al., "Gender Verification of Female Athletes," *Genetics in Medicine* 2, no. 4 (July/Aug. 2000): 249–54, https://www.gimjournal.org/article/S1098 -3600(21)00234-3/pdf.

12. Fiona Alice Miller, "'Your True and Proper Gender': The Barr Body as a Good Enough Science of Sex," *Studies in History and Philosophy of Biological and Biomedical Sciences* 37 (Jan. 2006): 459–83, https://www.thebloodproject.com/wp-content/uploads /2021/10/BARR-BODY.pdf.

13. Louis J. Elsas et al., "Gender Verification of Female Athletes," *Genetics in Medicine* 2, no. 4 (July/Aug. 2000): 249–54, https://www.gimjournal.org/article/S1098-3600 (21)00234-3/pdf.

14. Jon Holmes, "Caster Semenya Does Not Call Herself Intersex: 'I'm a Different Kind of Woman,'" *Outsports*, Oct. 26, 2023, https://www.outsports.com/2023/10/26 /23933175/caster-semenya-autobiography-athletics-intersex-awareness-day/.

15. Caster Semenya, *The Race to Be Myself* (New York: W. W. Norton, 2023).

16. Stewart Maclean, "Is She Really a HE? Women's 800m Runner Shrugs Off Gender Storm to Take Gold," *Daily Mail*, Aug. 19, 2009, https://www.dailymail.co.uk/news /article-1207653/Womens-800m-gold-medal-favourite-Caster-Semenya-takes-gender -test-hours-World-Championship-race.html.

17. Maclean, "Is She Really a HE?"

18. Semenya, *The Race to Be Myself*.

19. William Lee Adams, "Could This Woman's World Champ Be a Man?" *Time*, Aug. 21, 2009, https://content.time.com/time/world/article/0,8599,1917767,00.html.

20. Paul Waldie and Geoffrey York, "Semenya's Battle Against the IAAF Has Become a Rallying Cry for Human Rights Activists," *Globe and Mail*, Mar. 22, 2019, https://www.theglobeandmail.com/sports/article-semenyas-battle-against-the-iaaf-has -become-a-rallying-cry-for-human/.

21. Semenya, *The Race to Be Myself*.

22. Anna Kessel, "Rivals 'Laughed and Stared' at Caster Semenya, Says Jenny Meadows," *The Guardian*, July 21, 2010, https://www.theguardian.com/sport/2010/jul /21/caster-semenya-jenny-meadows.

23. Semenya, *The Race to Be Myself*.

24. Ruth Padawer, "The Humiliating Practice of Sex-Testing Female Athletes," *New York Times*, June 28, 2016, https://www.nytimes.com/2016/07/03/magazine/the -humiliating-practice-of-sex-testing-female-athletes.html.

25. Juliet Macur, "Fighting for the Body She Was Born With," *New York Times*, Aug. 19, 2009, https://www.nytimes.com/2014/10/07/sports/sprinter-dutee-chand-fights -ban-over-her-testosterone-level.html.

26. "IAAF to Introduce Eligibility Rules for Females with Hyperandrogenism," World Athletics, Apr. 12, 2011, https://worldathletics.org/news/iaaf-news/iaaf-to -introduce-eligibility-rules-for-femal-1.

27. Macur, "Fighting for the Body She Was Born With."

28. Manu Joseph, "The Definition of a Female Athlete," *Hindustan Times*, July 21, 2014, https://www.hindustantimes.com/columns/the-definition-of-a-female-athlete /story-Si0bkalblOjjJJHP1HudRO.html.

29. Ronald S. Katz, "INSIGHT: Discrimination in Athletics—Eligibility of Intersex Runner a Prime Example," *Bloomberg Law*, May 13, 2019, https://news.bloomberglaw

.com/us-law-week/insight-discrimination-in-athletics-eligibility-of-intersex-runner-a
-prime-example.

30. "Report: Women's 800m Final—Rio 2016 Olympic Games," World Athletics,
Aug. 20, 2016, https://worldathletics.org/competitions/olympic-games/news/rio-2016
-women-800m-final.

31. Tylyn Wells, "Intersex, Hyperandrogenism, Female Athletes: A Legal Perspective on the IAAF Doping Regulations and Where Hyperandrogenic Female Athletes Fit
In," *Santa Clara Journal of International Law* 17, no. 2 (Jan. 2019): 1–18, https://digital
commons.law.scu.edu/cgi/viewcontent.cgi?article=1233&context=scujil.

32. Nick Said, "Semenya Accuses IAAF of Using Her as a 'Human Guinea Pig,'"
Reuters, June 18, 2019, https://www.reuters.com/article/us-athletics-semenya/semenya
-accuses-World%20Athletics-of-using-her-as-a-human-guinea-pig-idUSKCN1TJ22P.

33. Ashfak Mohamed, "Caster Semenya: I Will Not Allow the IAAF to Use Me and
My Body Again," *IOL*, June 18, 2019, https://www.iol.co.za/sport/athletics/caster
-semenya-i-will-not-allow-the-iaaf-to-use-me-and-my-body-again-26619809.

34. Hida Viloria, "Lobbying the IOC on Behalf of Intersex Women Athletes," Hida
Viloria (website), Apr. 11, 2011, https://hidaviloria.com/lobbying-the-ioc-on-behalf
-of-intersex-women-athletes/.

35. Gerald Imray, "Semenya Listed to Run at World Athletics Championships in Potential Surprise Return," Associated Press, July 8, 2022, https://www.cbc.ca/sports/olympics
/summer/trackandfield/caster-semanya-listed-to-run-2022-worlds-july-8–1.6515158.

36. Gerald Imray, "Olympic Champion Caster Semenya Wins Appeal Against Testosterone Rules at Human Rights Court," Associated Press, July 11, 2023, https://www
.cbc.ca/sports/olympics/summer/trackandfield/caster-semenya-wins-appeal-against
-testosterone-rules-1.6902816.

37. Vanessa Heggie, "Testing Sex and Gender in Sports: Reinventing, Reimagining
and Reconstructing Histories," *Endeavour* 34, no. 4 (Dec. 2010), https://www.ncbi.nlm
.nih.gov/pmc/articles/PMC3007680/.

38. Kathryn Henne, "The 'Science' of Fair Play in Sport: Gender and the Politics of
Testing," *Journal of Women in Culture and Society* 39, no. 3 (Spring 2014), https://www
.journals.uchicago.edu/doi/full/10.1086/674208.

39. Semenya, *The Race to Be Myself*.

40. Sabi Hussain, "Don't Ban Transgender Women Athletes from Competing: Dutee Chand," *Times of India*, June 23, 2022, https://timesofindia.indiatimes.com/sports
/more-sports/athletics/dont-ban-transgender-women-athletes-from-competing-dutee
-chand/articleshow/92401397.cms.

41. Dave Zirin and Jules Boykoff, "Why There Are No Trans Women Competing at
the Paris Games," *The Nation*, July 25, 2024, https://www.thenation.com/article/society
/trans-athletes-paris-olympics/.

42. Li Zhou, "The Misleading Controversy over an Olympic Women's Boxing Match,
Briefly Explained," *Vox*, Aug. 2, 2024, https://www.vox.com/sports/364856/olympics
-boxing-imane-khelif-angela-carini.

43. Kiki Intarasuwan, "Fact Check: Olympics Boxing Gender Testing Controversy
Explained," NBC New York, Aug. 2, 2024, https://www.nbcnewyork.com/paris-2024
-summer-olympics/olympics-boxing-imane-khalif-xy-chromosome-italian-boxer-quit
/5662035/.

44. Becca Longmire, "Boxer Imane Khelif Urges Public to 'Refrain from Bullying Athletes' amid Olympics Gender Controversy," *People*, Aug. 5, 2024, https://people.com /boxer-imane-khelif-urges-public-refrain-bullying-gender-controversy-paris-olympics.

CHAPTER 6: THE MYTH OF SAVING WOMEN'S SPORTS

1. Tigerlily Hopson and Toia Conde Rodrigues da Cunha, "Swimming & Diving: 'It Feels Like Flying': Iszac Henig '23 Soars on Women's Swim Team," *Yale Daily News*, Feb. 3, 2022, https://yaledailynews.com/blog/2022/02/03/swimming-diving-it-feels -like-flying-iszac-henig-23-soars-on-womens-swim-team.

2. Iszac Henig, Zoom interview with the authors, 2023.

3. Henig, Zoom interview.

4. Danne Diamond, Zoom interview with the authors, 2023.

5. Jeré Longman, "New Study Bolsters Idea of Athletic Differences Between Men and Trans Women," *New York Times*, Apr. 23, 2024, https://www.nytimes.com/2024/04 /23/world/europe/paris-olympics-transgender-athletes.html.

6. Martina Navratilova, "The Rules on Trans Athletes Reward Cheats and Punish the Innocent," *Times of London*, Feb. 17, 2019, https://www.thetimes.co.uk/article/the -rules-on-trans-athletes-reward-cheats-and-punish-the-innocent-klsrq6h3x.

7. Jo Yurcaba, "Trump Promises to Ban Transgender Women from Sports If Re-elected," NBC News, Jan. 31, 2022, https://www.nbcnews.com/nbc-out/out-politics -and-policy/trump-promises-ban-transgender-women-sports-re-elected-rcna14248.

8. John Lohn, "The Protection of Women's Sports at the Heart of Lia Thomas Situation," *Swimming World Magazine*, Feb. 28, 2022, https://www.swimmingworldmagazine .com/news/protection-of-womens-sports-at-the-heart-of-lia-thomas-situation.

9. "Video Lia Thomas, the First Openly Transgender Swimmer to Win the NCAA D1: Part 1," *ABC News/Nightline*, June 1, 2022, https://abcnews.go.com/Nightline/video /lia-thomas-openly-transgender-swimmer-win-ncaa-d1-85103883.

10. Rohith Nair, "Caitlyn Jenner Says FINA Made Right Decision to Change Transgender Policy," Reuters, June 22, 2022, https://www.reuters.com/lifestyle/sports/caitlyn -jenner-says-fina-made-right-decision-change-transgender-policy-2022–06–22.

11. "PHF Transgender and Non-Binary Inclusion Policy," Premier Hockey Federation website (now discontinued), https://www.premierhockeyfederation.com/phf -transgender-and-non-binary-policy.

12. "Men's Swim Top Times," Penn Athletics, Nov. 14, 2019, https://pennathletics .com/sports/2019/11/14/mens-swim-top-times.aspx.

13. Daily Blast LIVE, "Former Penn Swimmer Lia Thomas: 'Trans People Don't Transition for Athletics,'" YouTube, May 31, 2022, https://www.youtube.com/watch?v =eX2R2zwb8eA.

14. Schuyler Bailar, *He/She/They: How We Talk About Gender and Why It Matters* (New York: Hachette, 2023).

15. "2021-22 Women's Swimming and Diving Roster," Penn Athletics, https:// pennathletics.com/sports/womens-swimming-and-diving/roster/lia-thomas/19456.

16. Anna Baeth, Zoom interview with authors, 2023.

17. Adriana Diaz, "It's Impossible to Beat Her . . . ," *Daily Mail*, Dec. 14, 2021, https://www.dailymail.co.uk/news/article-10310305/Female-competitor-speaks-saying -IMPOSSIBLE-beat-UPenn-transgender-swimmer-Lia-Thomas.html.

18. Schuyler Bailar, "How Do We Bring Our Authentic Selves to Sport?" *Dear Schuyler*, podcast, Sept. 18, 2023.

19. "Women's NCAA DI Records (SCY)," Swim Swam, https://swimswam.com /records/womens-ncaa-di-records-scy, accessed Aug. 16, 2024.

20. Jo Yurcaba, "Amid Trans Athlete Debate, Penn's Lia Thomas Loses to Trans Yale Swimmer," NBC News, Jan. 10, 2022, https://www.nbcnews.com/nbc-out/out-news /trans-athlete-debate-penns-lia-thomas-loses-trans-yale-swimmer-rcna11622.

21. "FINA Votes to Restrict Transgender Athletes in Elite Women's Events," CBC News, 2022, https://www.cbc.ca/player/play/2044816963586.

22. Elana Redfield et al., *Prohibiting Gender-Affirming Medical Care for Youth*, Williams Institute, Mar. 2023, https://williamsinstitute.law.ucla.edu/publications/bans -trans-youth-health-care.

23. "Fina Bars Transgender Swimmers from Women's Elite Events If They Went Through Male Puberty," BBC Sport, June 20, 2022, https://www.bbc.com/sport /swimming/61853450.

24. "Statement of the Stockholm Consensus on Sex Reassignment in Sports," Paris 2024 Olympics, https://stillmed.olympic.org/Documents/Reports/EN/en_report_905.pdf.

25. Valeri Guevarra, "Penn Women's Swimming Breaks Program, Conference, Pool Records at Ivy Championships," *Daily Pennsylvanian*, Feb. 20, 2023, https://www.thedp .com/article/2023/02/penn-womens-swimming-and-diving-ivy-league-championships -anna-kalandadze.

26. Melissa Cunningham, "FINA Ruling Based on 'Opinion Not Science,' Australian Researchers Say," *Sydney Morning Herald*, June 21, 2022, https://www.smh.com .au/national/fina-ruling-based-on-opinion-not-science-australian-researchers-say -20220620-p5av3o.html.

27. Shireen Ahmed, "FINA Trans Swim Policy Shows 'Equal but Separate' Is Actually Exclusion," CBC News, June 22, 2022, https://www.cbc.ca/sports/fina-transgender -swim-opinion-shireen-ahmed-1.6495697.

28. "Jessica Platt," Elite Prospects, https://www.eliteprospects.com/player/521043 /jessica-platt, accessed Aug. 16, 2024.

29. Cyd Zeigler, "Meet Some Trans Athletes Who Work Hard, Train Like Mad and (Almost) Never Win," *Outsports*, Dec. 3, 2019, https://www.outsports.com/2019/12 /3/20990763/trans-women-athlete-sports-winning-losing-transgender/.

30. "Emily Bridges: Cyclist Says Transgender Women Are the 'Punching Bag' in Society," BBC, May 26, 2022, https://www.bbc.com/sport/cycling/61563551.

31. "Emily Bridges."

32. PA Media, "Boris Johnson's Comments Led to Threats Against Me, Says Emily Bridges," *The Guardian*, June 7, 2022, https://www.theguardian.com/sport/2022/jun/07 /boris-johnsons-comments-led-to-threats-against-me-says-emily-bridges.

33. Emily Bridges, "Why I've Made a Documentary About My Transgender Journey," *ITVX*, Nov. 29, 2022, https://www.itv.com/news/wales/2022-11-29/emily-bridges -why-ive-made-a-documentary-about-my-transgender-journey.

34. "Swimmer Lia Thomas Breaks Silence About Backlash, Future Plans," *Good Morning America*, May 31, 2022, https://www.goodmorningamerica.com/news/video /swimmer-lia-thomas-breaks-silence-backlash-future-plans-85081325.

35. Donna Lopiano, Zoom interview with authors, 2023.

36. Will Hobson, "The Fight for the Future of Transgender Athletes," *Washington Post*, Apr. 15, 2021, https://www.washingtonpost.com/sports/2021/04/15/transgender-athletes-womens-sports-title-ix.

37. Nancy Hogshead-Makar, "Nancy Hogshead-Makar Explains Problems with Lia Thomas Situation," *Swimming World*, Dec. 25, 2021, https://www.swimmingworld magazine.com/news/nancy-hogshead-makar-explains-problems-with-lia-thomas-situation/.

38. Jo Yurcaba, "16 Penn Swimmers Issue Letter in Support of New Transgender Athlete Rules," NBC News, Feb. 4, 2022, https://www.nbcnews.com/nbc-out/out-news/16-penn-swimmers-issue-letter-support-new-transgender-athlete-rules-rcna14928.

39. Karleigh Chardonnay Webb, Twitter/X, Dec. 26, 2022, https://twitter.com/ChardonnayM/status/1607276640689860608?s=20.

40. Nancy Hogshead-Makar, Twitter/X, Dec. 12, 2022, https://twitter.com/Hogshead 3Au/status/1602384748596297731?s=20.

41. Diana Nyad, "Celebrate Trans Athletes. But Give Cisgender Women a Fair Shot," *Washington Post*, Feb. 9, 2022, https://www.washingtonpost.com/opinions/2022/02/09/celebrate-trans-athletes-give-cisgender-women-fair-shot-victory/.

42. Frankie de La Cretaz, "The IOC Has a New Trans-Inclusion Framework, but Is the Damage Already Done?" *Sports Illustrated*, Mar. 23, 2022, https://www.si.com/olympics/2022/03/23/transgender-athletes-testosterone-policies-ioc-framework.

43. Katie Barnes, "The Battle over Title IX and Who Gets to Be a Woman in Sports: Inside the Raging National Debate," ESPN, June 23, 2020, https://www.espn.com/espnw/story/_/id/29347507/the-battle-title-ix-gets-woman-sports-raging-national-debate.

44. Lopiano, Zoom interview.

45. Lopiano, Zoom interview.

46. Lopiano, Zoom interview.

47. Lopiano, Zoom interview.

48. Johanna Mellis, "Now More Than Ever, Cis Female Athletes Must Show Solidarity with Trans Athletes," *The Guardian*, July 7, 2023, https://www.theguardian.com/sport/2023/jul/07/cisgender-female-athletes-solidarity-trans-athletes.

49. Karleigh Webb, "Helen Carroll's Still in the Game for Inclusion," *Outsports*, Nov. 1, 2020, https://www.outsports.com/2020/11/1/21543114/helen-carroll-nclr-athletics-inclusion-lgbtq-title-ix-legislation-election-2020.

50. Lopiano, Zoom interview.

51. Peter Brand, "Why Some Calgary Elite Female Hockey Players Are Frustrated with Bodychecking Bans," *Calgary Journal*, Mar. 31, 2018, https://calgaryjournal.ca/2018/03/31/why-some-calgary-elite-female-hockey-players-are-frustrated-with-bodychecking-bans/.

52. "NHL—Team Comparison," Elite Prospects, https://www.eliteprospects.com/league/nhl/teams-physical-stats/2019–2020, accessed Dec. 2023.

53. George Kosziwka et al., "Risk of Head Injury Associated with Distinct Head Impact Events in Elite Women's Hockey," *Journal of Concussion* 5 (Dec. 2021), https://journals.sagepub.com/doi/10.1177/20597002211058894.

54. Greg Wyshynski, "Swedish Women's Hockey League to OK Bodychecking for 2022–23 Season," ESPN, May 20, 2022, https://www.espn.com/olympics/hockey/story/_/id/33951467/swedish-women-hockey-league-ok-body-checking-2022–23-season.

55. Ian Kennedy, "Sweden Extends Body Checking Pilot Project," *Hockey News*, June 15, 2023, https://thehockeynews.com/womens/international/sweden-extends -body-checking-pilot-project.

56. Ashley Burke, "Federal Government Launching Commission to Probe Systemic Abuse in Sports," CBC News, Dec. 11, 2023, https://www.cbc.ca/news/politics/ottawa -independent-mechanism-review-abuse-canadian-sport-1.7054257.

57. N'dea Yancey-Bragg, "1 in 4 College Athletes Say They Experienced Sexual Abuse from an Authority Figure, Survey Finds," *USA Today*, Aug. 26, 2021, https:// www.usatoday.com/story/news/nation/2021/08/26/college-athlete-report-sexual -assault-common-survey/8253766002.

58. Scott M. Reid, "100s of USA Swimmers Were Sexually Abused for Decades and the People in Charge Knew and Ignored It, Investigation Finds," Southern California News Group, Feb. 16, 2018, https://www.ocregister.com/2018/02/16/investigation-usa -swimming-ignored-sexual-abuse-for-decades.

59. Kristina Rutherford, "PWHL Drops the Puck: 24 Details on the New League for 2024," Sportsnet, Dec. 30, 2023, https://www.sportsnet.ca/pwhl/article/the-pwhl-drops -the-puck-24-details-on-the-new-league-for-2024; John Wawrow, "Grant-Mentis to Become 1st in Women's Pro Hockey to Earn $80K US in Deal with Buffalo Beauts: Reports," CBC News, May 8, 2022, https://www.cbc.ca/sports/hockey/phf-hockey -grant-mentis-womens-pro-hockeys-first-80k-player-1.6446273.

60. Sandro Azerrad, "Average NHL Salary (Updated for 2023–2024)," *Gaimday* (blog), https://www.gaimday.com/blog/average-nhl-salary.

61. E. J. Staurowsky et al., *Chasing Equity: The Triumphs, Challenges, and Opportunities in Sports for Girls and Women*, Women's Sports Foundation, 2020, https://www.womens sportsfoundation.org/wp-content/uploads/2020/01/Chasing-Equity-Full-Report-Web.pdf.

62. Sara Tidwell, "WNBA Salary, Contracts: How Much Money Do Women's Basketball Players Make?" *Sporting News*, Apr. 10, 2023, https://www.sportingnews.com /ca/wnba/news/wnba-salaries-2023-rookies-compared-nba/aaz024nlakdbvi0x91rfoir.

63. Megan McCluskey, "NCAA Accused of 'Disrespectful' Treatment Towards Women's March Madness Teams in Viral TikTok," *Time*, Mar. 19, 2021, https://time .com/5948127/sedona-prince-womens-basketball-march-madness.

64. Becky Sullivan, "Under Fire, the NCAA Apologizes and Unveils New Weight Room for Women's Tournament," NPR, Mar. 20, 2021, https://www.npr.org/2021/03 /20/979596524/under-fire-the-ncaa-apologizes-and-unveils-new-weight-room-for -womens-tournament.

65. Patt Field, "FIFA Upholds Hijab Ban in Soccer," *Globe and Mail*, Mar. 4, 2007, https://www.theglobeandmail.com/sports/fifa-upholds-hijab-ban-in-soccer/article 1071519.

66. Olivia Cleal, "The First Woman to Play Wearing a Hijab at the FIFA Women's World," *Women's Agenda*, July 25, 2023, https://womensagenda.com.au/latest/nouhaila -benzina-the-first-woman-to-play-wearing-a-hijab-at-the-fifa-womens-world-cup/.

67. "FIFA Lifts Ban on Head Covers," *Al Jazeera*, Mar. 1, 2014, https://www.aljazeera .com/sports/2014/3/1/fifa-lifts-ban-on-head-covers.

68. Constant Méheut, "The Female Soccer Players Challenging France's Hijab Ban," *New York Times*, Apr. 18, 2022, https://www.nytimes.com/2022/04/18/sports/soccer /france-hijab-ban-soccer.html.

CHAPTER 7: SCHOOL BATTLEGROUND

1. Chelsea Mitchell, "I Was the Fastest Girl in Connecticut. But Transgender Athletes Made It an Unfair Fight," ADF, May 26, 2021, https://adflegal.org/article/i-was-fastest-girl-connecticut-transgender-athletes-made-it-unfair-fight.

2. Gerry deSimas Jr., "Mitchell, the Fastest Girl in Connecticut, Wins State Open Title in 55 Meters," *Collinsville Press*, Feb. 28, 2020, https://collinsvillepress.com/2020/02/mitchell-the-fastest-girl-in-connecticut-wins-state-open-title-in-55-meters/23496.

3. Mirin Fader, "Andraya Yearwood Knows She Has the Right to Compete," *Bleacher Report*, Dec. 17, 2018, https://bleacherreport.com/articles/2810857-andraya-yearwood-knows-she-has-the-right-to-compete.

4. Mary Albl, "Beyond the Labels: Meet Terry Miller," DyeStat.com, May 26, 2019, https://www.runnerspace.com/gprofile.php?mgroup_id=44531&do=news&news_id=576791.

5. Albl, "Beyond the Labels: Meet Terry Miller."

6. Jeremy W. Peters, "Fighting Gay Rights and Abortion with the First Amendment," *New York Times*, Nov. 22, 2017, https://www.nytimes.com/2017/11/22/us/politics/alliance-defending-freedom-gay-rights.html.

7. David D. Kirkpatrick, "The Next Targets for the Group That Overturned Roe," *New Yorker*, Oct. 2, 2023, https://www.newyorker.com/magazine/2023/10/09/alliance-defending-freedoms-legal-crusade.

8. Associated Press, "Female Student Behind Trans Lawsuit Beats Trans Athlete in High School Race," ESPN, Feb. 15, 2020, https://www.espn.com/high-school/story/_/id/28710289/female-student-trans-lawsuit-beats-trans-athlete-high-school-race.

9. Associated Press, "Justice Department Withdraws Support for Lawsuit Seeking to Ban Transgender Athletes from Girls' High School Sports," ESPN, Feb. 23, 2021, https://www.espn.com/espn/story/_/id/30953477/justice-department-withdraws-support-lawsuit-seeking-ban-transgender-athletes-girls-high-school-sports.

10. Julia Mueller, "Former Connecticut Athletes Ask Appeals Court to Resurrect Their Challenge to State's Trans-Inclusive Sports Policy," *The Hill*, Mar. 23, 2023, https://thehill.com/homenews/3915487-former-connecticut-athletes-ask-appeals-court-to-resurrect-their-challenge-to-states-trans-inclusive-sports-policy.

11. Brooke Migdon, "Transgender Athletes Score Legal Victory in Connecticut case," *The Hill*, Dec. 16, 2022, https://thehill.com/regulation/court-battles/3778160-transgender-athletes-score-legal-victory-in-connecticut-case.

12. "Odds of a US High School Male Athlete Playing College," ScholarshipStats.com, https://scholarshipstats.com/varsityodds, accessed Aug. 16, 2024.

13. Sunny Bryant and Rebekah Bryant, Zoom interview with authors, 2023.

14. Bryant and Bryant, Zoom interview.

15. Jo Yurcaba, "Texas Has Considered Dozens of Anti-Trans Bills. These Moms Have Helped Stop Them," NBC News, Sept. 30, 2021, https://www.nbcnews.com/nbc-out/out-politics-and-policy/texas-considered-dozens-anti-trans-bills-moms-helped-stop-rcna2355.

16. Bryant and Bryant, Zoom interview.

17. Bryant and Bryant, Zoom interview.

18. Gonzales family, in-person meeting with authors, Apr. 2023.

19. Lily Durwood et al., "Mental Health and Self-Worth in Socially Transitioned Transgender Youth," *Journal of the American Academy of Child and Adolescent Psychiatry* 52, no. 2 (Feb. 2017), https://pubmed.ncbi.nlm.nih.gov/28117057/.

20. Alex Ura, "Despite Losing Bathroom Bill Fight, a Transgender Girl Gets Her Two Minutes," *Texas Tribune*, July 22, 2017, https://www.texastribune.org/2017/07/22 /transgender-girl-gets-her-two-minutes-bathroom-bill.

21. Ura, "Despite Losing Bathroom Bill Fight, a Transgender Girl Gets Her Two Minutes."

22. Nick Valencia, "Transgender and 7 Years Old, a Strong Voice Against Texas' 'Bathroom Bill,' CNN, Aug. 4, 2017, https://www.cnn.com/2017/08/03/health/trans -youth-texas-bathroom-bill/index.html.

23. Alex Ura, "After Months of Controversy, Texas Bathroom Bill Dies Quietly," *Texas Tribune*, Aug. 16, 2017, https://www.texastribune.org/2017/08/16/after-months -controversy-texas-bathroom-bill-dies-quiet-death.

24. David Montgomery, "Texas Transgender Bathroom Bill Falters amid Mounting Opposition," *New York Times*, Aug. 8, 2017, https://www.nytimes.com/2017/08/08/us /time-is-running-out-on-texas-bathroom-bill.html.

25. Associated Press, "'Bathroom Bill' to Cost North Carolina $3.76 Billion," CNBC, Mar. 27, 2017, https://www.cnbc.com/2017/03/27/bathroom-bill-to-cost -north-carolina-376-billion.html; Marc Tracy, "N.C.A.A. Ends Boycott of North Carolina After So-Called Bathroom Bill Is Repealed," *New York Times*, Apr. 4, 2017, https://www.nytimes.com/2017/04/04/sports/ncaa-hb2-north-carolina-boycott -bathroom-bill.html.

26. Rachel Gonzales, meeting with authors, Apr. 2023.

27. Gonzales, meeting with authors.

28. Jonah P. DeChants et al., "'I Get Treated Poorly in Regular School—Why Add to It?': Transgender Girls' Experiences Choosing to Play or Not Play Sports," *Transgender Health* 9, no. 1 (Oct. 2022), http://doi.org/10.1089/trgh.2022.0066.

29. Elliot Sylvester, "New Poll Emphasizes Negative Impacts of Anti-LGBTQ Policies on LGBTQ Youth," The Trevor Project, Jan. 19, 2023, https://www.thetrevor project.org/blog/new-poll-emphasizes-negative-impacts-of-anti-lgbtq-policies-on -lgbtq-youth.

30. Alexander Sin et al., "Sports Participation and Transgender Youth," *JAMA Pediatrics* 177, no. 11 (Sept. 2023): 1121–22, https://jamanetwork.com/journals/jamapediatrics /article-abstract/2809312.

31. Nina Golgowski, "Florida Students Protest After Principal, Staff Are Reassigned over Trans Athlete," *HuffPost*, Nov. 29, 2023, https://ca.finance.yahoo.com/news/florida -students-protest-principal-staff-184314162.html.

32. "Broward High School Principal Reassigned amid Investigation Involving Transgender Athlete: Sources," NBC6, Nov. 27, 2023, https://www.nbcmiami.com/news/local /broward-high-school-principal-and-staffers-reassigned-amid-investigation-into -student-sports-transgender-athlete/3169376.

33. Carlos Suarez, "Florida Athletic Officials Punish Transgender Student-Athlete and High School over Participation on Girls' Team," CNN, Dec. 12, 2023, https:// www.cnn.com/2023/12/12/us/florida-transgender-high-school-student-athlete -probation-fine/index.html.

34. Hogan Gore, "Texas Gov. Greg Abbott Signs Ban on 'Sexually Explicit' Books in School Libraries into Law," *Austin-American Statesman*, June 12, 2023, https://www .statesman.com/story/news/2023/06/12/hb-900-texas-book-ban-gov-greg-abbott-sign -banning-sexually-explicit-content-public-school-libraries/70314516007.

35. Gore, "Texas Gov. Greg Abbott Signs Ban."

36. Candy Gwyn, Zoom call with authors, 2023.

37. Gwyn, Zoom call.

38. Gwyn, Zoom call.

39. Gwyn, Zoom call.

40. Shireen Ahmed, "Hot Take: Trans Triathlete Chris Mosier on the Importance of Trans Inclusion in Sport," *Burn It All Down*, podcast, Mar. 7, 2022, https://www.burnit alldownpod.com/episodes/hot-take-trans-triathlete-chris-mosier-on-the-importance -of-trans-inclusion-in-sport.

41. Office of the Attorney General, Commonwealth of Massachusetts, "AG Campbell Co-leads Coalition in Support of Furthering Federal Antidiscrimination Protections for Transgender Athletes," press release, May 18, 2023, https://www.mass.gov/news/ag -campbell-co-leads-coalition-in-support-of-furthering-federal-antidiscrimination -protections-for-transgender-athletes.

42. Brian, Zoom meeting with authors, 2023.

43. Brian, Zoom meeting.

44. Tommy and Brian, Zoom interview with authors, 2023.

45. Tommy and Brian, Zoom interview.

46. Tommy and Brian, Zoom interview.

CHAPTER 8: VOICES FROM INSIDE THE LOCKER ROOM

1. Colin Perkel, "Transgender Minor Hockey Players Win Right to Choose Dressing Room," *Global News*, Sept. 15, 2014, https://globalnews.ca/news/1564826 /transgender-minor-hockey-players-win-right-to-choose-dressing-room.

2. Perkel, "Transgender Minor Hockey Players Win Right to Choose Dressing Room."

3. Laura Newberry, "Long Beach School Pauses Gender-Neutral Locker Room Proposal amid Anti-transgender Climate," *Los Angeles Times*, Mar. 4, 2022, https:// www.latimes.com/california/story/2022–03–04/long-beach-gender-neutral-locker -room-proposal-paused.

4. J. G. Kosciw, C. M. Clark, and L. Menard, *The 2021 National School Climate Survey: The Experiences of Lesbian, Gay, Bisexual, Transgender, and Queer Youth in Our Nation's Schools* (New York: GLSEN, 2022), https://www.glsen.org/research/2021 -national-school-climate-survey.

5. W. Burlette Carter, "Sexism in the 'Bathroom Debates': How Bathrooms Really Became Separated by Sex," *Yale Law & Policy Review* 37, no. 227 (2018): 227–97, https://openyls.law.yale.edu/bitstream/handle/20.500.13051/17285/WBurletteCarter Sexisminth.pdf.

6. Gillian Frank, "The Anti-trans Bathroom Nightmare Has Its Roots in Racial Segregation," *Slate*, https://slate.com/human-interest/2015/11/anti-trans-bathroom -propaganda-has-roots-in-racial-segregation.html.

7. "What Is the Americans with Disabilities Act (ADA)?" Americans with Disabilities Act, https://adata.org/learn-about-ada, accessed Aug. 16, 2024.

8. "Facts About Suicide Among LGBTQ+ Young People," The Trevor Project, Jan. 1, 2024, https://www.thetrevorproject.org/resources/article/facts-about-lgbtq-youth-suicide/.

9. "Statistics on Homophobia and Transphobia in Sport," Out on the Fields, 2019, https://outonthefields.com/media/.

10. "Facts About Suicide Among LGBTQ+ Young People," The Trevor Project.

11. Jessica Platt, in-person meeting with authors, 2023.

12. Katie Barnes, "CWHL's First Transgender Woman Finds Comfort, Confidence in Professional Hockey," ESPN, Jan. 10, 2018, https://www.espn.com/espnw/culture/story/_/id/22029536/cwhl-first-transgender-woman-finds-comfort-confidence-professional-hockey.

13. Platt, in-person meeting.

14. "We Are Here: Understanding the Size of the LGBTQ+ Community," Human Rights Campaign, 2021, https://hrc-prod-requests.s3-us-west-2.amazonaws.com/We-Are-Here-120821.pdf.

15. Jeffrey M. Jones, "LGBT Identification in U.S. Ticks Up to 7.1%," Gallup, Feb. 17, 2022, https://news.gallup.com/poll/389792/lgbt-identification-ticks-up.aspx.

16. Erin Anderssen and Jeff Blair, "Throwing in the Towel on Homophobia," *Globe and Mail*, Nov. 27, 2009, https://www.theglobeandmail.com/news/national/throwing-in-the-towel-on-homophobia/article4357030.

17. NHL, "Brendan Burke Feature," Facebook, June 18, 2021, https://www.facebook.com/watch/?v=1170946440050884.

18. Ryan Dixon, "A Decade of Difference," *Sportsnet*, https://www.sportsnet.ca/hockey/longform/inside-you-can-plays-fight-to-make-sports-more-inclusive/, accessed Aug. 16, 2024.

19. Kristopher Wells, Zoom interview with authors, 2023.

20. Mike Chiari, "Flyers' Ivan Provorov Doesn't Wear Pride Night Jersey, Cites Religious Beliefs," *Bleacher Report*, Jan. 18, 2023, https://bleacherreport.com/articles/10062100-flyers-ivan-provorov-doesnt-wear-pride-night-jersey-cites-religious-beliefs.

21. Human Rights Watch, "Russia: Supreme Court Bans 'LGBT Movement' as 'Extremist,'" Human Rights Watch, Nov. 30, 2023, https://www.hrw.org/news/2023/11/30/russia-supreme-court-bans-lgbt-movement-extremist.

22. Stephen Whyno, "NHL Issues Updated Theme Night Guidance, Which Includes a Ban on Players Using Pride Tape on the Ice," Associated Press, Oct. 11, 2023, https://apnews.com/article/nhl-theme-nights-pride-tape-1617bcf9a3deba43b9d39e935222089f.

23. Bill Chappell, "The NHL Bans Pride Tape, Setting Off a Backlash from Players and Fans," NPR, Oct. 12, 2023, https://www.npr.org/2023/10/12/1205476006/nhl-bans-pride-tape-backlash.

24. Joshua Clipperton, "'Had to Be Done': Coyotes' Travis Dermott on Using Pride Tape, Forcing NHL's Hand," CBC, Oct. 27, 2023, https://www.cbc.ca/sports/hockey/nhl/nhl-pride-tape-dermott-had-to-be-done-1.7010556.

25. Jessica Platt, in-person meeting with authors, 2023.

26. Jessica Platt, Instagram, https://www.instagram.com/p/Bdy5ji-F-1P.

27. Jay Forster, "Jessica Platt: 'My Team-Mates Told Me They Were Proud of Me,'" *Sports Media LGBT+*, Feb. 2, 2021, https://sportsmedialgbt.com/jessica-platt-my-team-mates-told-me-they-were-proud-of-me.

28. "Rule of Two," Coaching Association of Canada, https://coach.ca/responsible-coaching-movement/rule-of-two, accessed Aug. 16, 2024.

29. George B. Cunningham et al., "Inclusive Spaces and Locker Rooms for Transgender Athletes," *Kineseiology Review* 7, no. 4 (2018): 365–74, https://journals.humankinetics.com/view/journals/krj/7/4/article-p365.xml.

30. Kellie Zhao, "Gensler and Athlete Ally Team Up to Imagine More Inclusive Locker Rooms," *Architect's Newspaper*, Aug. 16, 2021, https://www.archpaper.com/2021/08/gensler-and-athlete-ally-team-up-to-imagine-more-inclusive-locker-rooms.

31. Zhao, "Gensler and Athlete Ally Team Up to Imagine More Inclusive Locker Rooms."

32. Zhao, "Gensler and Athlete Ally Team Up to Imagine More Inclusive Locker Rooms."

CHAPTER 9: THE TRIALS AND TRIBULATIONS OF THE NCAA AND COLLEGE SPORTS

1. CeCé Telfer as told to Josey Murray, "Athlete CeCe Telfer Says Sports Allow Trans Youth to Be Seen as People First," *Women's Health Magazine*, June 17, 2021, https://www.womenshealthmag.com/fitness/a36677707/cece-telfer-transgender-athlete-essay.

2. Telfer, "Athlete CeCe Telfer Says Sports Allow Trans Youth to Be Seen as People First."

3. Telfer, "Athlete CeCe Telfer Says Sports Allow Trans Youth to Be Seen as People First."

4. Peter Hasson, "Biological Male Is Top-Ranked NCAA Women's Track Star," *Daily Caller*, Feb. 25, 2019, https://dailycaller.com/2019/02/25/ncaa-transgender-franklin-pierce.

5. Donald Trump Jr., X, Feb. 26, 2019, https://x.com/DonaldJTrumpJr/status/1100384478894149633.

6. "Northeast-10 Indoor Track & Field Championships," TFRRS, Feb. 16–17, 2019, https://www.tfrrs.org/results/58362/3844506/Northeast-10_Indoor_Track__Field_Championships/Womens-60-Meters.

7. Dawn Ennis, "Cecé Telfer Is a Trans Athlete Who Doesn't Win Every Time," *Outsports*, Mar. 10, 2019, https://www.outsports.com/2019/3/10/18257930/ncaa-cece-telfer-trans-woman-athlete-track-field.

8. Dawn Ennis, "NCAA Champion CeCé Telfer Says 'I Have No Benefit' by Being Trans," *Outsports*, June 3, 2019, https://www.outsports.com/2019/6/3/18649927/ncaa-track-champion-cece-telfer-transgender-athlete-fpu-trans-testosterone.

9. Danne Diamond, Zoom interview with authors, 2023.

10. NPR Staff, "Transgender Athlete Competes for Olympic Spot," NPR, May 24, 2012, https://www.npr.org/2012/05/24/153589689/transgender-athlete-competes-for-olympic-spot.

11. Erin Buzuvis, "What's Wrong with NCAA's New Transgender Athlete Policy?" *William & Mary Journal of Race, Gender, and Social Justice* 29, no. 1 (Oct. 2022): 155–317, https://scholarship.law.wm.edu/wmjowl/vol29/iss1/5; David Moltz, "NCAA Considers Transgender Policy," *Inside Higher Ed*, Dec. 14, 2010, https://www.insidehighered.com/news/2010/12/15/ncaa-considers-transgender-policy.

12. International Olympic Committee, "IOC Approves Consensus with Regard to Athletes Who Have Changed Sex," press release, May 17, 2004, https://olympics

.com/ioc/news/ioc-approves-consensus-with-regard-to-athletes-who-have-changed
-sex-1.

13. Cyd Zeigler, "NCAA Adopts Official Policy Opening the Door for Transgender Athletes," *Outsports*, Sept. 13, 2011, https://www.outsports.com/2011/9/13/4051836 /ncaa-adopts-official-policy-opening-the-door-for-transgender-athletes.

14. Ethan Moreland, "Implications of Gender-Affirming Endocrine Care for Sports Participation," *Therapeutic Advances in Endocrinology and Metabolism* 14 (2023).

15. Matt Lavietes, "International Olympic Committee Issues New Guidelines on Transgender Athletes," NBC News, Nov. 16, 2021, https://www.nbcnews.com/nbc-out /out-news/international-olympic-committee-issues-new-guidelines-transgender-athl -rcna5775.

16. Lavietes, "International Olympic Committee Issues New Guidelines on Transgender Athletes."

17. NCAA, "Board of Governors Updates Transgender Participation Policy," press release, Jan. 19, 2022, https://www.ncaa.org/news/2022/1/19/media-center-board-of -governors-updates-transgender-participation-policy.aspx.

18. Joanna Harper, "Understanding New Olympic Guidelines for Trans Athletes," *The Hill*, Nov. 22, 2021, https://thehill.com/opinion/international/582651-understanding -new-olympic-guidelines-for-trans-athletes.

19. Athlete Ally, "Athlete Ally & Chris Mosier Respond to NCAA New Trans Inclusion Policy," press release, Jan. 20, 2022, https://www.athleteally.org/athlete-ally-mosier -respond-ncaa-new-trans-policy.

20. Julie Kliegman, "Diversity Facilitator Withdraws from NCAA Program in Wake of Association's Trans Eligibility Change," *Sports Illustrated*, Jan. 24, 2022, https:// www.si.com/college/2022/01/24/lgbtq-one-withdrawal-letter-dorian-rhea-debussy -transgender-eligibility.

21. NCAA, "Board of Governors Updates Transgender Participation Policy."

22. CL Viloria, Zoom interview with authors, 2023.

23. Viloria, Zoom interview.

24. Viloria, Zoom interview.

25. "Transgender Athlete Inspires Teammates and Policy Changes," Seneca Polytechnic, Apr. 12, 2022, https://www.senecapolytechnic.ca/news-and-events/seneca -news/transgender-athlete-inspires-teammates-and-policy-changes.html.

26. Canadian Centre for Ethics in Sport, "CCES Releases Guide to Creating Inclusive Environments for Trans Participants in Canadian Sport," press release, May 4, 2016, https://cces.ca/news/cces-releases-guide-creating-inclusive-environments-trans -participants-canadian-sport.

27. "Transgender Athlete Inspires Teammates and Policy Changes."

28. Viloria, Zoom interview.

29. Brett Finger, "NHL Scouting Combine: Does It Matter?" *Canes Country*, June 14, 2018, https://www.canescountry.com/2018/6/14/17445762/nhl-scouting-combine -does-it-matter-carolina-hurricanes-hockey-training-casey-mittelstadt-sabres.

CHAPTER 10: THE FUTURE IS TRANS

1. Aidan Cleary, Zoom interview with authors, 2023.

2. MGHA, https://www.madisongayhockey.org/.

3. Jamie Wareham, "Beaten, Stabbed and Shot: 320 Trans People Killed in 2023—New Monitoring Report," *Forbes*, Nov. 13, 2023, https://www.forbes.com/sites/jamie wareham/2023/11/13/beaten-stabbed-and-shot-320-trans-people-murdered-in-2023 /?sh=1c5c18001646.

4. Katie Barnes, "Premier Hockey Federation Updates Participation Policy for Transgender and Non-binary Athletes," ESPN, Oct. 15, 2021, https://www.espn.com /nhl/story/_/id/32405923/premier-hockey-federation-updates-participation-policy -transgender-nonbinary-athletes.

5. Barnes, "Premier Hockey Federation Updates Participation Policy for Transgender and Non-binary Athletes."

6. Mike Murphy, "Breaking Down the PHF's Trans Inclusion Policy," The Ice Garden, Oct. 15, 2021, https://www.theicegarden.com/breaking-down-the-phfs-trans -inclusion-policy.

7. Murphy, "Breaking Down the PHF's Trans Inclusion Policy."

8. Stefica Nicol Bikes, "Australian Sports Set Guidelines for Inclusion of Trans Athletes," Reuters, Oct. 1, 2020, https://www.reuters.com/article/sports-australia -transgender-idINKBN26M4IG.

9. Bikes, "Australian Sports Set Guidelines for Inclusion of Trans Athletes."

10. Bikes, "Australian Sports Set Guidelines for Inclusion of Trans Athletes."

11. Australian Football League, "Gender Diversity Policy – Companion Guide," https://resources.afl.com.au/afl/document/2021/02/18/d6ed1dab-f21b-4d36–924b -6cac89687e8e/AM-7411–0920-AFL-GDP-Companion-Booklet-D5.pdf.

12. Stephanie Convery, "Trans Participation in Sport Is Happening Now—Not Only Is It a Non-issue, It Makes Clubs Better," *The Guardian*, Apr. 23, 2022, https:// www.theguardian.com/society/2022/apr/24/trans-participation-in-sport-is-happening -now-not-only-is-it-a-non-issue-it-makes-clubs-better.

13. River Butcher, Zoom interview with authors, 2023.

14. Butcher, Zoom interview.

15. Jake McKee, "World Aquatics to Trial 'Open' Category for Trans Swimmers: 'Our Sport Must Be Open to Everybody,'" *Pink News*, July 27, 2023, https://www.the pinknews.com/2023/07/27/world-aquatics-open-category-trans-swimmers.

16. Associated Press, "Plans to Allow for Transgender Swimmers at World Cup Meet Scrapped Due to No Entries," CBC, Oct. 3, 2023, https://www.cbc.ca/sports /olympics/summer/aquatics/open-category-transgender-swimmers-world-cup-meet -fina-1.6985344.

17. World Aquatics, "Update on the Open Category Competitions at the World Aquatics Swimming World Cup – Berlin 2023," Oct. 3, 2023, https://www.world aquatics.com/news/3715191/update-on-the-open-category-competitions-at-the -world-aquatics-swimming-world-cup-berlin-2023.

18. Maggie Baska, "World Boxing Council to Put Trans Boxers in Separate Category After Ban on Fighting Cis Athletes," *Pink News*, Dec. 29, 2022, https://www.the pinknews.com/2022/12/29/world-boxing-council-transgender-category.

19. Ben Wyatt, "Trans Boxers Are Stepping into the Ring. Will the Sport Let Them Play?" *Rolling Stone*, Sept. 23, 2023, https://www.rollingstone.com/culture/culture -features/trans-boxers-patricio-manuel-compete-1234822106.

20. Robert Sanchez, "'I Am Lia': The Trans Swimmer Dividing America Tells Her Story," *Sports Illustrated*, Mar. 3, 2022, https://www.si.com/college/2022/03/03/lia -thomas-penn-swimmer-transgender-woman-daily-cover.

21. Butcher, Zoom interview.

22. Dave Zirin, "Banning Trans Athletes Is Just the Beginning," *The Nation*, Mar. 7, 2023, https://www.thenation.com/article/society/congress-sports-federal-ban-trans -athletes.

INDEX

Abbott, Greg, 113
abuse of women in sports, 98–99
accessing sport, 35, 42–44; financial
    barriers to, 35–38; LGBTQ+ people,
    40–41; parental advantage and,
    41–42; relative age theory and, 38–40
ACON, 153
activism for trans rights, 106–13
ADF (Alliance Defending Freedom), 92,
    94, 104–6
administrators, inspiration for action,
    161
Aguilar, Hugo, 29
Air Force study (2020), 54, 57–58
Ali, Laila, 42
Ali, Muhammad, 42
Alliance Defending Freedom (ADF), 92,
    94, 104–6
Allums, Kye, x
Al-Musallam, Husain, 157
American Principles Project, 7
Americans with Disabilities Act, 121
androgen insensitivity, 66
anti-trans oppression, 2, 4, 6, 82;
    bathroom restriction bills, 108–11,
    121–22; Fox News and right-wing
    outlets, 11–12, 76; legislation, 4, 7, 9;
    resultant as diversion from political
    situations, 9–10, 16; in Texas, 106–10;
    Donald Trump and Republican base,
    82; violence, 150, 159, 162
Arkansas, 10
Armchair Expert (podcast), 163
Asian Games (2014), 71

Athlete Ally, xii–xiii, 11–12, 80, 131–32
Australia, 153–54
Australian Football League, 153–54

Baby, This Is Keke Palmer (podcast), 163
Baeth, Anna, xiii, 11–12, 84
Bailar, Schuyler, 13, 50, 60, 83, 162
Bailey, Andrew, 13
bans against trans athletic participa-
    tion, 10, 14, 15, 53–54, 74, 76, 86, 87,
    100–101, 110–11
Barnes, Katie, 13, 162
Barnsley, Roger, 38
"base layer rule" policy (Hockey Can-
    ada), 130
basketball, 99
bathroom restriction bills, 108–11,
    121–22
Ben-Yehuda, Nachman, 3
Beshear, Andy, 7
"biological" males and females, 90
birthdate effect, 38–40
boxing, 27–30, 76–77
Bridges, Emily, 89–90
British Cycling, 89–90, 157
British Rowing, 157
British Triathlon, 157
Broward, Florida, 111–12
Browne, Harrison: biographical, ix–xviii,
    33, 99; Friendship Series, 147–51;
    and Donna Lopiano, 96; motivations
    to play sports, 114–15; perceived
    by others, 57; physical transitioning
    and locker room culture, 123, 129,

130; reflections on hormone therapy, inclusion, and athletic ability, 143–45; testosterone therapy and, 58–59
Browne, Rachel, xvii
Bryant, Sunny, 106–8
Buffalo Beauts, xv
Bullingham, Rachael, 18
Burke, Brendan, 125–26
Burke, Brian, 125–26
Burke, Patrick, 125–26
Burns, Katelyn, 13, 162
Butcher, River, 154–56, 159
Butler, Judith, 10

Canada: age barriers to fairness in sport, 38–39; financial barriers to sport fairness, 35–38; Ontario Colleges Athletics Association (OCAA), 141–44
Canadian Centre for Ethics in Sport, 142
Canadian Women's Hockey League (CWHL), 99, 128–29
Carini, Angela, 76–77
Carlson, Tucker, 11, 135
Carroll, Helen, 95
Chand, Dutee, 70–72, 74–76
chess, 14
Cheung, Ada, 87–88
children, trans, 106–11
Children's Rights in Sport declaration (Norway), 43
chromosomal analysis for gender verification, 66–67
chromosomal discrepancies, 66
cisgender men: and athletic superiority, 80–81; gender and biology stereotypes, 80; poverty rates of, 40; social conditioning of, 154–55; as threat to cisgender women, xix, 98–99; toxic masculinity and, 120
cisgender women: advantage over trans women in some athletic ability categories, 81; athletic variation among, 90; harm to, from competitive advantage rhetoric, 76; poverty rates of, 40; psychology or athletic mindset conditioning, 59; trans women as opportunity threat to, 92–93; trans

women as threat to, 12; as victims, 94–95
Cleary, Adam, 147
coaches, inspiration for action, 161
co-ed locker rooms, 120
Cohen, Stanley, 3, 9, 11–12
Commonwealth Games (1966), 65
Commonwealth Games (2014), 71
Connecticut, 93–94, 103–6
conspiracy theories, 5
Coughlin, Ricki, 153
Court of Arbitration for Sport, 71
Curry, Dell, 41
Curry, Steph, 41
Cusma, Elisa, 69
CWHL (Canadian Women's Hockey League), 99, 128–29
cycling, 89–90

Debussy, Dorian Rhea, 139
de Courbertin, Pierre, 64
Dermott, Travis, 128
de Varona, Donna, 91
Diamond, Danne, 80, 136
"Don't Ask, Don't Tell," 18
"Don't Say Gay" bill, 1
drag performances, 6
Drag Story Hour events, 6
"Draw the Line Against Transphobic Violence in Schools" (Egale Canada), 162
duathlon, 31–32
Dunn, Parker, 56–57

Eastwood, Juniper "June," 57
elite athleticism, 59
Emmert, Mark, 140
Erin in the Morning (newsletter), 3–4
ESPN The Magazine Body Issue, 31
estradiol, 47
estrogen, 47

FAA (Football Athletic Association), 56–57
fairness, in sport, 33–35, 42–44, 159–60; financial barriers to, 35–38; gender segregation and, 155; LGBTQ+

people accessing sport, 40–41; parental advantage and, 41–42; relative age theory and, 38–40

Fairness in Women's Sports Act (US), 34

"Fairness in Women's Sports Act" (Florida), 112

Fair Play For Women, xix, 91, 92

fascist movements, 10

Fédération Internationale de Natation (FINA), 86, 87–88, 139, 157

Fédération Internationale des Échecs (FIDE), 14

Ference, Andrew, 126

FIDE (Fédération Internationale des Échecs), 14

figure skating, 36

FINA (Fédération Internationale de Natation), 86, 87–88, 139, 157

financial barriers to fairness, 35–38

financial disparities in women's sports, 99

Florida, 112

Football Athletic Association (FAA), 56–57

Fox News, 11

Frackman, Kyle, 2–3

Friendship Series, 147–51

gender-affirming healthcare, 10, 150

gender and fairness in sport, 35–36

gender dysphoria, xvi

gender segregation, 5, 121, 154–56

gender verification procedures and exams, 66–77

GLAAD, 12–13

Gladwell, Malcolm, 38

Godsey, Keelin, 137

Gonzales, Libby, 108–11, 113–14, 121

Goode, Erich, 3

Goorevich, Anna, 11–12

Greene, Marjorie Taylor, 4

Gwyn, Candy, 113–14

gymnastics, 99

Harper, Joanna, 45–46, 60, 139

healthcare, transgender, xvi; Arkansas ban on gender-affirming for minors, 10

Heggie, Vanessa, 74

Henig, Iszac, 79–80, 85–86

Henne, Kathryn, 75

He/She/They (Bailar), 83

high school athletics, 93–94

hijab prohibition, soccer, 100

hockey, men's: body checking, 96–97; fairness and access, 36–39; Friendship Series, 147–51; Hockey Canada, 119–20, 130–32; homophobia and transphobia in, 124–29; locker room culture, 122–24; Pride Nights (NHL) controversies, 126–29; toxic masculinity in, 147; women's hockey, xiv, 123, 127–28

hockey, women's, xiv, 99, 123, 127–28, 161

Hockey Canada, 119–20, 130–32

Hogshead-Makar, Nancy, 91–92

homophobia, 18, 28, 122, 124–29

homosexuality: as barrier to athletic participation, 18–19; presumed of women athletes, 18

hormones, 47

hormone suppression effects, 45–46

hormone therapy, xiii–xiv, xvi, 23; age at advent of, 48; feminizing hormone therapy, 49; linked to participation policies, 151–52; reasons for, 47–48; testosterone therapy, 48–49; training difficulties, 89; and trans men in women's sports, 55–60

hormone therapy policies: International Olympic Committee (IOC), 29, 137–39; NCAA, x–xi, 57, 136–40, 142–43; Ontario Colleges Athletics Association, 141–44; Premier Hockey Federation, 151–54

Hubbard, Laurel, xvii, 21–24

hyperandrogenism, 70–71, 72, 75–76

hyperfemininity, 17

IAAF European Track and Field Championships (1966), 65

IAAF/World Athletics, 69, 71–73

IBA (International Boxing Association), 77

ICONS (Independent Council on Women's Sports) conference, 92
inclusive design, 132
inspiration for action, 161–63
International Boxing Association (IBA), 77
International Chess Organization (FIDE), 14
International Olympic Committee (IOC), 65; 2003 transgender policies, 23, 86–87, 137–38; 2021 framework, 138–39; competition criteria for trans athletes, 23, 32; gender-confirmation surgery requirement, 32, 138; gender verification procedures and exams, 66–77; testosterone guidelines, 29; trans inclusion policies, 137–38; World Conference on Women and Sport, 67
intersexuality, 68, 75–76
IOC. See International Olympic Committee (IOC)

Jackson, Victoria, 92–93
Jenner, Caitlyn, 82–83
Johnson, David K., 5
Jordan-Young, Rebecca, 50, 51, 52, 60, Joseph, Manu, 71
Justice for Trans Athletes (Baeth and Goorevich), 11–12, 41

Karkazis, Katrina, 88
Khelif, Imane, 76–77
King, Billie Jean, 18, 20
Kirshner, Alex, 8
Klobukowska, Ewa, 66
Knowles, Michael, 4

"Lavender Scare," 4–5
The Lavender Scare (Johnson), 5
law enforcement, and news media, 9
Ledecky, Katie, 87
legislation, anti-LGBTQ+, 4, 7, 9
LGBTQ+ people: accessing sport, 40–41; legislation targeting, 4, 7, 9
locker room culture: Hockey Canada policy initiatives, 129–32;

homophobia and transphobia in hockey, 124–29; inclusion and exclusion, 119–24
Lopiano, Donna, 91, 93, 94–95
low-dose testosterone therapy, 56–57

Madison Gay Hockey Association, 147–50
Magrath, Rory, 18
Manning, Archie, 41
Manning, Eli, 41
Manning, Peyton, 41
Mansour, Asmahan, 100
Manuel, Patricio, 27–30, 59, 60, 158
Marshall, Roger, 55
Massachusetts, 117
Masterpiece Cakeshop, Ltd. v. Colorado Civil Rights Commission, 104
"Matthew effect," 38–40
McCullough, Gillian, 142
McLean, Jeff, 126
media: and law enforcement, 9; and moral panics, 9, 10–15; trans-skeptical media coverage, 12
mental health, and hormone therapy, 48
Miller, Terry, 93–94, 103–6
misogyny, 9
Mitchell, Christina and Chelsea, 93, 94, 103–6
Mittelstadt, Casey, 145
mixed-gender sports, 154–56
moral panics: about, 2–5, 6; architecture of, 8–10; impacts for families and others, 15–16; role of media in, 10–15
Mosier, Chris, 31–32, 115, 139

National Hockey League (NHL), 37, 127–29
National Women's Hockey League (NWHL), xv, xvi, 99. See also Premier Hockey Federation (PHF)
National Women's Soccer League (NWSL), 26
Navratilova, Martina, 18, 20, 21, 81–82
NCAA (National Collegiate Athletic Association): Office for Inclusion, 137; scholarships and trans women

athletes, 105; trans inclusion policies, x–xi, 57, 136–40
New York Times, 12–13
NHL (National Hockey League), 37, 127–29
NHL Pride Nights, 126–29
Niehoff, Karissa, 42
nonbinary people, 152; as athletes, 24–27; and hormone therapy, 48–49
Norway, youth sports participation in, 43
NWHL (National Women's Hockey League), xv, xvi, 99. *See also* Premier Hockey Federation (PHF)
NWSL (National Women's Soccer League), 26
Nyad, Diana, 92

Obergefell v. Hodges, 104
OCAA (Ontario Colleges Athletics Association), 141–44
Ohio: legislation, 52–55
OJHL (Ontario Junior Hockey League), 38–39
Olympics: 1936, 63–64; 2016, 72; 2021, 73; 2024, 76; Dutee Chand, 70–72, 74–76; gender verification procedures and exams, 65–66; Caster Semenya, 67–70, 72–76. *See also* International Olympic Committee (IOC)
Ontario Colleges Athletics Association (OCAA), 141–44
Ontario Junior Hockey League (OJHL), 38–39
Organisation Intersex International, 73
Out in Sport (Anderson, Magrath, and Bullingham), 18
Outliers (Gladwell), 38
Outsports, 89

Palmer, Keke, 163
Pan American Games (1967), 65–66
parental advantage, 41–42
parents, 117
parents, inspiration for action, 162
patriarchic systems, dangers of, 120
"penis panics," 5
perceived threat, 9

phalloplasty, 48
PHF (Premier Hockey Federation), xvi, 99, 124–29, 151–54
physicality, and fairness, 33–34
Pitsiladis, Yannis, 81
Platt, Jessica, 88–89, 124–25, 128–29, 161
Policing the Crisis: Mugging, the State and Law and Order, 8–9
Poulin, Marie-Philip, 33
Premier Hockey Federation (PHF), xvi, 99, 124–29, 151–54
prepubescence, 49–51
Pride Nights (NHL), 126–29
Pride Tape, 126, 127–28
Prince, Sedona, 99
progesterone, 47
Prokop, Luke, 125
Provorov, Ivan, 127
psychology of elite athleticism, 59
puberty, physiological changes, 50–51

QAnon, 5
Quinn, 24–27, 138

race, and fairness in sport, 35–36, 37–38, 75
Race to Be Me (documentary), 90
Ratjen, Dora, 63
recreational sport, financial barrier in, 35–38
Reczek, Wlodzimierz, 66
Reed, Erin, 3–4
relative age theory, 38–40
Republican Party influencers, 5
Richards, Renée, 19–21, 37–38
Roberts, Timothy, 55
Rogan, Joe, 4
Romano, Aja, 13
Royal Canadian Mounted Police (RCMP), 2
Rugby Australia, 153
Rule of Two policy (Hockey Canada), 130

safety preoccupations, misguided and arbitrary, 96–97, 120
Sam, Michael, 18

Satanic Panic, 5
Save Women's Sports (bill) (Australia), 34
"Save Women's Sports Act" (Texas), 110–11
Savinova, Maria, 70
scapegoating, 9–10
Schilling, Terry, 7
school dropout rates, 122
SDHL (Svenska damhockeyligan), 97
segregation, gender, 5, 121, 154–56
Seidler, Maren, 66
Semenya, Caster, 46, 67–70, 72–76
Seplavy, Tara, 89
sexism, 8
sexual abuse, 98–99
Sherman, Texas, 13–14
Sipaia, Iuniarra, 22
Snoop Dogg, 36
soccer, 24–27
social conditioning, 155
social media, as instruments of moral panics, 11
social transitioning, xi–xii
Sonoma, Serena, 12–13
sports, importance of, 113–15
Starr, Heidi and Kari, 1–2
Stephens, Helen, 17, 63–64
Stonewall riots, 11
Strangio, Chase, 162
Sulaimán, Mauricio, 30, 158
Sullivan, Erica, 85
surgeries, gender-affirming, 48
Svenska damhockeyligan (SDHL), 97
Swim England, 157
swimming, 79–80, 83–88, 98–99, 139–40

Tea, Michelle, 6
teachers, inspiration for action, 162
Team Trans, 147–51, 156, 163
team *versus* individual sports, 144
Telfer, CeCé, 133–36
tennis, 19–21
Tennis Australia, 153
testosterone, xi, 47; and athletic performance, 50–55; Harrison's experience, 144–45; hyperandrogenism and,

70–74; levels involved in policy positions, 87; limits for cisgender men, 74
Testosterone: An Unauthorized Biography (Karkazis and Jordan-Young), 50, 51–52, 88
testosterone therapy, 48–49, 56–57; low-dose advent, 56–57
Texas, 110–11, 113
Thom, Kai Cheng, 16
Thomas, Lia, 82, 83–87, 90, 91–92, 94, 95, 135, 136, 157, 159
Thompson, A. H., 38
Thompson, Jesse, 119–20
Title IX, 18, 92–93, 154
Tommy (pseudonym), 115–17
top surgery, 25, 48
transgender boys as athletes, 115–17
Transgender Day of Remembrance, 150
transgender men as athletes: Air Force study (2020), 54, 57–58; Bailar, Schuyler, 13, 50, 60, 83, 162; hormone therapy and women's sports, 51, 54, 57–60; Patricio Manuel, 27–30, 59, 60, 158; PHF (Premier Hockey Federation), 151–54; seen as not a threat to cisgender men athletes, 58, 59–60; sit up performance compared to cisgender men, 58; social transitioning, xi. *see also* Browne, Harrison
transgender persons as athletes: "living" their identity, 152–53; percent of high schoolers, 3–4; at risk of victimization and abuse, 120–21; and separate gender-neutral locker rooms, 131; social effects of transitioning, 49
transgender women as athletes: advocating for trans inclusion, 106–11; Air Force study (2020), 54, 57–58; at competitive disadvantage in key areas of athletics, 81; difficulties and hurdles to competition, 83; embodying worst of the patriarchy, 95; exoticization of bodies, 95; presumed competitive advantages of, 21, 22, 34–35, 55–60, 80–81, 84–85; variation in athletic ability, 88–89; vilified as "men," 82–83
Trans Health Research, 87–88

TransLash Media, 12
transphobia, 122, 158–59, 162; in boxing, 28; incidents, 1–3
trans-specific sports teams, 156–58
Trump, Donald, 82
Trump, Donald, Jr., 135
Tucker, Ross, 46

UCI (Union Cycliste Internationale), 89–90
UK Athletics, 157
Union Cycliste Internationale (UCI), 89–90
United Kingdom (UK), 157
United States Tennis Association (USTA), 20, 37–38
USA Boxing, 29–30
USA Gymnastics, 99
USA Swimming, 98–99
US Open (tennis), 20

vaginoplasty, 48
Van Ness, Jonathan, 163
Viloria, CL, 140–43
Viloria, Hida, 73
violence, 159, 162
volleyball, 140–44

Walsh, James P., 11
Walsh, Matt, 4, 15
Walsh, Stella, 63–64

Wambach, Abby, 18
"washroom wars," 5
WBC (World Boxing Council), 30, 157–58
weightlifting, 21–24
Wells, Kristopher, 126
Williams, Serena, 41, 88
Williams, Venus, 41
Willis, Raquel, 162
Wisconsin, 150
women's hockey, xiv, 99, 123, 127–28, 161
women's sports, barriers in: abuse, 98–99; access, 17–18; financial disparities, 99; misguided and arbitrary safety preoccupations, 96–97
Women's Sports Foundation, 67
Women's Sports Policy Working Group (WSPWG), 91–93, 94
Women's Tennis Association, 20
World Aquatics, 86, 87–88, 139, 157
World Athletics, 87
World Boxing Council (WBC), 30, 157–58

Yearwood, Andraya, xvii, 93–94, 103–6
You Can Play, 125–26
Yu-ting, Lin, 76–77

Zelch, Ember, 53
Zirin, Dave, 159